FREDERICK DOUGLASS

SELECTED WRITINGS AND SPEECHES

FREDERICK DOUGLASS

SELECTED WRITINGS AND SPEECHES

a *Broadview Anthology of American Literature* edition

General Editors, *The Broadview Anthology of American Literature*:

Derrick R. Spires, Cornell University
Rachel Greenwald Smith, Saint Louis University
Christina Roberts, Seattle University
Joseph Rezek, Boston University
Justine S. Murison, University of Illinois, Urbana-Champaign
Laura L. Mielke, University of Kansas
Christopher Looby, University of California, Los Angeles
Rodrigo Lazo, University of California, Irvine
Alisha Knight, Washington College
Hsuan L. Hsu, University of California, Davis
Michael Everton, Simon Fraser University
Christine Bold, University of Guelph

broadview press

BROADVIEW PRESS – www.broadviewpress.com
Peterborough, Ontario, Canada

Founded in 1985, Broadview Press remains a wholly independent publishing house. Broadview's focus is on academic publishing: our titles are accessible to university and college students as well as scholars and general readers. With over 800 titles in print, Broadview has become a leading international publisher in the humanities, with world-wide distribution. Broadview is committed to environmentally responsible publishing and fair business practices.

Library and Archives Canada Cataloguing in Publication

Title: Frederick Douglass : selected writings and speeches / general editors, The Broadview anthology of American literature: Derrick R. Spires (Cornell University), Rachel Greenwald Smith (Saint Louis University), Christina Roberts (Seattle University), Joseph Rezek (Boston University), Justine S. Murison (University of Illinois, Urbana-Champaign), Laura L. Mielke (University of Kansas), Christopher Looby (University of California, Los Angeles), Rodrigo Lazo (University of California, Irvine), Alisha Knight (Washington College), Hsuan L. Hsu (University of California, Davis), Michael Everton (Simon Fraser University), Christine Bold (University of Guelph).
Other titles: Works. Selections (Spires)
Names: Douglass, Frederick, 1818-1895, author. | Container of (work): Douglass, Frederick, 1818-1895. Narrative of the life of Frederick Douglass, an American slave. | Container of (work): Douglass, Frederick, 1818-1895. Heroic slave. | Spires, Derrick Ramon, editor.
Description: Series statement: A Broadview anthology of American literature edition | Includes bibliographical references.
Identifiers: Canadiana (print) 20230198015 | Canadiana (ebook) 20230198023 | ISBN 9781554816316 (softcover) | ISBN 9781770489028 (PDF) | ISBN 9781460408346 (EPUB)
Subjects: LCSH: Douglass, Frederick, 1818-1895. | LCSH: Abolitionists—United States—Biography. | LCSH: African American abolitionists—Biography. | LCSH: Antislavery movements—United States—History—19th century. | LCGFT: Autobiographies.
Classification: LCC E499 .D58 2023 | DDC 973.8092—dc23

Broadview Press handles its own distribution in North America:
PO Box 1243, Peterborough, Ontario K9J 7H5, Canada
555 Riverwalk Parkway, Tonawanda, NY 14150, USA
Tel: (705) 743-8990; Fax: (705) 743-8353
email: customerservice@broadviewpress.com

For all territories outside of North America, distribution is handled by Eurospan Group.

Broadview Press acknowledges the financial support of the Government of Canada for our publishing activities.

Canada

Developmental Editor: Maxwell Uphaus
Cover Designer: Lisa Brawn
Typesetter: Alexandria Stuart

PRINTED IN CANADA

Contents

Introduction

Frederick Douglass
1818 – 1895

Author of the most powerfully written and most widely read slave narrative of the antebellum era, Frederick Douglass became the foremost voice in the abolitionist movement, and, following the Civil War, one of the foremost critics of the horrors of the new "Jim Crow" system of oppression. He spoke up too against the oppression of women and against all forms of prejudice and inequality, and he spoke up consistently in favor of speaking up—in favor of resistance. "Power concedes nothing without a demand," he famously wrote. "It never did and it never will." He occupies a unique place in American literature, American history, and American political thought.

Douglass was born Frederick Augustus Washington Bailey in Talbot County, Maryland. A degree of mystery surrounds the circumstances of Douglass's birth; like many enslaved people, he was denied full knowledge of his parentage or date of birth. He inherited the enslavement of his mother, Harriet Bailey, but his father was almost certainly a white man, quite likely his enslaver, Aaron Anthony (though other possibilities have been suggested). Douglass came to accept a tentative birth year of 1817; however, we now know that he was born in February 1818.

In 1826 Douglass was acquired by the slaveholder Thomas Auld, and was sent to live in Baltimore with Auld's brother and sister-in-law. In 1833 Douglass was removed from his situation in Baltimore and forced to work on Thomas Auld's plantation. Emboldened by his growing consciousness of slavery's injustice, Douglass grew increasingly rebellious, and was sent to work for a man named Edward Covey, locally famous as a so-called slave-breaker. Douglass attempted escape twice. In 1836 he was part of a failed plot organized by several enslaved companions, and was briefly jailed for his participation. Two years later, Douglass's second attempt was successful. Douglass left unexplained in the first and second versions of his autobiography any of the details of this escape, on the grounds—as he explains in Chapter 11—that telling the story would probably cause "difficulties" for those who helped him and "would most undoubtedly induce greater vigilance on the part of slaveholders"; it is only the third and final version—the 1881 *Life and Times of Frederick Douglass*—that includes the story of his escape.

Douglass presents the escape very largely as a solo endeavor; as we now know, he was in fact aided by several people—very much including the free black woman Anna Murray, to whom he had become engaged shortly before the escape. It was largely from Anna that Douglass obtained the funds that enabled him to travel from slavery in Baltimore to freedom in New York on 3 September 1838. Anna made the same trip a week later, and on 15 September the two were married in the home of David Ruggles, a black grocer and printer who led an organization devoted to assisting fugitive slaves. It was Ruggles who suggested that Frederick Bailey change his name—as was often done by those wishing to minimize the chances of being captured and returned to bondage. For a few days Douglass called himself Frederick Johnson, and it was under that name that he and Anna were married.

Ruggles also suggested that the couple move to New Bedford, Massachusetts, a community more friendly than was New York to fugitives who had been enslaved, and one where he felt Douglass would be able to find employment. There the Douglasses stayed initially at the home of an abolitionist named Nathan Johnson—evidently one of many Johnsons in New Bedford. Feeling that another name was necessary to distinguish himself from the other Johnsons, Frederick asked Nathan Johnson to suggest a new name; according to the narrative, it was Johnson who suggested the name under which Douglass would become famous.

In the North Douglass found a land of remarkable prosperity but also of profound contradiction; though an ordinary white laborer might enjoy a more luxurious existence and higher education level than an upper-class southern slaveholder, a free black citizen could expect continual discrimination from employers, church congregations, and other groups. Eventually Douglass—whose religious conversion experiences are given more emphasis in his two later memoirs—found employment as a licensed preacher in the African Methodist Episcopal Zion Church. Douglass also became a regular reader of the *Liberator*, an antislavery newspaper founded by leading white abolitionist William Lloyd Garrison. Douglass began attending antislavery meetings, where he soon began to share his own story and to make a local name for himself. In August 1841 he delivered his first formal speech before an antislavery audience in Nantucket. His moving story and evident oratorical talents caught Garrison's attention; Douglass became a valued contributor to the *Liberator*, and was appointed to a paid position with the Massachusetts Anti-Slavery Society not long thereafter.

Over the following years Douglass traveled widely and delivered speech after speech to audiences throughout the Northern states; he came to occupy a central place in the abolitionist movement. When the famous philosopher and orator Ralph Waldo Emerson was invited to deliver a major speech on slavery in August 1844, for example, Frederick Douglass was among the three others rounding out the program. People everywhere found something extraordinary about him. Nathaniel P. Rogers, editor of the *Herald of Freedom* abolitionist newspaper, described in 1843 the effect of Douglass's words when the speaker was in full flight as "sterner, darker, deeper" than oratory or eloquence. "It was the volcanic outbreak of human nature, long pent up in slavery and at last bursting its imprisonment. It was the storm of insurrection."

Douglass's celebrated status also often made him a target; he endured egg- and brick-throwing and, in Pennsylvania in 1843, a mob attack resulted in a permanent injury to his right hand. Even those who ostensibly supported Douglass's goals were often unable or unwilling to reconcile the distinguished and eloquent speaker they saw with the enslaved life he described, and insisted that his story must have been falsified. (Douglass averred in the second version of his autobiography that "prejudice against color is stronger in the north than [in the] south; it hangs around my neck like a heavy weight.")

Emboldened rather than intimidated by the challenges to his story, Douglass began work on an autobiography in which he would provide factual details to corroborate his claims. Written in the space of just a few months beginning in December 1844, *Narrative of the Life of Frederick Douglass, an American Slave. Written by Himself* was published in the spring of 1845 by the Anti-Slavery Office in Boston. The book was welcomed with enthusiasm in the abolitionist press; most notably, the *New York Tribune* on 10 June 1845 printed on its front page a long and highly favorable review (written by Margaret Fuller), along with a substantial excerpt from the book. By contrast, the *New York Herald* accorded it only a few words—"a neatly printed volume, which abolitionists may find interesting"—and most mainstream newspapers in northern states ignored it altogether. (In most southern states the dissemination of such works was strictly prohibited; a *Richmond Enquirer* article from April 1849 details a case in which a preacher named Jarvis C. Bacon was prosecuted for having circulated copies of Douglass's *Narrative* and another antislavery publication.)

By the 1840s the "slave narrative" was a well-established literary genre; in America alone at least ten such volumes were published between 1830 and 1845. Douglass's *Narrative* closely follows the conventions of the genre in several respects. The inclusion of a prefatory address by a white activist attesting to the book's authorship; the repeated assertions, near the beginning of the text, of un-hyperbolic truthfulness; the visceral descriptions of whippings, auction blocks, and other gruesome realities of enslaved life—all these are typical of the genre. Yet from the beginning Douglass's work was recognized as extraordinary in the quality of its writing and the depth of feeling it conveys; Fuller was not alone in finding the *Narrative* to be "glowing with … life and fertile in invention," "more simple, true, coherent, and warm with genuine feeling" than any other work of its kind. Writing in the 1860s, black abolitionist William Wells Brown reminisced that "the narrative of [Douglass's] life ... gave a new impetus to the black man's literature. All other stories of fugitive slaves faded away before the beautifully written, highly descriptive, and thrilling memoir of Frederick Douglass." Within less than four months the *Narrative* had sold almost 5,000 copies, and by 1850 some 30,000 copies had been printed.

The book's broad readership and Douglass's increasing fame, however, did nothing to alter his legal status. With the threat of discovery and capture by fugitive-slave hunters in mind, Douglass embarked in late 1845 on a lecture tour of Great Britain—a tour that broadened Douglass's readership and led to several European editions of his *Narrative*. While he was abroad a group of English friends purchased his manumission for a sum of £150; Douglass returned to the United States a legally free man in 1847, and moved with his family to Rochester, New York.

That same year Douglass established a new antislavery weekly newspaper, *The North Star* (a collaboration with the free-born black abolitionist Martin Delany). The ideals emblazoned on its masthead—"Right is of no Sex—Truth is of no Color—God is the Father of us all, and we are all Brethren"—may seem unexceptionable today, but in 1847 they were revolutionary on several fronts. Douglass struggled to build a readership (in 1851 he merged *The North Star* with another weekly to form *Frederick Douglass' Paper*, and in 1858 he began to publish monthly rather than weekly), but he managed in one form or another to keep publishing a newspaper until 1863, and each issue is believed to have had several thousand readers.

William Lloyd Garrison did not entirely welcome the competition with his *Liberator*. By 1851, Douglass and Garrison had reached a formal parting of the ways, with issues of principle having come to separate the two. Garrison was an uncompromising believer in "immediatism"—the doctrine that slavery should be abolished immediately rather than gradually—but he remained reluctant to countenance the use of force to overcome the evils of slavery; Douglass, by contrast, was more and more strongly convinced that the use of force in certain circumstances was entirely justified. Douglass's revised and expanded 1855 autobiography, *My Bondage and My Freedom*, puts forward even more powerfully than the *Narrative* the case for forceful resistance to such evils as slavery. (A passage from the 1855 autobiography is provided for comparison in this edition.)

Douglass had also begun to feel a desire to distance himself from the sometimes patronizing guidance of white abolitionists such as Garrison; his declared goal in founding *The North Star* had been to provide "a printing-press and paper, permanently established, under the complete control and direction of the immediate victims of slavery and oppression." Increasingly, questions about the appropriate means of resisting oppression became matters not only of the moral imperatives involved, but also matters of character formation; like Emerson, Douglass took the idea of self-reliance very much to heart. As early as 1848, in an essay entitled "What Are the Colored People Doing for Themselves?," Douglass had written against "that lazy, mean, and cowardly spirit that robs us of all self-reliance, and teaches us to depend upon others for the accomplishment of that which we should achieve with our own hands." For Douglass, the principle of self-reliance had a special resonance for African Americans.

In many of Douglass's writings, self-reliance (and self-fashioning) appears to be heavily gendered; "manhood" is given a central place. But Douglass was also involved in the fight for women's rights. In 1848 he spoke at both the Rochester and the Seneca Falls Women's Rights Conventions. One of Douglass's most celebrated speeches, commonly titled "What to the Slave Is the Fourth of July?," was given at an Independence Day event hosted by the Rochester Ladies' Anti-Slavery Society. During this period, then, Douglass saw activism on behalf of African Americans and activism for women's rights as connected causes. "When the true history of the antislavery cause shall be written," he wrote, "woman will occupy a large space in its pages, for the cause of the slave has been peculiarly a woman's cause." In the wake of the Civil War, however, there was for some years a significant rift between Douglass and leading campaigners for women's rights such as Elizabeth Cady Stanton and Susan B. Anthony, as debate intensified over the 1868 Fourteenth Amendment (affirming citizenship for all people born in the United States, regardless of color, but affirming the right to vote only for *male* citizens) and the 1870 Fifteenth Amendment (affirming that the right to vote was not to "be denied ... on account of race"). Anthony and Stanton were among those who opposed the Fifteenth Amendment; they saw no reason why the vote should be granted to black men before it had been granted to white women. Douglass, on the other hand, was outspoken in his belief that the former was a more urgent imperative than the latter. (Throughout the controversy, the voices of black women activists such as Frances Harper and Mary Ann Shadd Cary were too seldom heard.)

In addition to his autobiographical writings, Douglass published hundreds of speeches and essays—and one novella, *The Heroic Slave*

(1852). After the Civil War he became a prominent member of the Republican Party (which remained for many decades after Lincoln's death a party sympathetic to and supportive of African Americans). He received several government appointments, including United States Marshall for the District of Columbia and Minister (ambassador) to Haiti. In 1884, two years after Anna Murray-Douglass's death, he married Helen Pitts, a college-educated activist who had been working with Douglass in the office of the Recorder of Deeds. That she was white and he black led to accusations of betrayal and to her estrangement from several members of her family, but the two weathered the storm, and their marriage was a happy one.

Douglass lived for thirty years after the end of the Civil War, received many honors, and continued to speak out powerfully on a wide variety of topics. But in the years following the Compromise of 1877 and the rebirth of legalized oppression in the southern states, the tide was running against Douglass. His eloquence could do little to stop the spread of revisionist versions of the Civil War that downplayed the centrality of slavery to the struggle and framed the Confederacy as a noble "lost cause." As the years went by the slave narrative genre received less and less attention. Douglass's final great act of self-fashioning—his 1881 *Life and Times of Frederick Douglass*—sold poorly. By 1900 such writing had been nearly forgotten by mainstream white America. That year saw the publication of *A Literary History of America* by Harvard Professor of English Barrett Wendell; Wendell's eighteen-page chapter on the literature of the antislavery movement makes no mention whatsoever of Douglass—or of any other African American author. Douglass remained more consistently renowned among black readers in the late nineteenth and early twentieth centuries. He was honored in a long elegy by popular African American poet Paul Laurence Dunbar upon his death in 1895, and in 1899 was the subject of a biography written by black novelist Charles Chesnutt for the popular series Beacon Biographies of Eminent Americans; in 1906 Booker T. Washington wrote, "No negro can read and study the life of Frederick Douglass without deriving from it courage to look up and forward."

Nevertheless, in the first half of the twentieth century Douglass's *Narrative* went out of print. Not until 1960 did Harvard University Press bring out a new edition of the work—and even then with some timidity, the editor suggesting in his introduction that "perhaps Douglass seemed to protest too much in making slavery out as a 'soul-killing' institution." Only in the twenty-first century has Douglass come once again to be acknowledged without apology or equivocation as a uniquely towering presence, of enduring importance to America.

Note on the Texts

The texts of the works included in this edition are, in most cases, based on the first published version of the work in question. The text of *Narrative of the Life of Frederick Douglass* is based on that of the book's first published edition (1845). The text of the excerpt from "To My Old Master" is based on the letter's first printing in the 8 September 1848 issue of *The North Star*. The text of "What to the Slave Is the Fourth of July?" is based on the version of the speech published in pamphlet form in 1852. The text of *The Heroic Slave* is based on the version published in the first edition of *Autographs for Freedom* (1853). The excerpt from *My Bondage and My Freedom* is based on the first published edition (1855). The excerpt from "The Dred Scott Decision" is based on the text of the speech as printed in *Two Speeches by Frederick Douglass* (1857). The excerpt from "Self-Made Men" is based on the published text of the speech as delivered at the Indian Industrial School, Carlisle, Pennsylvania, in March 1893, available on the website of the Frederick Douglass Papers collection, Library of Congress. The text of "Men of Color, to Arms!" is based on the published broadside included in the Rare Books and Special Collections Division of the Library of Congress. The excerpt from "The Composite Nation" is based on the typescript of the speech available on the website of the Frederick Douglass Papers collection, Library of Congress. The excerpt from "Oration in Memory of Abraham Lincoln" is based on the text of the speech included as an appendix to the first edition of *Life and Times of Frederick Douglass* (1881). The excerpt from *Life and Times of Frederick Douglass* is based on the book's expanded 1893 edition. Spelling and punctuation have been modernized throughout in accordance with the editorial practices of *The Broadview Anthology of American Literature*.

Narrative of the Life of Frederick Douglass, an American Slave. Written by Himself

PREFACE[1]

In the month of August, 1841, I attended an anti-slavery convention in Nantucket, at which it was my happiness to become acquainted with Frederick Douglass, the writer of the following Narrative. He was a stranger to nearly every member of that body; but, having recently made his escape from the southern prison-house of bondage, and feeling his curiosity excited to ascertain the principles and measures of the abolitionists—of whom he had heard a somewhat vague description while he was a slave—he was induced to give his attendance, on the occasion alluded to, though at that time a resident in New Bedford.[2]

Fortunate, most fortunate occurrence!—fortunate for the millions of his manacled brethren, yet panting for deliverance from their awful thraldom!—fortunate for the cause of negro emancipation, and of universal liberty!—fortunate for the land of his birth, which he has already done so much to save and bless!—fortunate for a large circle of friends and acquaintances, whose sympathy and affection he has strongly secured by the many sufferings he has endured, by his virtuous traits of character, by his ever-abiding remembrance of those who are in bonds, as being bound with them!—fortunate for the multitudes, in various parts of our republic, whose minds he has enlightened on the subject of slavery, and who have been melted to tears by his pathos, or roused to virtuous indignation by his stirring eloquence against the enslavers of men!—fortunate for himself, as it at once brought him into the field of public usefulness, "gave the

1 *PREFACE* Written by prominent white abolitionist William Lloyd Garrison (1805–79). It was common practice for the slave narratives of black authors to be prefaced by white authors, whose testimonials were thought to authenticate the text. This practice was not followed with Douglass's two subsequent autobiographies.

2 *New Bedford* Douglass settled in New Bedford, Massachusetts with his wife after his self-emancipation in 1838.

world assurance of a MAN,"[1] quickened the slumbering energies of his soul, and consecrated him to the great work of breaking the rod of the oppressor, and letting the oppressed go free!

I shall never forget his first speech at the convention—the extraordinary emotion it excited in my own mind—the powerful impression it created upon a crowded auditory, completely taken by surprise—the applause which followed from the beginning to the end of his felicitous remarks. I think I never hated slavery so intensely as at that moment; certainly, my perception of the enormous outrage which is inflicted by it, on the godlike nature of its victims, was rendered far more clear than ever. There stood one, in physical proportion and stature commanding and exact—in intellect richly endowed—in natural eloquence a prodigy—in soul manifestly "created but a little lower than the angels"[2]—yet a slave, ay, a fugitive slave—trembling for his safety, hardly daring to believe that on the American soil, a single white person could be found who would befriend him at all hazards, for the love of God and humanity! Capable of high attainments as an intellectual and moral being—needing nothing but a comparatively small amount of cultivation to make him an ornament to society and a blessing to his race—by the law of the land, by the voice of the people, by the terms of the slave code, he was only a piece of property, a beast of burden, a chattel[3] personal, nevertheless!

A beloved friend[4] from New Bedford prevailed on Mr. DOUGLASS to address the convention: He came forward to the platform with a hesitancy and embarrassment, necessarily the attendants of a sensitive mind in such a novel position. After apologizing for his ignorance, and reminding the audience that slavery was a poor school for the human intellect and heart, he proceeded to narrate some of the facts in his own history as a slave, and in the course of his speech gave utterance to many noble thoughts and thrilling reflections. As soon as he had taken his seat, filled with hope and admiration, I rose, and

---

1 *gave the world ... a MAN* See Shakespeare's *Hamlet* 3.4.72.

2 *created but ... the angels* See Psalm 8.5: "For thou hast made him [humankind] a little lower than the angels"; and Hebrews 2.7: "But we see Jesus, who was made a little lower than the angels."

3 *chattel* Property.

4 *A beloved friend* William C. Coffin, prominent white abolitionist in and around New Bedford and a supporter of Douglass.

declared that Patrick Henry,[1] of revolutionary fame, never made a speech more eloquent in the cause of liberty, than the one we had just listened to from the lips of that hunted fugitive. So I believed at that time—such is my belief now. I reminded the audience of the peril which surrounded this self-emancipated young man at the North—even in Massachusetts, on the soil of the Pilgrim Fathers, among the descendants of revolutionary sires;[2] and I appealed to them, whether they would ever allow him to be carried back into slavery—law or no law, constitution or no constitution. The response was unanimous and in thunder-tones—"NO!" "Will you succor and protect him as a brother-man—a resident of the old Bay State?"[3] "YES!" shouted the whole mass, with an energy so startling, that the ruthless tyrants south of Mason and Dixon's line[4] might almost have heard the mighty burst of feeling, and recognized it as the pledge of an invincible determination, on the part of those who gave it, never to betray him that wanders, but to hide the outcast, and firmly to abide the consequences.

It was at once deeply impressed upon my mind, that, if Mr. Douglass could be persuaded to consecrate his time and talents to the promotion of the anti-slavery enterprise, a powerful impetus would be given to it, and a stunning blow at the same time inflicted on northern prejudice against a colored complexion. I therefore endeavored to instil hope and courage into his mind, in order that he might dare to engage in a vocation so anomalous and responsible for a person in his situation; and I was seconded in this effort by warm-hearted friends, especially by the late General Agent of the Massachusetts Anti-Slavery Society, Mr. John A. Collins,[5] whose judgment in this instance entirely coincided with

1 *Patrick Henry* American revolutionary orator (1736–99), famous for the speech in which he proclaimed: "Forbid it, Almighty God! I know not what course others may take; but as for me, give me liberty or give me death!"

2 *Pilgrim Fathers … revolutionary sires* "Pilgrim Fathers" refers to the English colonists who arrived in Plymouth, Massachusetts in 1620; *revolutionary sires* Ancestors who participated in the American Revolution.

3 *old Bay State* Massachusetts.

4 *Mason and Dixon's line* Drawn in the 1760s by English surveyors Charles Mason and Jeremiah Dixon, the Mason-Dixon line separated parts of Pennsylvania and Delaware from parts of Maryland and Virginia; it came to signify the border between the American North and South, and thereby the literal and symbolic border between the free states and the slave states.

5 *John A. Collins* White antislavery activist (1810–79).

my own. At first, he could give no encouragement; with unfeigned diffidence, he expressed his conviction that he was not adequate to the performance of so great a task; the path marked out was wholly an untrodden one; he was sincerely apprehensive that he should do more harm than good. After much deliberation, however, he consented to make a trial; and ever since that period, he has acted as a lecturing agent, under the auspices either of the American or the Massachusetts Anti-Slavery Society.[1] In labors he has been most abundant; and his success in combating prejudice, in gaining proselytes, in agitating the public mind, has far surpassed the most sanguine expectations that were raised at the commencement of his brilliant career. He has borne himself with gentleness and meekness, yet with true manliness of character. As a public speaker, he excels in pathos, wit, comparison, imitation, strength of reasoning, and fluency of language. There is in him that union of head and heart, which is indispensable to an enlightenment of the heads and a winning of the hearts of others. May his strength continue to be equal to his day! May he continue to "grow in grace, and in the knowledge of God,"[2] that he may be increasingly serviceable in the cause of bleeding humanity, whether at home or abroad!

It is certainly a very remarkable fact, that one of the most efficient advocates of the slave population, now before the public, is a fugitive slave, in the person of FREDERICK DOUGLASS; and that the free colored population of the United States are as ably represented by one of their own number, in the person of CHARLES LENOX REMOND,[3] whose eloquent appeals have extorted the highest applause of multitudes on both sides of the Atlantic. Let the calumniators[4] of the colored race despise themselves for their baseness and illiberality of spirit, and henceforth cease to talk of the natural inferiority of those who require nothing but time and opportunity to attain to the highest point of human excellence.

---

1 *American or … Society* The Massachusetts Anti-Slavery Society was an auxiliary of the American Anti-Slavery Society; both were associated with William Lloyd Garrison.

2 *grow in grace … of God* See 2 Peter 3:18: "But grow in grace, and in the knowledge of our Lord and Saviour Jesus Christ."

3 *CHARLES LENOX REMOND* Free-born African American abolitionist from Salem, Massachusetts (1810–73), a close friend of Douglass after whom Douglass named his youngest son.

4 *calumniators* Slanderers.

It may, perhaps, be fairly questioned, whether any other portion of the population of the earth could have endured the privations, sufferings and horrors of slavery, without having become more degraded in the scale of humanity than the slaves of African descent. Nothing has been left undone to cripple their intellects, darken their minds, debase their moral nature, obliterate all traces of their relationship to mankind; and yet how wonderfully they have sustained the mighty load of a most frightful bondage, under which they have been groaning for centuries! To illustrate the effect of slavery on the white man—to show that he has no powers of endurance, in such a condition, superior to those of his black brother—DANIEL O'CONNELL,[1] the distinguished advocate of universal emancipation, and the mightiest champion of prostrate but not conquered Ireland, relates the following anecdote in a speech delivered by him in the Conciliation Hall, Dublin, before the Loyal National Repeal Association,[2] March 31, 1845. "No matter," said Mr. O'CONNELL, "under what specious term it may disguise itself, slavery is still hideous. It has a natural, an inevitable tendency to brutalize every noble faculty of man. An American sailor, who was cast away on the shore of Africa, where he was kept in slavery for three years, was, at the expiration of that period, found to be imbruted and stultified—he had lost all reasoning power; and having forgotten his native language, could only utter some savage gibberish between Arabic and English, which nobody could understand, and which even he himself found difficulty in pronouncing. So much for the humanizing influence of THE DOMESTIC INSTITUTION!" Admitting this to have been an extraordinary case of mental deterioration, it proves at least that the white slave can sink as low in the scale of humanity as the black one.

Mr. DOUGLASS has very properly chosen to write his own Narrative, in his own style, and according to the best of his ability, rather than to employ someone else. It is, therefore, entirely his own production; and, considering how long and dark was the career he had to

1 *DANIEL O'CONNELL* Irish politician (1775–1847) who fought to obtain equal rights for Catholics (a goal that was partially achieved with the so-called "Catholic Emancipation" of 1829) and to obtain for Ireland a degree of independence from English rule.

2 *Repeal Association* Founded by O'Connell to call for repeal of the 1800 Acts of Union (which had abolished the Irish Parliament in order to bring Ireland under the direct control of Britain).

run as a slave—how few have been his opportunities to improve his mind since he broke his iron fetters—it is, in my judgment, highly creditable to his head and heart. He who can peruse it without a tearful eye, a heaving breast, an afflicted spirit—without being filled with an unutterable abhorrence of slavery and all its abettors, and animated with a determination to seek the immediate overthrow of that execrable system—without trembling for the fate of this country in the hands of a righteous God, who is ever on the side of the oppressed, and whose arm is not shortened that it cannot save—must have a flinty heart, and be qualified to act the part of a trafficker "in slaves and the souls of men."[1] I am confident that it is essentially true in all its statements; that nothing has been set down in malice, nothing exaggerated, nothing drawn from the imagination; that it comes short of the reality, rather than overstates a single fact in regard to SLAVERY AS IT IS.[2] The experience of FREDERICK DOUGLASS, as a slave, was not a peculiar one; his lot was not especially a hard one; his case may be regarded as a very fair specimen of the treatment of slaves in Maryland, in which State it is conceded that they are better fed and less cruelly treated than in Georgia, Alabama, or Louisiana. Many have suffered incomparably more, while very few on the plantations have suffered less, than himself. Yet how deplorable was his situation! what terrible chastisements were inflicted upon his person! what still more shocking outrages were perpetrated upon his mind! with all his noble powers and sublime aspirations, how like a brute was he treated, even by those professing to have the same mind in them that was in Christ Jesus! to what dreadful liabilities was he continually subjected! how destitute of friendly counsel and aid, even in his greatest extremities! how heavy was the midnight of woe which shrouded in blackness the last ray of hope, and filled the future with terror and gloom! what longings after freedom took possession of his breast, and how his misery augmented, in proportion as he grew reflective and intelligent—thus demonstrating that a happy slave is an extinct man! how he thought, reasoned, felt, under the lash of the driver, with the chains upon his limbs! what perils he encountered in his endeavors to escape from his horrible doom! and how signal

---

1 *in slaves ... souls of men* See Revelation 18.13.

2 *SLAVERY AS IT IS* Allusion to the influential antislavery book *American Slavery as It Is: Testimony of a Thousand Witnesses.*

have been his deliverance and preservation in the midst of a nation of pitiless enemies!

This Narrative contains many affecting incidents, many passages of great eloquence and power; but I think the most thrilling one of them all is the description Douglass gives of his feelings, as he stood soliloquizing respecting his fate, and the chances of his one day being a freeman, on the banks of the Chesapeake Bay—viewing the receding vessels as they flew with their white wings before the breeze, and apostrophizing[1] them as animated by the living spirit of freedom. Who can read that passage, and be insensible to its pathos and sublimity? Compressed into it is a whole Alexandrian library[2] of thought, feeling, and sentiment—all that can, all that need be urged, in the form of expostulation, entreaty, rebuke, against that crime of crimes—making man the property of his fellow-man! O, how accursed is that system, which entombs the godlike mind of man, defaces the divine image, reduces those who by creation were crowned with glory and honor to a level with four-footed beasts, and exalts the dealer in human flesh above all that is called God! Why should its existence be prolonged one hour? Is it not evil, only evil, and that continually? What does its presence imply but the absence of all fear of God, all regard for man, on the part of the people of the United States? Heaven speed its eternal overthrow!

So profoundly ignorant of the nature of slavery are many persons, that they are stubbornly incredulous whenever they read or listen to any recital of the cruelties which are daily inflicted on its victims. They do not deny that the slaves are held as property; but that terrible fact seems to convey to their minds no idea of injustice, exposure to outrage, or savage barbarity. Tell them of cruel scourgings, of mutilations and brandings, of scenes of pollution and blood, of the banishment of all light and knowledge, and they affect to be greatly indignant at such enormous exaggerations, such wholesale misstatements, such abominable libels on the character of the southern planters! As if all these direful outrages were not the natural results of slavery! As if it were less cruel to reduce a human being to the condition of a thing, than to give him a severe flagellation, or to deprive him of necessary

---

1 *apostrophizing* Addressing inanimate objects directly in a poetic fashion.
2 *Alexandrian library* Renowned ancient library located in Alexandria, Egypt.

food and clothing! As if whips, chains, thumb-screws, paddles, blood-hounds, overseers, drivers, patrols, were not all indispensable to keep the slaves down, and to give protection to their ruthless oppressors! As if, when the marriage institution is abolished, concubinage, adultery, and incest, must not necessarily abound; when all the rights of humanity are annihilated, any barrier remains to protect the victim from the fury of the spoiler; when absolute power is assumed over life and liberty, it will not be wielded with destructive sway! Skeptics of this character abound in society. In some few instances, their incredulity arises from a want of reflection; but, generally, it indicates a hatred of the light, a desire to shield slavery from the assaults of its foes, a contempt of the colored race, whether bond or free. Such will try to discredit the shocking tales of slaveholding cruelty which are recorded in this truthful Narrative; but they will labor in vain. Mr. DOUGLASS has frankly disclosed the place of his birth, the names of those who claimed ownership in his body and soul, and the names also of those who committed the crimes which he has alleged against them. His statements, therefore, may easily be disproved, if they are untrue.

In the course of his Narrative, he relates two instances of murderous cruelty—in one of which a planter deliberately shot a slave belonging to a neighboring plantation, who had unintentionally gotten within his lordly domain in quest of fish; and in the other, an overseer blew out the brains of a slave who had fled to a stream of water to escape a bloody scourging. Mr. DOUGLASS states that in neither of these instances was any thing done by way of legal arrest or judicial investigation. *The Baltimore American*, of March 17, 1845, relates a similar case of atrocity, perpetrated with similar impunity—as follows: "Shooting a slave.—We learn, upon the authority of a letter from Charles County, Maryland, received by a gentleman of this city, that a young man, named Matthews, a nephew of General Matthews, and whose father, it is believed, holds an office at Washington, killed one of the slaves upon his father's farm by shooting him. The letter states that young Matthews had been left in charge of the farm; that he gave an order to the servant, which was disobeyed, when he proceeded to the house, obtained a gun, and, returning, shot the servant. He immediately, the letter continues, fled to his father's residence, where he still remains unmolested." Let it never be forgotten, that no slaveholder or overseer can be convicted of any outrage perpetrated on the person of a slave, however diabolical it may be, on the testimony of colored witnesses, whether bond or free. By the slave code, they are adjudged to be as incompetent to testify against a white man, as though they were indeed a part of the brute creation. Hence, there is no legal protection in fact, whatever there may be in form, for the slave population; and any amount of cruelty may be inflicted on them with impunity. Is it possible for the human mind to conceive of a more horrible state of society?

The effect of a religious profession on the conduct of southern masters is vividly described in the following Narrative, and shown to be anything but salutary. In the nature of the case, it must be in the highest degree pernicious. The testimony of Mr. Douglass, on this point, is sustained by a cloud of witnesses, whose veracity is unimpeachable. "A slaveholder's profession of Christianity is a palpable imposture. He is a felon of the highest grade. He is a man-stealer. It is of no importance what you put in the other scale."

Reader! are you with the man-stealers in sympathy and purpose, or on the side of their down-trodden victims? If with the former, then are you the foe of God and man. If with the latter, what are you prepared to do and dare in their behalf? Be faithful, be vigilant, be untiring in your efforts to break every yoke, and let the oppressed go free. Come what may—cost what it may—inscribe on the banner which you unfurl to the breeze, as your religious and political motto—"NO COMPROMISE WITH SLAVERY! NO UNION WITH SLAVEHOLDERS!"

WM. LLOYD GARRISON.
BOSTON, May 1, 1845.

Letter from Wendell Phillips,[1] Esq

BOSTON, April 22, 1845

My Dear Friend

You remember the old fable of "The Man and the Lion,"[2] where the lion complained that he should not be so misrepresented "when the lions wrote history."

I am glad the time has come when the "lions write history." We have been left long enough to gather the character of slavery from the involuntary evidence of the masters. One might, indeed, rest sufficiently satisfied with what, it is evident, must be, in general, the results of such a relation, without seeking farther to find whether they have followed in every instance. Indeed, those who stare at the half-peck of corn a week, and love to count the lashes on the slave's back, are seldom the "stuff" out of which reformers and abolitionists are to be made. I remember that, in 1838, many were waiting for the results of the West India experiment,[3] before they could come into our ranks. Those "results" have come long ago; but, alas! few of that number have come with them, as converts. A man must be disposed to judge of emancipation by other tests than whether it has increased the produce of sugar—and to hate slavery for other reasons than because it starves men and whips women—before he is ready to lay the first stone of his anti-slavery life.

I was glad to learn, in your story, how early the most neglected of God's children waken to a sense of their rights, and of the injustice done them. Experience is a keen teacher; and long before you had mastered your A B C, or knew where the "white sails" of the Chesapeake were bound, you began, I see, to gauge the wretchedness of the

---

1 *Wendell Phillips* Massachusetts-based abolitionist and social activist (1811–84).

2 *The Man and the Lion* Allusion to one of Aesop's fables, in which a man gestures towards a sculpture of a male figure conquering a lion as evidence of human superiority; the lion counters that if lions could sculpt, they would be the ones depicted as victorious. Tradition has long held that the Greek storyteller Aesop was himself enslaved.

3 *West India experiment* Referring to the British West Indies Emancipation Act that formally abolished slavery in the British West Indies. It was enacted in 1833, and began to take effect a year later, but its provisions were for a phased abolition; until at least 1838 many previously enslaved people were still bound to their former enslavers as apprentices.

slave, not by his hunger and want, not by his lashes and toil, but by the cruel and blighting death which gathers over his soul.

In connection with this, there is one circumstance which makes your recollections peculiarly valuable, and renders your early insight the more remarkable. You come from that part of the country where we are told slavery appears with its fairest features. Let us hear, then, what it is at its best estate—gaze on its bright side, if it has one; and then imagination may task her powers to add dark lines to the picture, as she travels southward to that (for the colored man) Valley of the Shadow of Death,[1] where the Mississippi sweeps along.

Again, we have known you long, and can put the most entire confidence in your truth, candor, and sincerity. Everyone who has heard you speak has felt, and, I am confident, every one who reads your book will feel, persuaded that you give them a fair specimen of the whole truth. No one-sided portrait—no wholesale complaints—but strict justice done, whenever individual kindliness has neutralized, for a moment, the deadly system with which it was strangely allied. You have been with us, too, some years, and can fairly compare the twilight of rights, which your race enjoy at the North, with that "noon of night" under which they labor south of Mason and Dixon's line. Tell us whether, after all, the half-free colored man of Massachusetts is worse off than the pampered slave of the rice swamps!

In reading your life, no one can say that we have unfairly picked out some rare specimens of cruelty. We know that the bitter drops, which even you have drained from the cup, are no incidental aggravations, no individual ills, but such as must mingle always and necessarily in the lot of every slave. They are the essential ingredients, not the occasional results, of the system.

After all, I shall read your book with trembling for you. Some years ago, when you were beginning to tell me your real name and birthplace, you may remember I stopped you, and preferred to remain ignorant of all. With the exception of a vague description, so I continued, till the other day, when you read me your memoirs. I hardly knew, at the time, whether to thank you or not for the sight of them, when I reflected that it was still dangerous, in Massachusetts, for honest men to tell their names! They say the fathers, in 1776, signed

---

1 *Valley of the Shadow of Death* See Psalms 23.4.

the Declaration of Independence with the halter about their necks. You, too, publish your declaration of freedom with danger compassing you around. In all the broad lands which the Constitution of the United States overshadows, there is no single spot—however narrow or desolate—where a fugitive slave can plant himself and say, "I am safe." The whole armory of Northern Law has no shield for you. I am free to say that, in your place, I should throw the MS.[1] into the fire.

You, perhaps, may tell your story in safety, endeared as you are to so many warm hearts by rare gifts, and a still rarer devotion of them to the service of others. But it will be owing only to your labors, and the fearless efforts of those who, trampling the laws and Constitution of the country under their feet, are determined that they will "hide the outcast,"[2] and that their hearths shall be, spite of the law, an asylum for the oppressed, if, some time or other, the humblest may stand in our streets, and bear witness in safety against the cruelties of which he has been the victim.

Yet it is sad to think, that these very throbbing hearts which welcome your story, and form your best safeguard in telling it, are all beating contrary to the "statute in such case made and provided." Go on, my dear friend, till you, and those who, like you, have been saved, so as by fire, from the dark prison-house, shall stereotype these free, illegal pulses into statutes; and New England, cutting loose from a blood-stained Union, shall glory in being the house of refuge for the oppressed—till we no longer merely "hide the outcast," or make a merit of standing idly by while he is hunted in our midst; but, consecrating anew the soil of the Pilgrims as an asylum for the oppressed, proclaim our welcome to the slave so loudly, that the tones shall reach every hut in the Carolinas, and make the broken-hearted bondman leap up at the thought of old Massachusetts.

God speed the day!

Till then, and ever,
Yours truly,
WENDELL PHILLIPS

---

1 *MS* Manuscript.

2 *hide the outcast* See Isaiah 16.3.

Chapter 1

I was born in Tuckahoe, near Hillsborough, and about twelve miles from Easton, in Talbot county, Maryland. I have no accurate knowledge of my age, never having seen any authentic record containing it. By far the larger part of the slaves know as little of their ages as horses know of theirs, and it is the wish of most masters within my knowledge to keep their slaves thus ignorant. I do not remember to have ever met a slave who could tell of his birthday. They seldom come nearer to it than planting-time, harvest-time, cherry-time, spring-time, or fall-time. A want of information concerning my own was a source of unhappiness to me even during childhood. The white children could tell their ages. I could not tell why I ought to be deprived of the same privilege. I was not allowed to make any inquiries of my master concerning it. He deemed all such inquiries on the part of a slave improper and impertinent, and evidence of a restless spirit. The nearest estimate I can give makes me now between twenty-seven and twenty-eight years of age. I come to this, from hearing my master say, some time during 1835, I was about seventeen years old.[1]

My mother was named Harriet Bailey. She was the daughter of Isaac and Betsey Bailey, both colored, and quite dark. My mother was of a darker complexion than either my grandmother or grandfather.

My father was a white man. He was admitted to be such by all I ever heard speak of my parentage. The opinion was also whispered that my master was my father; but of the correctness of this opinion, I know nothing; the means of knowing was withheld from me. My mother and I were separated when I was but an infant—before I knew her as my mother. It is a common custom, in the part of Maryland from which I ran away, to part children from their mothers at a very early age. Frequently, before the child has reached its twelfth month, its mother is taken from it, and hired out on some farm a considerable distance off, and the child is placed under the care of an old woman, too old for field labor. For what this separation is done, I do not know, unless it be to hinder the development of the child's affection

---

1 *I have no accurate knowledge ... years old* Records made available after Douglass's death reveal that he was born in February 1818 (though the exact date remains unknown).

toward its mother, and to blunt and destroy the natural affection of the mother for the child. This is the inevitable result.

I never saw my mother, to know her as such, more than four or five times in my life; and each of these times was very short in duration, and at night. She was hired by a Mr. Stewart,[1] who lived about twelve miles from my home. She made her journeys to see me in the night, travelling the whole distance on foot, after the performance of her day's work. She was a field hand, and a whipping is the penalty of not being in the field at sunrise, unless a slave has special permission from his or her master to the contrary—a permission which they seldom get, and one that gives to him that gives it the proud name of being a kind master. I do not recollect of ever seeing my mother by the light of day. She was with me in the night. She would lie down with me, and get me to sleep, but long before I waked she was gone. Very little communication ever took place between us. Death soon ended what little we could have while she lived, and with it her hardships and suffering. She died when I was about seven years old, on one of my master's farms, near Lee's Mill. I was not allowed to be present during her illness, at her death, or burial. She was gone long before I knew any thing about it. Never having enjoyed, to any considerable extent, her soothing presence, her tender and watchful care, I received the tidings of her death with much the same emotions I should have probably felt at the death of a stranger.

Called thus suddenly away, she left me without the slightest intimation of who my father was. The whisper that my master was my father, may or may not be true; and, true or false, it is of but little consequence to my purpose whilst the fact remains, in all its glaring odiousness, that slaveholders have ordained, and by law established, that the children of slave women shall in all cases follow the condition of their mothers; and this is done too obviously to administer to their own lusts, and make a gratification of their wicked desires profitable as well as pleasurable; for by this cunning arrangement, the slaveholder, in cases not a few, sustains to his slaves the double relation of master and father.

---

1 *hired by a Mr. Stewart* I.e., her owner hired her out to a Mr. Stewart; the transaction would not have involved Douglass's mother being paid.

I know of such cases; and it is worthy of remark that such slaves invariably suffer greater hardships, and have more to contend with, than others. They are, in the first place, a constant offence to their mistress. She is ever disposed to find fault with them; they can seldom do anything to please her; she is never better pleased than when she sees them under the lash, especially when she suspects her husband of showing to his mulatto children favors which he withholds from his black slaves. The master is frequently compelled to sell this class of his slaves, out of deference to the feelings of his white wife; and, cruel as the deed may strike anyone to be, for a man to sell his own children to human flesh-mongers, it is often the dictate of humanity for him to do so; for, unless he does this, he must not only whip them himself, but must stand by and see one white son tie up his brother, of but few shades darker complexion than himself, and ply the gory lash to his naked back; and if he lisp one word of disapproval, it is set down to his parental partiality, and only makes a bad matter worse, both for himself and the slave whom he would protect and defend.

Every year brings with it multitudes of this class of slaves. It was doubtless in consequence of a knowledge of this fact, that one great statesman of the south predicted the downfall of slavery by the inevitable laws of population. Whether this prophecy is ever fulfilled or not, it is nevertheless plain that a very different-looking class of people are springing up at the south, and are now held in slavery, from those originally brought to this country from Africa; and if their increase do no other good, it will do away the force of the argument, that God cursed Ham, and therefore American slavery is right.[1] If the lineal descendants of Ham are alone to be scripturally enslaved, it is certain that slavery at the south must soon become unscriptural; for thousands are ushered into the world, annually, who, like myself, owe their existence to white fathers, and those fathers most frequently their own masters.

I have had two masters. My first master's name was Anthony. I do not remember his first name. He was generally called Captain Anthony—a title which, I presume, he acquired by sailing a craft on the Chesapeake Bay. He was not considered a rich slaveholder. He

1 *God cursed Ham ... is right* Some proslavery apologists claimed that a biblical justification for slavery could be found in Genesis 9.25, in which God curses Canaan, the son of Ham, declaring that "a servant of servants shall he be unto his brethren."

owned two or three farms, and about thirty slaves. His farms and slaves were under the care of an overseer. The overseer's name was Plummer. Mr. Plummer was a miserable drunkard, a profane swearer, and a savage monster. He always went armed with a cowskin[1] and a heavy cudgel. I have known him to cut and slash the women's heads so horribly, that even master would be enraged at his cruelty, and would threaten to whip him if he did not mind himself. Master, however, was not a humane slaveholder. It required extraordinary barbarity on the part of an overseer to affect him. He was a cruel man, hardened by a long life of slaveholding. He would at times seem to take great pleasure in whipping a slave. I have often been awakened at the dawn of day by the most heart-rending shrieks of an own aunt of mine, whom he used to tie up to a joist, and whip upon her naked back till she was literally covered with blood. No words, no tears, no prayers, from his gory victim, seemed to move his iron heart from its bloody purpose. The louder she screamed, the harder he whipped; and where the blood ran fastest, there he whipped longest. He would whip her to make her scream, and whip her to make her hush; and not until overcome by fatigue, would he cease to swing the blood-clotted cowskin. I remember the first time I ever witnessed this horrible exhibition. I was quite a child, but I well remember it. I never shall forget it whilst I remember anything. It was the first of a long series of such outrages, of which I was doomed to be a witness and a participant. It struck me with awful force. It was the blood-stained gate, the entrance to the hell of slavery, through which I was about to pass. It was a most terrible spectacle. I wish I could commit to paper the feelings with which I beheld it.

This occurrence took place very soon after I went to live with my old master, and under the following circumstances. Aunt Hester went out one night—where or for what I do not know—and happened to be absent when my master desired her presence. He had ordered her not to go out evenings, and warned her that she must never let him catch her in company with a young man, who was paying attention to her, belonging to Colonel Lloyd. The young man's name was Ned Roberts, generally called Lloyd's Ned. Why master was so careful of her, may be safely left to conjecture. She was a woman of noble form,

---

1 *cowskin* Whip made from cowhide.

and of graceful proportions, having very few equals, and fewer superiors, in personal appearance, among the colored or white women of our neighborhood.

Aunt Hester had not only disobeyed his orders in going out, but had been found in company with Lloyd's Ned; which circumstance, I found, from what he said while whipping her, was the chief offence. Had he been a man of pure morals himself, he might have been thought interested in protecting the innocence of my aunt; but those who knew him will not suspect him of any such virtue. Before he commenced whipping Aunt Hester, he took her into the kitchen, and stripped her from neck to waist, leaving her neck, shoulders, and back, entirely naked. He then told her to cross her hands, calling her at the same time a d——d b——h. After crossing her hands, he tied them with a strong rope, and led her to a stool under a large hook in the joist, put in for the purpose. He made her get upon the stool, and tied her hands to the hook. She now stood fair for his infernal purpose. Her arms were stretched up at their full length, so that she stood upon the ends of her toes. He then said to her, "Now, you d——d b——h, I'll learn[1] you how to disobey my orders!" and after rolling up his sleeves, he commenced to lay on the heavy cowskin, and soon the warm, red blood (amid heart-rending shrieks from her, and horrid oaths from him) came dripping to the floor. I was so terrified and horror-stricken at the sight, that I hid myself in a closet, and dared not venture out till long after the bloody transaction was over. I expected it would be my turn next. It was all new to me. I had never seen anything like it before. I had always lived with my grandmother on the outskirts of the plantation, where she was put to raise the children of the younger women. I had therefore been, until now, out of the way of the bloody scenes that often occurred on the plantation.

Chapter 2

My master's family consisted of two sons, Andrew and Richard; one daughter, Lucretia, and her husband, Captain Thomas Auld. They lived in one house, upon the home plantation of Colonel Edward Lloyd. My master was Colonel Lloyd's clerk and superintendent.

1 *learn* Teach.

He was what might be called the overseer of the overseers. I spent two years of childhood on this plantation in my old master's family. It was here that I witnessed the bloody transaction recorded in the first chapter; and as I received my first impressions of slavery on this plantation, I will give some description of it, and of slavery as it there existed. The plantation is about twelve miles north of Easton, in Talbot county, and is situated on the border of Miles River. The principal products raised upon it were tobacco, corn, and wheat. These were raised in great abundance; so that, with the products of this and the other farms belonging to him, he was able to keep in almost constant employment a large sloop,[1] in carrying them to market at Baltimore. This sloop was named Sally Lloyd, in honor of one of the colonel's daughters. My master's son-in-law, Captain Auld, was master of the vessel; she was otherwise manned by the colonel's own slaves. Their names were Peter, Isaac, Rich, and Jake. These were esteemed very highly by the other slaves, and looked upon as the privileged ones of the plantation; for it was no small affair, in the eyes of the slaves, to be allowed to see Baltimore.

Colonel Lloyd kept from three to four hundred slaves on his home plantation, and owned a large number more on the neighboring farms belonging to him. The names of the farms nearest to the home plantation were Wye Town and New Design. "Wye Town" was under the overseership of a man named Noah Willis. New Design was under the overseership of a Mr. Townsend. The overseers of these, and all the rest of the farms, numbering over twenty, received advice and direction from the managers of the home plantation. This was the great business place. It was the seat of government for the whole twenty farms. All disputes among the overseers were settled here. If a slave was convicted of any high misdemeanor, became unmanageable, or evinced a determination to run away, he was brought immediately here, severely whipped, put on board the sloop, carried to Baltimore, and sold to Austin Woolfolk, or some other slave-trader, as a warning to the slaves remaining.

Here, too, the slaves of all the other farms received their monthly allowance of food, and their yearly clothing. The men and women slaves received, as their monthly allowance of food, eight pounds of

1 *sloop* Small, single-masted sailing vessel.

pork, or its equivalent in fish, and one bushel of corn meal. Their yearly clothing consisted of two coarse linen shirts, one pair of linen trousers, like the shirts, one jacket, one pair of trousers for winter, made of coarse negro cloth,[1] one pair of stockings, and one pair of shoes; the whole of which could not have cost more than seven dollars. The allowance of the slave children was given to their mothers, or the old women having the care of them. The children unable to work in the field had neither shoes, stockings, jackets, nor trousers, given to them; their clothing consisted of two coarse linen shirts per year. When these failed them, they went naked until the next allowance-day. Children from seven to ten years old, of both sexes, almost naked, might be seen at all seasons of the year.

There were no beds given the slaves, unless one coarse blanket be considered such, and none but the men and women had these. This, however, is not considered a very great privation. They find less difficulty from the want of beds, than from the want of time to sleep; for when their day's work in the field is done, the most of them having their washing, mending, and cooking to do, and having few or none of the ordinary facilities for doing either of these, very many of their sleeping hours are consumed in preparing for the field the coming day; and when this is done, old and young, male and female, married and single, drop down side by side, on one common bed—the cold, damp floor—each covering himself or herself with their miserable blankets; and here they sleep till they are summoned to the field by the driver's horn. At the sound of this, all must rise, and be off to the field. There must be no halting; everyone must be at his or her post; and woe betides them who hear not this morning summons to the field; for if they are not awakened by the sense of hearing, they are by the sense of feeling: no age nor sex finds any favor. Mr. Severe, the overseer, used to stand by the door of the quarter, armed with a large hickory stick[2] and heavy cowskin, ready to whip anyone who was so unfortunate as not to hear, or, from any other cause, was prevented from being ready to start for the field at the sound of the horn.

Mr. Severe was rightly named: he was a cruel man. I have seen him whip a woman, causing the blood to run half an hour at the

---

1 *negro cloth* General term referring to the poor-quality fabric used to make clothing for enslaved people.

2 *hickory stick* Made from the tough wood of the hickory tree.

time; and this, too, in the midst of her crying children, pleading for their mother's release. He seemed to take pleasure in manifesting his fiendish barbarity. Added to his cruelty, he was a profane swearer. It was enough to chill the blood and stiffen the hair of an ordinary man to hear him talk. Scarce a sentence escaped him but that was commenced or concluded by some horrid oath. The field was the place to witness his cruelty and profanity. His presence made it both the field of blood and of blasphemy. From the rising till the going down of the sun, he was cursing, raving, cutting, and slashing among the slaves of the field, in the most frightful manner. His career was short. He died very soon after I went to Colonel Lloyd's; and he died as he lived, uttering, with his dying groans, bitter curses and horrid oaths. His death was regarded by the slaves as the result of a merciful providence.

Mr. Severe's place was filled by a Mr. Hopkins. He was a very different man. He was less cruel, less profane, and made less noise, than Mr. Severe. His course was characterized by no extraordinary demonstrations of cruelty. He whipped, but seemed to take no pleasure in it. He was called by the slaves a good overseer.

The home plantation of Colonel Lloyd wore the appearance of a country village. All the mechanical operations for all the farms were performed here. The shoemaking and mending, the blacksmithing, cartwrighting, coopering,[1] weaving, and grain-grinding, were all performed by the slaves on the home plantation. The whole place wore a business-like aspect very unlike the neighboring farms. The number of houses, too, conspired to give it advantage over the neighboring farms. It was called by the slaves the Great House Farm. Few privileges were esteemed higher, by the slaves of the out-farms, than that of being selected to do errands at the Great House Farm. It was associated in their minds with greatness. A representative could not be prouder of his election to a seat in the American Congress, than a slave on one of the out-farms would be of his election to do errands at the Great House Farm. They regarded it as evidence of great confidence reposed in them by their overseers; and it was on this account, as well as a constant desire to be out of the field from under the driver's lash, that they esteemed it a high privilege, one worth careful

---

1 *cartwrighting* Carpentry; *coopering* Making of wooden casks, barrels, and other vessels for storing goods.

living for. He was called the smartest and most trusty fellow, who had this honor conferred upon him the most frequently. The competitors for this office sought as diligently to please their overseers, as the office-seekers in the political parties seek to please and deceive the people. The same traits of character might be seen in Colonel Lloyd's slaves, as are seen in the slaves of the political parties.

The slaves selected to go to the Great House Farm, for the monthly allowance for themselves and their fellow-slaves, were peculiarly enthusiastic. While on their way, they would make the dense old woods, for miles around, reverberate with their wild songs, revealing at once the highest joy and the deepest sadness. They would compose and sing as they went along, consulting neither time nor tune. The thought that came up, came out—if not in the word, in the sound; and as frequently in the one as in the other. They would sometimes sing the most pathetic sentiment in the most rapturous tone, and the most rapturous sentiment in the most pathetic tone. Into all of their songs they would manage to weave something of the Great House Farm. Especially would they do this, when leaving home. They would then sing most exultingly the following words:

> "I am going away to the Great House Farm!
> O, yea! O, yea! O!"

This they would sing, as a chorus, to words which to many would seem unmeaning jargon, but which, nevertheless, were full of meaning to themselves. I have sometimes thought that the mere hearing of those songs would do more to impress some minds with the horrible character of slavery, than the reading of whole volumes of philosophy on the subject could do.

I did not, when a slave, understand the deep meaning of those rude and apparently incoherent songs. I was myself within the circle; so that I neither saw nor heard as those without might see and hear. They told a tale of woe which was then altogether beyond my feeble comprehension; they were tones loud, long, and deep; they breathed the prayer and complaint of souls boiling over with the bitterest anguish. Every tone was a testimony against slavery, and a prayer to God for deliverance from chains. The hearing of those wild notes always depressed my spirit, and filled me with ineffable sadness. I have frequently found myself in tears while hearing them. The mere recurrence to those songs, even now, afflicts me; and while I am writing these lines, an expression of feeling has already found its way down my cheek. To those songs I trace my first glimmering conception of the dehumanizing character of slavery. I can never get rid of that conception. Those songs still follow me, to deepen my hatred of slavery, and quicken my sympathies for my brethren in bonds. If any one wishes to be impressed with the soul-killing effects of slavery, let him go to Colonel Lloyd's plantation, and, on allowance-day, place himself in the deep pine woods, and there let him, in silence, analyze the sounds that shall pass through the chambers of his soul—and if he is not thus impressed, it will only be because "there is no flesh in his obdurate heart."[1]

I have often been utterly astonished, since I came to the north, to find persons who could speak of the singing, among slaves, as evidence of their contentment and happiness. It is impossible to conceive of a greater mistake. Slaves sing most when they are most unhappy. The songs of the slave represent the sorrows of his heart; and he is relieved by them, only as an aching heart is relieved by its tears. At least, such is my experience. I have often sung to drown my sorrow, but seldom to express my happiness. Crying for joy, and singing for joy, were alike uncommon to me while in the jaws of slavery. The singing of a man cast away upon a desolate island might be as appropriately considered as evidence of contentment and happiness, as the singing of a slave; the songs of the one and of the other are prompted by the same emotion.

---

1 *there is … obdurate heart* Douglass is quoting from an approximately 50-line passage dealing with slavery (sometimes printed as if it were a separate poem, and given the title "Slavery") that appears in Book 2 of English poet William Cowper's long poem *The Task* (1785). It reads in part as follows:

> My soul is sick, with every day's report
> Of wrong and outrage with which earth is filled.
> There is no flesh in man's obdurate heart …;
> He finds his fellow guilty of a skin
> Not colored like his own[.] …

In America as well as in Britain, editions of Cowper's poetic works remained very widely read well into the second half of the nineteenth century, often outselling poets such as Milton and Wordsworth; it is likely that many of Douglass's readers would have been familiar with this quotation.

CHAPTER 3

Colonel Lloyd kept a large and finely cultivated garden, which afforded almost constant employment for four men, besides the chief gardener, (Mr. M'Durmond). This garden was probably the greatest attraction of the place. During the summer months, people came from far and near—from Baltimore, Easton, and Annapolis—to see it. It abounded in fruits of almost every description, from the hardy apple of the north to the delicate orange of the south. This garden was not the least source of trouble on the plantation. Its excellent fruit was quite a temptation to the hungry swarms of boys, as well as the older slaves, belonging to the colonel, few of whom had the virtue or the vice to resist it. Scarcely a day passed, during the summer, but that some slave had to take the lash for stealing fruit. The colonel had to resort to all kinds of stratagems to keep his slaves out of the garden. The last and most successful one was that of tarring his fence all around; after which, if a slave was caught with any tar upon his person, it was deemed sufficient proof that he had either been into the garden, or had tried to get in. In either case, he was severely whipped by the chief gardener. This plan worked well; the slaves became as fearful of tar as of the lash. They seemed to realize the impossibility of touching tar without being defiled.

The colonel also kept a splendid riding equipage. His stable and carriage-house presented the appearance of some of our large city livery[1] establishments. His horses were of the finest form and noblest blood. His carriage-house contained three splendid coaches, three or four gigs, besides dearborns and barouches[2] of the most fashionable style.

This establishment was under the care of two slaves—old Barney and young Barney—father and son. To attend to this establishment was their sole work. But it was by no means an easy employment; for in nothing was Colonel Lloyd more particular than in the management of his horses. The slightest inattention to these was unpardonable, and was visited upon those, under whose care they were placed, with the severest punishment; no excuse could shield them, if the colonel only suspected any want of attention to his horses—a supposition which

---

1 *livery* Stable.

2 *gigs* Light two-wheeled, one-horse carriages; *dearborns* Light four-wheeled carriages; *barouches* Heavier, four-wheeled carriages, considered quite luxurious.

he frequently indulged, and one which, of course, made the office of old and young Barney a very trying one. They never knew when they were safe from punishment. They were frequently whipped when least deserving, and escaped whipping when most deserving it. Every thing depended upon the looks of the horses, and the state of Colonel Lloyd's own mind when his horses were brought to him for use. If a horse did not move fast enough, or hold his head high enough, it was owing to some fault of his keepers. It was painful to stand near the stable-door, and hear the various complaints against the keepers when a horse was taken out for use. "This horse has not had proper attention. He has not been sufficiently rubbed and curried, or he has not been properly fed; his food was too wet or too dry; he got it too soon or too late; he was too hot or too cold; he had too much hay, and not enough of grain; or he had too much grain, and not enough of hay; instead of old Barney's attending to the horse, he had very improperly left it to his son." To all these complaints, no matter how unjust, the slave must answer never a word. Colonel Lloyd could not brook any contradiction from a slave. When he spoke, a slave must stand, listen, and tremble; and such was literally the case. I have seen Colonel Lloyd make old Barney, a man between fifty and sixty years of age, uncover his bald head, kneel down upon the cold, damp ground, and receive upon his naked and toil-worn shoulders more than thirty lashes at the time. Colonel Lloyd had three sons—Edward, Murray, and Daniel—and three sons-in-law, Mr. Winder, Mr. Nicholson, and Mr. Lowndes. All of these lived at the Great House Farm, and enjoyed the luxury of whipping the servants when they pleased, from old Barney down to William Wilkes, the coach-driver. I have seen Winder make one of the house-servants stand off from him a suitable distance to be touched with the end of his whip, and at every stroke raise great ridges upon his back.

To describe the wealth of Colonel Lloyd would be almost equal to describing the riches of Job.[1] He kept from ten to fifteen house-servants. He was said to own a thousand slaves, and I think this estimate quite within the truth. Colonel Lloyd owned so many that he did not know them when he saw them; nor did all the slaves of the out-farms

1 *riches of Job* The biblical figure Job is best known for the brutal test of faith he is put under by God, but prior to these events he is described as wealthy and prosperous.

know him. It is reported of him, that, while riding along the road one day, he met a colored man, and addressed him in the usual manner of speaking to colored people on the public highways of the south: "Well, boy, whom do you belong to?" "To Colonel Lloyd," replied the slave. "Well, does the colonel treat you well?" "No, sir," was the ready reply. "What, does he work you too hard?" "Yes, sir." "Well, don't he give you enough to eat?" "Yes, sir, he gives me enough, such as it is."

The colonel, after ascertaining where the slave belonged, rode on; the man also went on about his business, not dreaming that he had been conversing with his master. He thought, said, and heard nothing more of the matter, until two or three weeks afterwards. The poor man was then informed by his overseer that, for having found fault with his master, he was now to be sold to a Georgia trader. He was immediately chained and handcuffed; and thus, without a moment's warning, he was snatched away, and forever sundered, from his family and friends, by a hand more unrelenting than death. This is the penalty of telling the truth, of telling the simple truth, in answer to a series of plain questions.

It is partly in consequence of such facts, that slaves, when inquired of as to their condition and the character of their masters, almost universally say they are contented, and that their masters are kind. The slaveholders have been known to send in spies among their slaves, to ascertain their views and feelings in regard to their condition. The frequency of this has had the effect to establish among the slaves the maxim, that a still tongue makes a wise head. They suppress the truth rather than take the consequences of telling it, and in so doing prove themselves a part of the human family. If they have anything to say of their masters, it is generally in their masters' favor, especially when speaking to an untried man. I have been frequently asked, when a slave, if I had a kind master, and do not remember ever to have given a negative answer; nor did I, in pursuing this course, consider myself as uttering what was absolutely false; for I always measured the kindness of my master by the standard of kindness set up among slaveholders around us. Moreover, slaves are like other people, and imbibe prejudices quite common to others. They think their own better than that of others. Many, under the influence of this prejudice, think their own masters are better than the masters of other slaves; and this, too, in some cases, when the very reverse is true. Indeed, it is not uncommon for slaves even to fall out and quarrel among themselves about the relative goodness of their masters, each contending for the superior goodness of his own over that of the others. At the very same time, they mutually execrate their masters when viewed separately. It was so on our plantation. When Colonel Lloyd's slaves met the slaves of Jacob Jepson, they seldom parted without a quarrel about their masters; Colonel Lloyd's slaves contending that he was the richest, and Mr. Jepson's slaves that he was the smartest, and most of a man. Colonel Lloyd's slaves would boast his ability to buy and sell Jacob Jepson. Mr. Jepson's slaves would boast his ability to whip Colonel Lloyd. These quarrels would almost always end in a fight between the parties, and those that whipped were supposed to have gained the point at issue. They seemed to think that the greatness of their masters was transferable to themselves. It was considered as being bad enough to be a slave; but to be a poor man's slave was deemed a disgrace indeed!

Chapter 4

Mr. Hopkins remained but a short time in the office of overseer. Why his career was so short, I do not know, but suppose he lacked the necessary severity to suit Colonel Lloyd. Mr. Hopkins was succeeded by Mr. Austin Gore, a man possessing, in an eminent degree, all those traits of character indispensable to what is called a first-rate overseer. Mr. Gore had served Colonel Lloyd, in the capacity of overseer, upon one of the out-farms, and had shown himself worthy of the high station of overseer upon the home or Great House Farm.

Mr. Gore was proud, ambitious, and persevering. He was artful, cruel, and obdurate. He was just the man for such a place, and it was just the place for such a man. It afforded scope for the full exercise of all his powers, and he seemed to be perfectly at home in it. He was one of those who could torture the slightest look, word, or gesture, on the part of the slave, into impudence, and would treat it accordingly. There must be no answering back to him; no explanation was allowed a slave, showing himself to have been wrongfully accused. Mr. Gore acted fully up to the maxim laid down by slaveholders, "It is better that a dozen slaves should suffer under the lash, than that the overseer should be convicted, in the presence of the slaves, of having been at fault." No matter how innocent a slave might be—it availed him nothing, when accused by Mr. Gore of any misdemeanor. To be accused was to be convicted, and to be convicted was to be punished; the one always following the other with immutable certainty. To escape punishment was to escape accusation; and few slaves had the fortune to do either, under the overseership of Mr. Gore. He was just proud enough to demand the most debasing homage of the slave, and quite servile enough to crouch, himself, at the feet of the master. He was ambitious enough to be contented with nothing short of the highest rank of overseers, and persevering enough to reach the height of his ambition. He was cruel enough to inflict the severest punishment, artful enough to descend to the lowest trickery, and obdurate enough to be insensible to the voice of a reproving conscience. He was, of all the overseers, the most dreaded by the slaves. His presence was painful; his eye flashed confusion; and seldom was his sharp, shrill voice heard, without producing horror and trembling in their ranks.

Mr. Gore was a grave man, and, though a young man, he indulged in no jokes, said no funny words, seldom smiled. His words were in perfect keeping with his looks, and his looks were in perfect keeping with his words. Overseers will sometimes indulge in a witty word, even with the slaves; not so with Mr. Gore. He spoke but to command, and commanded but to be obeyed; he dealt sparingly with his words, and bountifully with his whip, never using the former where the latter would answer as well. When he whipped, he seemed to do so from a sense of duty, and feared no consequences. He did nothing reluctantly, no matter how disagreeable; always at his post, never inconsistent. He never promised but to fulfil. He was, in a word, a man of the most inflexible firmness and stone-like coolness.

His savage barbarity was equalled only by the consummate coolness with which he committed the grossest and most savage deeds upon the slaves under his charge. Mr. Gore once undertook to whip one of Colonel Lloyd's slaves, by the name of Demby. He had given Demby but few stripes,[1] when, to get rid of the scourging, he ran and plunged himself into a creek, and stood there at the depth of his shoulders, refusing to come out. Mr. Gore told him that he would give him three calls, and that, if he did not come out at the third call, he would shoot him. The first call was given. Demby made no response, but stood his ground. The second and third calls were given with the same result.

---

1 *stripes* I.e., scars from having been whipped.

Mr. Gore then, without consultation or deliberation with anyone, not even giving Demby an additional call, raised his musket to his face, taking deadly aim at his standing victim, and in an instant poor Demby was no more. His mangled body sank out of sight, and blood and brains marked the water where he had stood.

A thrill of horror flashed through every soul upon the plantation, excepting Mr. Gore. He alone seemed cool and collected. He was asked by Colonel Lloyd and my old master, why he resorted to this extraordinary expedient. His reply was (as well as I can remember) that Demby had become unmanageable. He was setting a dangerous example to the other slaves—one which, if suffered to pass without some such demonstration on his part, would finally lead to the total subversion of all rule and order upon the plantation. He argued that if one slave refused to be corrected, and escaped with his life, the other slaves would soon copy the example; the result of which would be, the freedom of the slaves, and the enslavement of the whites. Mr. Gore's defence was satisfactory. He was continued in his station as overseer upon the home plantation. His fame as an overseer went abroad. His horrid crime was not even submitted to judicial investigation. It was committed in the presence of slaves, and they of course could neither institute a suit, nor testify against him; and thus the guilty perpetrator of one of the bloodiest and most foul murders goes unwhipped of justice, and uncensured by the community in which he lives. Mr. Gore lived in St. Michael's, Talbot county, Maryland, when I left there; and if he is still alive, he very probably lives there now; and if so, he is now, as he was then, as highly esteemed and as much respected as though his guilty soul had not been stained with his brother's blood.

I speak advisedly when I say this—that killing a slave, or any colored person, in Talbot county, Maryland, is not treated as a crime, either by the courts or the community. Mr. Thomas Lanman, of St. Michael's, killed two slaves, one of whom he killed with a hatchet, by knocking his brains out. He used to boast of the commission of the awful and bloody deed. I have heard him do so laughingly, saying, among other things, that he was the only benefactor of his country in the company, and that when others would do as much as he had done, we should be relieved of "the d——d niggers."[1]

---

1 *niggers* By the mid-nineteenth century, as the context here suggests, this word (today

The wife of Mr. Giles Hicks, living but a short distance from where I used to live, murdered my wife's cousin, a young girl between fifteen and sixteen years of age, mangling her person in the most horrible manner, breaking her nose and breastbone with a stick, so that the poor girl expired in a few hours afterward. She was immediately buried, but had not been in her untimely grave but a few hours before she was taken up and examined by the coroner, who decided that she had come to her death by severe beating. The offence for which this girl was thus murdered was this: She had been set that night to mind Mrs. Hicks's baby, and during the night she fell asleep, and the baby cried. She, having lost her rest for several nights previous, did not hear the crying. They were both in the room with Mrs. Hicks. Mrs. Hicks, finding the girl slow to move, jumped from her bed, seized an oak stick of wood by the fireplace, and with it broke the girl's nose and breastbone, and thus ended her life. I will not say that this most horrid murder produced no sensation in the community. It did produce sensation, but not enough to bring the murderess to punishment. There was a warrant issued for her arrest, but it was never served. Thus she escaped not only punishment, but even the pain of being arraigned before a court for her horrid crime.

Whilst I am detailing bloody deeds which took place during my stay on Colonel Lloyd's plantation, I will briefly narrate another, which occurred about the same time as the murder of Demby by Mr. Gore.

Colonel Lloyd's slaves were in the habit of spending a part of their nights and Sundays in fishing for oysters, and in this way made up the deficiency of their scanty allowance. An old man belonging to Colonel Lloyd, while thus engaged, happened to get beyond the limits of Colonel Lloyd's, and on the premises of Mr. Beal Bondly. At this trespass, Mr. Bondly took offence, and with his musket came down to the shore, and blew its deadly contents into the poor old man.

Mr. Bondly came over to see Colonel Lloyd the next day, whether to pay him for his property, or to justify himself in what he had done, I know not. At any rate, this whole fiendish transaction was soon hushed up. There was very little said about it at all, and nothing done. It was a common saying, even among little white boys, that it was worth a half-cent to kill a "nigger," and a half-cent to bury one.

---

universally acknowledged to be an utterly unacceptable expression of racism) had firmly established itself in white American vernacular as an emphatically pejorative alternative to the then-more neutral term "negro."

Chapter 5

As to my own treatment while I lived on Colonel Lloyd's plantation, it was very similar to that of the other slave children. I was not old enough to work in the field, and there being little else than field work to do, I had a great deal of leisure time. The most I had to do was to drive up the cows at evening, keep the fowls out of the garden, keep the front yard clean, and run of errands for my old master's daughter, Mrs. Lucretia Auld. The most of my leisure time I spent in helping Master Daniel Lloyd in finding his birds, after he had shot them. My connection with Master Daniel was of some advantage to me. He became quite attached to me, and was a sort of protector of me. He would not allow the older boys to impose upon me, and would divide his cakes with me.

I was seldom whipped by my old master, and suffered little from anything else than hunger and cold. I suffered much from hunger, but much more from cold. In hottest summer and coldest winter, I was kept almost naked—no shoes, no stockings, no jacket, no trousers, nothing on but a coarse tow linen[1] shirt, reaching only to my knees. I had no bed. I must have perished with cold, but that, the coldest nights, I used to steal a bag which was used for carrying corn to the mill. I would crawl into this bag, and there sleep on the cold, damp, clay floor, with my head in and feet out. My feet have been so cracked with the frost, that the pen with which I am writing might be laid in the gashes.

We were not regularly allowanced. Our food was coarse corn meal boiled. This was called mush. It was put into a large wooden tray or trough, and set down upon the ground. The children were then called, like so many pigs, and like so many pigs they would come and devour the mush; some with oyster-shells, others with pieces of shingle, some with naked hands, and none with spoons. He that ate fastest got most; he that was strongest secured the best place; and few left the trough satisfied.

I was probably between seven and eight years old when I left Colonel Lloyd's plantation. I left it with joy. I shall never forget the ecstasy

1 *tow linen* Material made from shorter, unworked strands of flax fibers, resulting in a coarser cloth than regular linen.

with which I received the intelligence that my old master (Anthony) had determined to let me go to Baltimore, to live with Mr. Hugh Auld, brother to my old master's son-in-law, Captain Thomas Auld. I received this information about three days before my departure. They were three of the happiest days I ever enjoyed. I spent the most part of all these three days in the creek, washing off the plantation scurf, and preparing myself for my departure.

The pride of appearance which this would indicate was not my own. I spent the time in washing, not so much because I wished to, but because Mrs. Lucretia had told me I must get all the dead skin off my feet and knees before I could go to Baltimore; for the people in Baltimore were very cleanly, and would laugh at me if I looked dirty. Besides, she was going to give me a pair of trousers, which I should not put on unless I got all the dirt off me. The thought of owning a pair of trousers was great indeed! It was almost a sufficient motive, not only to make me take off what would be called by pig-drovers the mange, but the skin itself. I went at it in good earnest, working for the first time with the hope of reward.

The ties that ordinarily bind children to their homes were all suspended in my case. I found no severe trial in my departure. My home was charmless; it was not home to me; on parting from it, I could not feel that I was leaving anything which I could have enjoyed by staying. My mother was dead, my grandmother lived far off, so that I seldom saw her. I had two sisters and one brother, that lived in the same house with me; but the early separation of us from our mother had well nigh blotted the fact of our relationship from our memories. I looked for home elsewhere, and was confident of finding none which I should relish less than the one which I was leaving. If, however, I found in my new home hardship, hunger, whipping, and nakedness, I had the consolation that I should not have escaped any one of them by staying. Having already had more than a taste of them in the house of my old master, and having endured them there, I very naturally inferred my ability to endure them elsewhere, and especially at Baltimore; for I had something of the feeling about Baltimore that is expressed in the proverb, that "being hanged in England is preferable to dying a natural death in Ireland." I had the strongest desire to see Baltimore. Cousin Tom, though not fluent in speech, had inspired me with that desire by his eloquent description of the place. I could never point out anything at the Great House, no matter how beautiful or powerful, but that he had seen something at Baltimore far exceeding, both in beauty and strength, the object which I pointed out to him. Even the Great House itself, with all its pictures, was far inferior to many buildings in Baltimore. So strong was my desire, that I thought a gratification of it would fully compensate for whatever loss of comforts I should sustain by the exchange. I left without a regret, and with the highest hopes of future happiness.

We sailed out of Miles River for Baltimore on a Saturday morning. I remember only the day of the week, for at that time I had no knowledge of the days of the month, nor the months of the year. On setting sail, I walked aft, and gave to Colonel Lloyd's plantation what I hoped would be the last look. I then placed myself in the bows of the sloop, and there spent the remainder of the day in looking ahead, interesting myself in what was in the distance rather than in things near by or behind.

In the afternoon of that day, we reached Annapolis, the capital of the State. We stopped but a few moments, so that I had no time to go on shore. It was the first large town that I had ever seen, and though it would look small compared with some of our New England factory villages, I thought it a wonderful place for its size—more imposing even than the Great House Farm!

We arrived at Baltimore early on Sunday morning, landing at Smith's Wharf, not far from Bowley's Wharf. We had on board the sloop a large flock of sheep; and after aiding in driving them to the slaughterhouse of Mr. Curtis on Louden Slater's Hill, I was conducted by Rich, one of the hands belonging on board of the sloop, to my new home in Alliciana Street, near Mr. Gardner's shipyard, on Fells Point.

Mr. and Mrs. Auld were both at home, and met me at the door with their little son Thomas, to take care of whom I had been given. And here I saw what I had never seen before; it was a white face beaming with the most kindly emotions; it was the face of my new mistress, Sophia Auld. I wish I could describe the rapture that flashed through my soul as I beheld it. It was a new and strange sight to me, brightening up my pathway with the light of happiness. Little Thomas was told, there was his Freddy—and I was told to take care of little Thomas; and thus I entered upon the duties of my new home with the most cheering prospect ahead.

I look upon my departure from Colonel Lloyd's plantation as one of the most interesting events of my life. It is possible, and even quite probable, that but for the mere circumstance of being removed from that plantation to Baltimore, I should have today, instead of being here seated by my own table, in the enjoyment of freedom and the happiness of home, writing this Narrative, been confined in the galling chains of slavery. Going to live at Baltimore laid the foundation, and opened the gateway, to all my subsequent prosperity. I have ever regarded it as the first plain manifestation of that kind providence which has ever since attended me, and marked my life with so many favors. I regarded the selection of myself as being somewhat remarkable. There were a number of slave children that might have been sent from the plantation to Baltimore. There were those younger, those older, and those of the same age. I was chosen from among them all, and was the first, last, and only choice.

I may be deemed superstitious, and even egotistical, in regarding this event as a special interposition of divine Providence in my favor. But I should be false to the earliest sentiments of my soul, if I suppressed the opinion. I prefer to be true to myself, even at the hazard of incurring the ridicule of others, rather than to be false, and incur my own abhorrence. From my earliest recollection, I date the entertainment of a deep conviction that slavery would not always be able to hold me within its foul embrace; and in the darkest hours of my career in slavery, this living word of faith and spirit of hope departed not from me, but remained like ministering angels to cheer me through the gloom. This good spirit was from God, and to him I offer thanksgiving and praise.

Chapter 6

My new mistress proved to be all she appeared when I first met her at the door—a woman of the kindest heart and finest feelings. She had never had a slave under her control previously to myself, and prior to her marriage she had been dependent upon her own industry for a living. She was by trade a weaver; and by constant application to her business, she had been in a good degree preserved from the blighting and dehumanizing effects of slavery. I was utterly astonished at her goodness. I scarcely knew how to behave towards her. She was entirely unlike any other white woman I had ever seen. I could not approach her as I was accustomed to approach other white ladies. My early instruction was all out of place. The crouching servility, usually so acceptable a quality in a slave, did not answer when manifested toward her. Her favor was not gained by it; she seemed to be disturbed by it. She did not deem it impudent or unmannerly for a slave to look her in the face. The meanest slave was put fully at ease in her presence, and none left without feeling better for having seen her. Her face was made of heavenly smiles, and her voice of tranquil music.

But, alas! this kind heart had but a short time to remain such. The fatal poison of irresponsible power was already in her hands, and soon commenced its infernal work. That cheerful eye, under the influence of slavery, soon became red with rage; that voice, made all of sweet accord, changed to one of harsh and horrid discord; and that angelic face gave place to that of a demon.

Very soon after I went to live with Mr. and Mrs. Auld, she very kindly commenced to teach me the A, B, C. After I had learned this, she assisted me in learning to spell words of three or four letters. Just at this point of my progress, Mr. Auld found out what was going on, and at once forbade Mrs. Auld to instruct me further, telling her, among other things, that it was unlawful, as well as unsafe, to teach a slave to read. To use his own words, further, he said, "If you give a nigger an inch, he will take an ell.[1] A nigger should know nothing but to obey his master—to do as he is told to do. Learning would spoil the best nigger in the world. Now," said he, "if you teach that nigger (speaking of myself) how to read, there would be no keeping him. It would forever unfit him to be a slave. He would at once become unmanageable, and of no value to his master. As to himself, it could do him no good, but a great deal of harm. It would make him discontented and unhappy." These words sank deep into my heart, stirred up sentiments within that lay slumbering, and called into existence an entirely new train of thought. It was a new and special revelation, explaining dark and mysterious things, with which my youthful understanding had struggled, but struggled in vain. I now understood what had been to me a most perplexing difficulty—to wit, the white man's power to enslave the black man. It was a grand

1 *an ell* Approximately 45 inches.

achievement, and I prized it highly. From that moment, I understood the pathway from slavery to freedom. It was just what I wanted, and I got it at a time when I the least expected it. Whilst I was saddened by the thought of losing the aid of my kind mistress, I was gladdened by the invaluable instruction which, by the merest accident, I had gained from my master. Though conscious of the difficulty of learning without a teacher, I set out with high hope, and a fixed purpose, at whatever cost of trouble, to learn how to read. The very decided manner with which he spoke, and strove to impress his wife with the evil consequences of giving me instruction, served to convince me that he was deeply sensible of the truths he was uttering. It gave me the best assurance that I might rely with the utmost confidence on the results which, he said, would flow from teaching me to read. What he most dreaded, that I most desired. What he most loved, that I most hated. That which to him was a great evil, to be carefully shunned, was to me a great good, to be diligently sought; and the argument which he so warmly urged, against my learning to read, only served to inspire me with a desire and determination to learn. In learning to read, I owe almost as much to the bitter opposition of my master, as to the kindly aid of my mistress. I acknowledge the benefit of both.

I had resided but a short time in Baltimore before I observed a marked difference, in the treatment of slaves, from that which I had witnessed in the country. A city slave is almost a freeman, compared with a slave on the plantation. He is much better fed and clothed, and enjoys privileges altogether unknown to the slave on the plantation. There is a vestige of decency, a sense of shame, that does much to curb and check those outbreaks of atrocious cruelty so commonly enacted upon the plantation. He is a desperate slaveholder, who will shock the humanity of his non-slaveholding neighbors with the cries of his lacerated slave. Few are willing to incur the odium attaching to the reputation of being a cruel master; and above all things, they would not be known as not giving a slave enough to eat. Every city slaveholder is anxious to have it known of him, that he feeds his slaves well; and it is due to them to say, that most of them do give their slaves enough to eat. There are, however, some painful exceptions to this rule. Directly opposite to us, on Philpot Street, lived Mr. Thomas Hamilton. He owned two slaves. Their names were Henrietta and Mary. Henrietta was about twenty-two years of age, Mary was about fourteen; and of all the mangled and emaciated creatures I ever looked upon, these two were the most so. His heart must be harder than stone, that could look upon these unmoved. The head, neck, and shoulders of Mary were literally cut to pieces. I have frequently felt her head, and found it nearly covered with festering sores, caused by the lash of her cruel mistress. I do not know that her master ever whipped her, but I have been an eye-witness to the cruelty of Mrs. Hamilton. I used to be in Mr. Hamilton's house nearly every day. Mrs. Hamilton used to sit in a large chair in the middle of the room, with a heavy cowskin always by her side, and scarce an hour passed during the day but was marked by the blood of one of these slaves. The girls seldom passed her without her saying, "Move faster, you black gip!" at the same time giving them a blow with the cowskin over the head or shoulders, often drawing the blood. She would then say, "Take that, you black gip!" continuing, "If you don't move faster, I'll move you!" Added to the cruel lashings to which these slaves were subjected, they were kept nearly half-starved. They seldom knew what it was to eat a full meal. I have seen Mary contending with the pigs for the offal thrown into the street. So much was Mary kicked and cut to pieces, that she was oftener called "pecked" than by her name.

Chapter 7

I lived in Master Hugh's family about seven years. During this time, I succeeded in learning to read and write. In accomplishing this, I was compelled to resort to various stratagems. I had no regular teacher. My mistress, who had kindly commenced to instruct me, had, in compliance with the advice and direction of her husband, not only ceased to instruct, but had set her face against my being instructed by anyone else. It is due, however, to my mistress to say of her, that she did not adopt this course of treatment immediately. She at first lacked the depravity indispensable to shutting me up in mental darkness. It was at least necessary for her to have some training in the exercise of irresponsible power, to make her equal to the task of treating me as though I were a brute.

My mistress was, as I have said, a kind and tender-hearted woman; and in the simplicity of her soul she commenced, when I first went to live with her, to treat me as she supposed one human being ought to treat another. In entering upon the duties of a slaveholder, she did not seem to perceive that I sustained to her the relation of a mere chattel, and that for her to treat me as a human being was not only wrong, but dangerously so. Slavery proved as injurious to her as it did to me. When I went there, she was a pious, warm, and tender-hearted woman. There was no sorrow or suffering for which she had not a tear. She had bread for the hungry, clothes for the naked, and comfort for every mourner that came within her reach. Slavery soon proved its ability to divest her of these heavenly qualities. Under its influence, the tender heart became stone, and the lamblike disposition gave way to one of tiger-like fierceness. The first step in her downward course was in her ceasing to instruct me. She now commenced to practise her husband's precepts. She finally became even more violent in her opposition than her husband himself. She was not satisfied with simply doing as well as he had commanded; she seemed anxious to do better. Nothing seemed to make her more angry than to see me with a newspaper. She seemed to think that here lay the danger. I have had her rush at me with a face made all up of fury, and snatch from me a newspaper, in a manner that fully revealed her apprehension. She was an apt woman; and a little experience soon demonstrated, to her satisfaction, that education and slavery were incompatible with each other.

From this time I was most narrowly[1] watched. If I was in a separate room any considerable length of time, I was sure to be suspected of having a book, and was at once called to give an account of myself. All this, however, was too late. The first step had been taken. Mistress, in teaching me the alphabet, had given me the inch, and no precaution could prevent me from taking the ell.

The plan which I adopted, and the one by which I was most successful, was that of making friends of all the little white boys whom I met in the street. As many of these as I could, I converted into teachers. With their kindly aid, obtained at different times and in different places, I finally succeeded in learning to read. When I was sent of errands, I always took my book with me, and by going one part of my errand quickly, I found time to get a lesson before my return. I used also to carry bread with me, enough of which was always in the house,

1 *narrowly* Closely.

and to which I was always welcome; for I was much better off in this regard than many of the poor white children in our neighborhood. This bread I used to bestow upon the hungry little urchins, who, in return, would give me that more valuable bread of knowledge. I am strongly tempted to give the names of two or three of those little boys, as a testimonial of the gratitude and affection I bear them; but prudence forbids;—not that it would injure me, but it might embarrass them; for it is almost an unpardonable offence to teach slaves to read in this Christian country. It is enough to say of the dear little fellows, that they lived on Philpot Street, very near Durgin and Bailey's ship-yard. I used to talk this matter of slavery over with them. I would sometimes say to them, I wished I could be as free as they would be when they got to be men. "You will be free as soon as you are twenty-one, but I am a slave for life! Have not I as good a right to be free as you have?" These words used to trouble them; they would express for me the liveliest sympathy, and console me with the hope that something would occur by which I might be free.

I was now about twelve years old, and the thought of being a slave for life began to bear heavily upon my heart. Just about this time, I got hold of a book entitled "The Columbian Orator."[1] Every opportunity I got, I used to read this book. Among much of other interesting matter, I found in it a dialogue between a master and his slave. The slave was represented as having run away from his master three times. The dialogue represented the conversation which took place between them, when the slave was retaken the third time. In this dialogue, the whole argument in behalf of slavery was brought forward by the master, all of which was disposed of by the slave. The slave was made to say some very smart as well as impressive things in reply to his master—things which had the desired though unexpected effect; for the conversation resulted in the voluntary emancipation of the slave on the part of the master.

1 *The Columbian Orator* Anthology of speeches and essays collected by New England educator Caleb Bingham (1757–1817), popular as a schoolbook.

In the same book, I met with one of Sheridan's[1] mighty speeches on and in behalf of Catholic emancipation. These were choice documents to me. I read them over and over again with unabated interest. They gave tongue to interesting thoughts of my own soul, which had frequently flashed through my mind, and died away for want of utterance. The moral which I gained from the dialogue was the power of truth over the conscience of even a slaveholder. What I got from Sheridan was a bold denunciation of slavery, and a powerful vindication of human rights. The reading of these documents enabled me to utter my thoughts, and to meet the arguments brought forward to sustain slavery; but while they relieved me of one difficulty, they brought on another even more painful than the one of which I was relieved. The more I read, the more I was led to abhor and detest my enslavers. I could regard them in no other light than a band of successful robbers, who had left their homes, and gone to Africa, and stolen us from our homes, and in a strange land reduced us to slavery. I loathed them as being the meanest as well as the most wicked of men. As I read and contemplated the subject, behold! that very discontentment which Master Hugh had predicted would follow my learning to read had already come, to torment and sting my soul to unutterable anguish. As I writhed under it, I would at times feel that learning to read had been a curse rather than a blessing. It had given me a view of my wretched condition, without the remedy. It opened my eyes to the horrible pit, but to no ladder upon which to get out. In moments of agony, I envied my fellow-slaves for their stupidity. I have often wished myself a beast. I preferred the condition of the meanest reptile to my own. Anything, no matter what, to get rid of thinking! It was this everlasting thinking of my condition that tormented me. There was no getting rid of it. It was pressed upon me by every object within sight or hearing, animate or inanimate. The silver trump of freedom had roused my soul to eternal wakefulness. Freedom now appeared,

---

1 *Sheridan* Douglass is misremembering here. Richard Brinsley Sheridan (1751–1816) was an Irish poet, playwright, and politician; a short parliamentary speech by Sheridan is included in the contents of the *Orator*, but it bears little resemblance to what Douglass describes here. The text to which he likely meant to refer is the speech for Catholic Emancipation given by United Irishman Arthur O'Connor in 1795, which directly follows the "Dialogue between a Master and Slave." (This speech is often further misidentified as having been given by Daniel O'Connell.)

to disappear no more forever. It was heard in every sound, and seen in every thing. It was ever present to torment me with a sense of my wretched condition. I saw nothing without seeing it, I heard nothing without hearing it, and felt nothing without feeling it. It looked from every star, it smiled in every calm, breathed in every wind, and moved in every storm.

I often found myself regretting my own existence, and wishing myself dead; and but for the hope of being free, I have no doubt but that I should have killed myself, or done something for which I should have been killed. While in this state of mind, I was eager to hear anyone speak of slavery. I was a ready listener. Every little while, I could hear something about the abolitionists. It was some time before I found what the word meant. It was always used in such connections as to make it an interesting word to me. If a slave ran away and succeeded in getting clear, or if a slave killed his master, set fire to a barn, or did anything very wrong in the mind of a slaveholder, it was spoken of as the fruit of abolition. Hearing the word in this connection very often, I set about learning what it meant. The dictionary afforded me little or no help. I found it was "the act of abolishing"; but then I did not know what was to be abolished. Here I was perplexed. I did not dare to ask anyone about its meaning, for I was satisfied that it was something they wanted me to know very little about. After a patient waiting, I got one of our city papers, containing an account of the number of petitions from the north, praying for the abolition of slavery in the District of Columbia, and of the slave trade between the States. From this time I understood the words abolition and abolitionist, and always drew near when that word was spoken, expecting to hear something of importance to myself and fellow-slaves. The light broke in upon me by degrees. I went one day down on the wharf of Mr. Waters; and seeing two Irishmen unloading a scow of stone, I went, unasked, and helped them. When we had finished, one of them came to me and asked me if I were a slave. I told him I was. He asked, "Are ye a slave for life?" I told him that I was. The good Irishman seemed to be deeply affected by the statement. He said to the other that it was a pity so fine a little fellow as myself should be a slave for life. He said it was a shame to hold me. They both advised me to run away to the north; that I should find friends there, and that I should be free. I pretended not to be interested in what they said, and treated them as if I did not understand them; for I feared they might be treacherous. White men have been known to encourage slaves to escape, and then, to get the reward, catch them and return them to their masters. I was afraid that these seemingly good men might use me so; but I nevertheless remembered their advice, and from that time I resolved to run away. I looked forward to a time at which it would be safe for me to escape. I was too young to think of doing so immediately; besides, I wished to learn how to write, as I might have occasion to write my own pass. I consoled myself with the hope that I should one day find a good chance. Meanwhile, I would learn to write.

The idea as to how I might learn to write was suggested to me by being in Durgin and Bailey's shipyard, and frequently seeing the ship carpenters, after hewing, and getting a piece of timber ready for use, write on the timber the name of that part of the ship for which it was intended. When a piece of timber was intended for the larboard[1] side, it would be marked thus—"L." When a piece was for the starboard side, it would be marked thus—"S." A piece for the larboard side forward, would be marked thus—"L. F." When a piece was for starboard side forward, it would be marked thus—"S. F." For larboard aft, it would be marked thus—"L. A." For starboard aft, it would be marked thus—"S. A." I soon learned the names of these letters, and for what they were intended when placed upon a piece of timber in the ship-yard. I immediately commenced copying them, and in a short time was able to make the four letters named. After that, when I met with any boy who I knew could write, I would tell him I could write as well as he. The next word would be, "I don't believe you. Let me see you try it." I would then make the letters which I had been so fortunate as to learn, and ask him to beat that. In this way I got a good many lessons in writing, which it is quite possible I should never have gotten in any other way. During this time, my copy-book was the board fence, brick wall, and pavement; my pen and ink was a lump of chalk. With these, I learned mainly how to write. I then commenced and continued copying

1 *larboard* Left (or "port") side of a ship; the right side is referred to as the "starboard."

the italics in Webster's Spelling Book,[1] until I could make them all without looking on the book. By this time, my little Master Thomas had gone to school, and learned how to write, and had written over a number of copy-books. These had been brought home, and shown to some of our near neighbors, and then laid aside. My mistress used to go to class meeting at the Wilk Street meetinghouse every Monday afternoon, and leave me to take care of the house. When left thus, I used to spend the time in writing in the spaces left in Master Thomas's copy-book, copying what he had written. I continued to do this until I could write a hand very similar to that of Master Thomas. Thus, after a long, tedious effort for years, I finally succeeded in learning how to write.

Chapter 8

In a very short time after I went to live at Baltimore, my old master's youngest son Richard died; and in about three years and six months after his death, my old master, Captain Anthony, died, leaving only his son, Andrew, and daughter, Lucretia, to share his estate. He died while on a visit to see his daughter at Hillsborough. Cut off thus unexpectedly, he left no will as to the disposal of his property. It was therefore necessary to have a valuation of the property, that it might be equally divided between Mrs. Lucretia and Master Andrew. I was immediately sent for, to be valued with the other property. Here again my feelings rose up in detestation of slavery. I had now a new conception of my degraded condition. Prior to this, I had become, if not insensible to my lot, at least partly so. I left Baltimore with a young heart overborne with sadness, and a soul full of apprehension. I took passage with Captain Rowe, in the schooner Wild Cat, and, after a sail of about twenty-four hours, I found myself near the place of my birth. I had now been absent from it almost, if not quite, five years. I, however, remembered the place very well. I was only about five years old when I left it, to go and live with my old master on Colonel Lloyd's plantation; so that I was now between ten and eleven years old.

---

1 *Webster's Spelling Book* Refers to *The American Spelling Book* by American educator Noah Webster (1758–1843); first published in 1783, the book was a steady bestseller into the second half of the nineteenth century.

We were all ranked together at the valuation. Men and women, old and young, married and single, were ranked with horses, sheep, and swine. There were horses and men, cattle and women, pigs and children, all holding the same rank in the scale of being, and were all subjected to the same narrow examination. Silvery-headed age and sprightly youth, maids and matrons, had to undergo the same indelicate inspection. At this moment, I saw more clearly than ever the brutalizing effects of slavery upon both slave and slaveholder.

After the valuation, then came the division. I have no language to express the high excitement and deep anxiety which were felt among us poor slaves during this time. Our fate for life was now to be decided. We had no more voice in that decision than the brutes among whom we were ranked. A single word from the white men was enough—against all our wishes, prayers, and entreaties—to sunder forever the dearest friends, dearest kindred, and strongest ties known to human beings. In addition to the pain of separation, there was the horrid dread of falling into the hands of Master Andrew. He was known to us all as being a most cruel wretch—a common drunkard, who had, by his reckless mismanagement and profligate dissipation, already wasted a large portion of his father's property. We all felt that we might as well be sold at once to the Georgia traders, as to pass into his hands; for we knew that that would be our inevitable condition—a condition held by us all in the utmost horror and dread.

I suffered more anxiety than most of my fellow-slaves. I had known what it was to be kindly treated; they had known nothing of the kind. They had seen little or nothing of the world. They were in very deed men and women of sorrow, and acquainted with grief. Their backs had been made familiar with the bloody lash, so that they had become callous; mine was yet tender; for while at Baltimore I got few whippings, and few slaves could boast of a kinder master and mistress than myself; and the thought of passing out of their hands into those of Master Andrew—a man who, but a few days before, to give me a sample of his bloody disposition, took my little brother by the throat, threw him on the ground, and with the heel of his boot stamped upon his head till the blood gushed from his nose and ears—was well calculated to make me anxious as to my fate. After he had committed this savage outrage upon my brother, he turned to me, and said that was the way he meant to serve me one of these days—meaning, I suppose, when I came into his possession.

Thanks to a kind Providence, I fell to the portion of Mrs. Lucretia, and was sent immediately back to Baltimore, to live again in the family of Master Hugh. Their joy at my return equalled their sorrow at my departure. It was a glad day to me. I had escaped a worse than lion's jaws. I was absent from Baltimore, for the purpose of valuation and division, just about one month, and it seemed to have been six.

Very soon after my return to Baltimore, my mistress, Lucretia, died, leaving her husband and one child, Amanda; and in a very short time after her death, Master Andrew died. Now all the property of my old master, slaves included, was in the hands of strangers—strangers who had had nothing to do with accumulating it. Not a slave was left free. All remained slaves, from the youngest to the oldest. If any one thing in my experience, more than another, served to deepen my conviction of the infernal character of slavery, and to fill me with unutterable loathing of slaveholders, it was their base ingratitude to my poor old grandmother. She had served my old master faithfully from youth to old age. She had been the source of all his wealth; she had peopled his plantation with slaves; she had become a great grandmother in his service. She had rocked him in infancy, attended him in childhood, served him through life, and at his death wiped from his icy brow the cold death-sweat, and closed his eyes forever. She was nevertheless left a slave—a slave for life—a slave in the hands of strangers; and in their hands she saw her children, her grandchildren, and her great-grandchildren, divided, like so many sheep, without being gratified with the small privilege of a single word, as to their or her own destiny. And, to cap the climax of their base ingratitude and fiendish barbarity, my grandmother, who was now very old, having outlived my old master and all his children, having seen the beginning and end of all of them, and her present owners finding she was of but little value, her frame already racked with the pains of old age, and complete helplessness fast stealing over her once active limbs, they took her to the woods, built her a little hut, put up a little mud-chimney, and then made her welcome to the privilege of supporting herself there in perfect loneliness; thus virtually turning her out to die! If my poor old grandmother now lives, she lives to suffer in utter loneliness; she lives to remember and mourn over the loss of children, the loss of grandchildren, and the loss of great-grandchildren. They are, in the language of the slave's poet, Whittier,[1]

Gone, gone, sold and gone
To the rice swamp dank and lone,
Where the slave-whip ceaseless swings,
Where the noisome insect stings,
Where the fever-demon strews
Poison with the falling dews,
Where the sickly sunbeams glare
Through the hot and misty air:—
  Gone, gone, sold and gone
  To the rice swamp dank and lone,
  From Virginia hills and waters—
  Woe is me, my stolen daughters!

The hearth is desolate. The children, the unconscious children, who once sang and danced in her presence, are gone. She gropes her way, in the darkness of age, for a drink of water. Instead of the voices of her children, she hears by day the moans of the dove, and by night the screams of the hideous owl. All is gloom. The grave is at the door. And now, when weighed down by the pains and aches of old age, when the head inclines to the feet, when the beginning and ending of human existence meet, and helpless infancy and painful old age combine together—at this time, this most needful time, the time for the exercise of that tenderness and affection which children only can exercise towards a declining parent—my poor old grandmother, the devoted mother of twelve children, is left all alone, in yonder little hut, before a few dim embers. She stands—she sits—she staggers—she falls—she groans—she dies—and there are none of her children or grandchildren present, to wipe from her wrinkled brow the cold sweat of death, or to place beneath the sod her fallen remains. Will not a righteous God visit for these things?[2]

---

1 *the slave's poet, Whittier* John Greenleaf Whittier (1807–92), white Quaker poet and abolitionist who was associated with William Lloyd Garrison. The quotation is from "The Farewell of a Virginia Slave Mother to Her Daughters Sold into Southern Bondage."

2 *Will not … these things?* See Jeremiah 5.29: "Shall I not visit for these things? saith the Lord: shall not my soul be avenged on such a nation as this?"

In about two years after the death of Mrs. Lucretia, Master Thomas married his second wife. Her name was Rowena Hamilton. She was the eldest daughter of Mr. William Hamilton. Master now lived in St. Michael's. Not long after his marriage, a misunderstanding took place between himself and Master Hugh; and as a means of punishing his brother, he took me from him to live with himself at St. Michael's. Here I underwent another most painful separation. It, however, was not so severe as the one I dreaded at the division of property; for, during this interval, a great change had taken place in Master Hugh and his once kind and affectionate wife. The influence of brandy upon him, and of slavery upon her, had effected a disastrous change in the characters of both; so that, as far as they were concerned, I thought I had little to lose by the change. But it was not to them that I was attached. It was to those little Baltimore boys that I felt the strongest attachment. I had received many good lessons from them, and was still receiving them, and the thought of leaving them was painful indeed. I was leaving, too, without the hope of ever being allowed to return. Master Thomas had said he would never let me return again. The barrier betwixt himself and brother he considered impassable.

I then had to regret that I did not at least make the attempt to carry out my resolution to run away; for the chances of success are tenfold greater from the city than from the country.

I sailed from Baltimore for St. Michael's in the sloop Amanda, Captain Edward Dodson. On my passage, I paid particular attention to the direction which the steamboats took to go to Philadelphia. I found, instead of going down, on reaching North Point they went up the bay, in a north-easterly direction. I deemed this knowledge of the utmost importance. My determination to run away was again revived. I resolved to wait only so long as the offering of a favorable opportunity. When that came, I was determined to be off.

Chapter 9

I have now reached a period of my life when I can give dates. I left Baltimore, and went to live with Master Thomas Auld, at St. Michael's, in March, 1832. It was now more than seven years since I lived with him in the family of my old master, on Colonel Lloyd's plantation. We of course were now almost entire strangers to each other. He was to me a new master, and I to him a new slave. I was ignorant of his temper and disposition; he was equally so of mine. A very short time, however, brought us into full acquaintance with each other. I was made acquainted with his wife not less than with himself. They were well matched, being equally mean[1] and cruel. I was now, for the first time during a space of more than seven years, made to feel the painful gnawings of hunger—a something which I had not experienced before since I left Colonel Lloyd's plantation. It went hard enough with me then, when I could look back to no period at which I had enjoyed a sufficiency. It was tenfold harder after living in Master Hugh's family, where I had always had enough to eat, and of that which was good. I have said Master Thomas was a mean man. He was so. Not to give a slave enough to eat, is regarded as the most aggravated development of meanness even among slaveholders. The rule is, no matter how coarse the food, only let there be enough of it. This is the theory; and in the part of Maryland from which I came, it is the general practice—though there are many exceptions. Master Thomas gave us enough of neither coarse nor fine food. There were four slaves of us in the kitchen—my sister Eliza, my aunt Priscilla, Henny, and myself; and we were allowed less than a half of a bushel of corn-meal per week, and very little else, either in the shape of meat or vegetables. It was not enough for us to subsist upon. We were therefore reduced to the wretched necessity of living at the expense of our neighbors. This we did by begging and stealing, whichever came handy in the time of need, the one being considered as legitimate as the other. A great many times have we poor creatures been nearly perishing with hunger, when food in abundance lay mouldering in the safe and smoke-house,[2] and our pious mistress was aware of the fact; and yet that mistress and her husband would kneel every morning, and pray that God would bless them in basket and store!

Bad as all slaveholders are, we seldom meet one destitute of every element of character commanding respect. My master was one of this rare sort. I do not know of one single noble act ever performed by him. The leading trait in his character was meanness; and if there were any other element in his nature, it was made subject to this. He was

---

1 *mean* Lowly and undignified; also, miserly.

2 *safe and smoke-house* Storage-places for meat.

mean; and, like most other mean men, he lacked the ability to conceal his meanness. Captain Auld was not born a slaveholder. He had been a poor man, master only of a Bay craft. He came into possession of all his slaves by marriage; and of all men, adopted slaveholders are the worst. He was cruel, but cowardly. He commanded without firmness. In the enforcement of his rules, he was at times rigid, and at times lax. At times, he spoke to his slaves with the firmness of Napoleon and the fury of a demon; at other times, he might well be mistaken for an inquirer who had lost his way. He did nothing of himself. He might have passed for a lion, but for his ears. In all things noble which he attempted, his own meanness shone most conspicuous. His airs, words, and actions, were the airs, words, and actions of born slaveholders, and, being assumed, were awkward enough. He was not even a good imitator. He possessed all the disposition to deceive, but wanted the power. Having no resources within himself, he was compelled to be the copyist of many, and being such, he was forever the victim of inconsistency; and of consequence he was an object of contempt, and was held as such even by his slaves. The luxury of having slaves of his own to wait upon him was something new and unprepared for. He was a slaveholder without the ability to hold slaves. He found himself incapable of managing his slaves either by force, fear, or fraud. We seldom called him "master"; we generally called him "Captain Auld," and were hardly disposed to title him at all. I doubt not that our conduct had much to do with making him appear awkward, and of consequence fretful. Our want of reverence for him must have perplexed him greatly. He wished to have us call him master, but lacked the firmness necessary to command us to do so. His wife used to insist upon our calling him so, but to no purpose. In August, 1832, my master attended a Methodist camp-meeting[1] held in the Bay-side, Talbot county, and there experienced religion. I indulged a faint hope that his conversion would lead him to emancipate his slaves, and that, if he did not do this, it would, at any rate, make him more kind and humane. I was disappointed in both these respects. It neither made him to be humane to his slaves, nor to emancipate them. If it had any effect on his character, it made him more cruel and hateful in all his ways; for I believe him to have

---

1 *camp-meeting* Outdoor meeting.

been a much worse man after his conversion than before. Prior to his conversion, he relied upon his own depravity to shield and sustain him in his savage barbarity; but after his conversion, he found religious sanction and support for his slaveholding cruelty. He made the greatest pretensions to piety. His house was the house of prayer. He prayed morning, noon, and night. He very soon distinguished himself among his brethren, and was soon made a class-leader and exhorter. His activity in revivals was great, and he proved himself an instrument in the hands of the church in converting many souls. His house was the preachers' home. They used to take great pleasure in coming there to put up; for while he starved us, he stuffed them. We have had three or four preachers there at a time. The names of those who used to come most frequently while I lived there, were Mr. Storks, Mr. Ewery, Mr. Humphry, and Mr. Hickey. I have also seen Mr. George Cookman[1] at our house. We slaves loved Mr. Cookman. We believed him to be a good man. We thought him instrumental in getting Mr. Samuel Harrison, a very rich slaveholder, to emancipate his slaves; and by some means got the impression that he was laboring to effect the emancipation of all the slaves. When he was at our house, we were sure to be called in to prayers. When the others were there, we were sometimes called in and sometimes not. Mr. Cookman took more notice of us than either of the other ministers. He could not come among us without betraying his sympathy for us, and, stupid as we were, we had the sagacity to see it.

While I lived with my master in St. Michael's, there was a white young man, a Mr. Wilson, who proposed to keep a Sabbath school for the instruction of such slaves as might be disposed to learn to read the New Testament. We met but three times, when Mr. West and Mr. Fairbanks, both class-leaders, with many others, came upon us with sticks and other missiles, drove us off, and forbade us to meet again. Thus ended our little Sabbath school in the pious town of St. Michael's.

I have said my master found religious sanction for his cruelty. As an example, I will state one of many facts going to prove the charge. I have seen him tie up a lame young woman, and whip her with a heavy

---

1 *Mr. George Cookman* Methodist minister (1800–41) who served as Chaplain to the Senate and promoted emancipation.

cowskin upon her naked shoulders, causing the warm red blood to drip; and, in justification of the bloody deed, he would quote this passage of Scripture—"He that knoweth his master's will, and doeth it not, shall be beaten with many stripes."[1]

Master would keep this lacerated young woman tied up in this horrid situation four or five hours at a time. I have known him to tie her up early in the morning, and whip her before breakfast; leave her, go to his store, return at dinner, and whip her again, cutting her in the places already made raw with his cruel lash. The secret of master's cruelty toward "Henny" is found in the fact of her being almost helpless. When quite a child, she fell into the fire, and burned herself horribly. Her hands were so burnt that she never got the use of them. She could do very little but bear heavy burdens. She was to master a bill of expense; and as he was a mean man, she was a constant offence to him. He seemed desirous of getting the poor girl out of existence. He gave her away once to his sister; but, being a poor gift, she was not disposed to keep her. Finally, my benevolent master, to use his own words, "set her adrift to take care of herself." Here was a recently-converted man, holding on upon the mother, and at the same time turning out her helpless child, to starve and die! Master Thomas was one of the many pious slaveholders who hold slaves for the very charitable purpose of taking care of them.

My master and myself had quite a number of differences. He found me unsuitable to his purpose. My city life, he said, had had a very pernicious effect upon me. It had almost ruined me for every good purpose, and fitted me for every thing which was bad. One of my greatest faults was that of letting his horse run away, and go down to his father-in-law's farm, which was about five miles from St. Michael's. I would then have to go after it. My reason for this kind of carelessness, or carefulness, was, that I could always get something to eat when I went there. Master William Hamilton, my master's father-in-law, always gave his slaves enough to eat. I never left there hungry, no matter how great the need of my speedy return. Master Thomas at length said he would stand it no longer. I had lived with him nine months, during which time he had given me a number of severe whippings, all to no good purpose. He resolved to put me out, as he said,

---

1 *He that knoweth ... many stripes* See Luke 12.47.

to be broken; and, for this purpose, he let me for one year to a man named Edward Covey. Mr. Covey was a poor man, a farm-renter. He rented the place upon which he lived, as also the hands with which he tilled it. Mr. Covey had acquired a very high reputation for breaking young slaves, and this reputation was of immense value to him. It enabled him to get his farm tilled with much less expense to himself than he could have had it done without such a reputation. Some slaveholders thought it not much loss to allow Mr. Covey to have their slaves one year, for the sake of the training to which they were subjected, without any other compensation. He could hire young help with great ease, in consequence of this reputation. Added to the natural good qualities of Mr. Covey, he was a professor of religion—a pious soul—a member and a class-leader in the Methodist church. All of this added weight to his reputation as a "nigger-breaker." I was aware of all the facts, having been made acquainted with them by a young man who had lived there. I nevertheless made the change gladly; for I was sure of getting enough to eat, which is not the smallest consideration to a hungry man.

Chapter 10

I had left Master Thomas's house, and went to live with Mr. Covey, on the 1st of January, 1833. I was now, for the first time in my life, a field hand. In my new employment, I found myself even more awkward than a country boy appeared to be in a large city. I had been at my new home but one week before Mr. Covey gave me a very severe whipping, cutting my back, causing the blood to run, and raising ridges on my flesh as large as my little finger. The details of this affair are as follows: Mr. Covey sent me, very early in the morning of one of our coldest days in the month of January, to the woods, to get a load of wood. He gave me a team of unbroken oxen. He told me which was the in-hand ox, and which the off-hand one.[1] He then tied the end of a large rope around the horns of the in-hand ox, and gave me the other end of it, and told me, if the oxen started to run, that I must hold on upon the rope. I had never driven oxen before, and of course I was very awkward. I, however, succeeded in getting to the edge of

---

1 *in-hand ox ... off-hand one* Oxen on the right- and left-hand sides of a pair, respectively.

the woods with little difficulty; but I had got a very few rods into the woods, when the oxen took fright, and started full tilt, carrying the cart against trees, and over stumps, in the most frightful manner. I expected every moment that my brains would be dashed out against the trees. After running thus for a considerable distance, they finally upset the cart, dashing it with great force against a tree, and threw themselves into a dense thicket. How I escaped death, I do not know. There I was, entirely alone, in a thick wood, in a place new to me. My cart was upset and shattered, my oxen were entangled among the young trees, and there was none to help me. After a long spell of effort, I succeeded in getting my cart righted, my oxen disentangled, and again yoked to the cart. I now proceeded with my team to the place where I had, the day before, been chopping wood, and loaded my cart pretty heavily, thinking in this way to tame my oxen. I then proceeded on my way home. I had now consumed one half of the day. I got out of the woods safely, and now felt out of danger. I stopped my oxen to open the woods gate; and just as I did so, before I could get hold of my ox-rope, the oxen again started, rushed through the gate, catching it between the wheel and the body of the cart, tearing it to pieces, and coming within a few inches of crushing me against the gate-post. Thus twice, in one short day, I escaped death by the merest chance. On my return, I told Mr. Covey what had happened, and how it happened. He ordered me to return to the woods again immediately. I did so, and he followed on after me. Just as I got into the woods, he came up and told me to stop my cart, and that he would teach me how to trifle away my time, and break gates. He then went to a large gum-tree, and with his axe cut three large switches, and, after trimming them up neatly with his pocketknife, he ordered me to take off my clothes. I made him no answer, but stood with my clothes on. He repeated his order. I still made him no answer, nor did I move to strip myself. Upon this he rushed at me with the fierceness of a tiger, tore off my clothes, and lashed me till he had worn out his switches, cutting me so savagely as to leave the marks visible for a long time after. This whipping was the first of a number just like it, and for similar offences.

I lived with Mr. Covey one year. During the first six months, of that year, scarce a week passed without his whipping me. I was seldom free from a sore back. My awkwardness was almost always his excuse for whipping me. We were worked fully up to the point of endurance.

Long before day we were up, our horses fed, and by the first approach of day we were off to the field with our hoes and ploughing teams. Mr. Covey gave us enough to eat, but scarce time to eat it. We were often less than five minutes taking our meals. We were often in the field from the first approach of day till its last lingering ray had left us; and at saving-fodder time, midnight often caught us in the field binding blades.[1]

Covey would be out with us. The way he used to stand it, was this. He would spend the most of his afternoons in bed. He would then come out fresh in the evening, ready to urge us on with his words, example, and frequently with the whip. Mr. Covey was one of the few slaveholders who could and did work with his hands. He was a hard-working man. He knew by himself just what a man or a boy could do. There was no deceiving him. His work went on in his absence almost as well as in his presence; and he had the faculty of making us feel that he was ever present with us. This he did by surprising us. He seldom approached the spot where we were at work openly, if he could do it secretly. He always aimed at taking us by surprise. Such was his cunning, that we used to call him, among ourselves, "the snake." When we were at work in the cornfield, he would sometimes crawl on his hands and knees to avoid detection, and all at once he would rise nearly in our midst, and scream out, "Ha, ha! Come, come! Dash on, dash on!" This being his mode of attack, it was never safe to stop a single minute. His comings were like a thief in the night. He appeared to us as being ever at hand. He was under every tree, behind every stump, in every bush, and at every window, on the plantation. He would sometimes mount his horse, as if bound to St. Michael's, a distance of seven miles, and in half an hour afterwards you would see him coiled up in the corner of the wood-fence, watching every motion of the slaves. He would, for this purpose, leave his horse tied up in the woods. Again, he would sometimes walk up to us, and give us orders as though he was upon the point of starting on a long journey, turn his back upon us, and make as though he was going to the house to get ready; and, before he would get half way thither, he would turn short and crawl into a fence-corner, or behind some tree, and there watch us till the going down of the sun.

1 *saving-fodder time* Harvest time; *binding blades* Binding wheat sheaves.

Mr. Covey's *forte*[1] consisted in his power to deceive. His life was devoted to planning and perpetrating the grossest deceptions. Every thing he possessed in the shape of learning or religion, he made conform to his disposition to deceive. He seemed to think himself equal to deceiving the Almighty. He would make a short prayer in the morning, and a long prayer at night; and, strange as it may seem, few men would at times appear more devotional than he. The exercises of his family devotions were always commenced with singing; and, as he was a very poor singer himself, the duty of raising the hymn generally came upon me. He would read his hymn, and nod at me to commence. I would at times do so; at others, I would not. My non-compliance would almost always produce much confusion. To show himself independent of me, he would start and stagger through with his hymn in the most discordant manner. In this state of mind, he prayed with more than ordinary spirit. Poor man! such was his disposition, and success at deceiving, I do verily believe that he sometimes deceived himself into the solemn belief, that he was a sincere worshipper of the most high God; and this, too, at a time when he may be said to have been guilty of compelling his woman slave to commit the sin of adultery. The facts in the case are these: Mr. Covey was a poor man; he was just commencing in life; he was only able to buy one slave; and, shocking as is the fact, he bought her, as he said, for a breeder. This woman was named Caroline. Mr. Covey bought her from Mr. Thomas Lowe, about six miles from St. Michael's. She was a large, able-bodied woman, about twenty years old. She had already given birth to one child, which proved her to be just what he wanted. After buying her, he hired a married man of Mr. Samuel Harrison, to live with him one year; and him he used to fasten up with her every night! The result was, that, at the end of the year, the miserable woman gave birth to twins. At this result Mr. Covey seemed to be highly pleased, both with the man and the wretched woman. Such was his joy, and that of his wife, that nothing they could do for Caroline during her confinement was too good, or too hard, to be done. The children were regarded as being quite an addition to his wealth.

If at any one time of my life more than another, I was made to drink the bitterest dregs of slavery, that time was during the first six

1 *forte* Italian: strength; particular ability.

months of my stay with Mr. Covey. We were worked in all weathers. It was never too hot or too cold; it could never rain, blow, hail, or snow, too hard for us to work in the field. Work, work, work, was scarcely more the order of the day than of the night. The longest days were too short for him, and the shortest nights too long for him. I was somewhat unmanageable when I first went there, but a few months of this discipline tamed me. Mr. Covey succeeded in breaking me. I was broken in body, soul, and spirit. My natural elasticity was crushed, my intellect languished, the disposition to read departed, the cheerful spark that lingered about my eye died; the dark night of slavery closed in upon me; and behold a man transformed into a brute!

Sunday was my only leisure time. I spent this in a sort of beast-like stupor, between sleep and wake, under some large tree. At times I would rise up, a flash of energetic freedom would dart through my soul, accompanied with a faint beam of hope, that flickered for a moment, and then vanished. I sank down again, mourning over my wretched condition. I was sometimes prompted to take my life, and that of Covey, but was prevented by a combination of hope and fear. My sufferings on this plantation seem now like a dream rather than a stern reality.

Our house stood within a few rods of the Chesapeake Bay, whose broad bosom was ever white with sails from every quarter of the habitable globe. Those beautiful vessels, robed in purest white, so delightful to the eye of freemen, were to me so many shrouded ghosts, to terrify and torment me with thoughts of my wretched condition. I have often, in the deep stillness of a summer's Sabbath, stood all alone upon the lofty banks of that noble bay, and traced, with saddened heart and tearful eye, the countless number of sails moving off to the mighty ocean. The sight of these always affected me powerfully. My thoughts would compel utterance; and there, with no audience but the Almighty, I would pour out my soul's complaint, in my rude way, with an apostrophe[1] to the moving multitude of ships:

"You are loosed from your moorings, and are free; I am fast in my chains, and am a slave! You move merrily before the gentle gale, and I sadly before the bloody whip! You are freedom's swift-winged angels,

---

1 *apostrophe* Exclamatory speech made either to one or more people who are unable to respond (whether because they are not present or because they are not alive) or to one or more inanimate objects.

that fly round the world; I am confined in bands of iron! O that I were free! O, that I were on one of your gallant decks, and under your protecting wing! Alas! betwixt me and you, the turbid waters roll. Go on, go on. O that I could also go! Could I but swim! If I could fly! O, why was I born a man, of whom to make a brute! The glad ship is gone; she hides in the dim distance. I am left in the hottest hell of unending slavery. O God, save me! God, deliver me! Let me be free! Is there any God? Why am I a slave? I will run away. I will not stand it. Get caught, or get clear, I'll try it. I had as well die with ague as the fever.[1] I have only one life to lose. I had as well be killed running as die standing. Only think of it; one hundred miles straight north, and I am free! Try it? Yes! God helping me, I will. It cannot be that I shall live and die a slave. I will take to the water. This very bay shall yet bear me into freedom. The steamboats steered in a north-east course from North Point. I will do the same; and when I get to the head of the bay, I will turn my canoe adrift, and walk straight through Delaware into Pennsylvania. When I get there, I shall not be required to have a pass; I can travel without being disturbed. Let but the first opportunity offer, and, come what will, I am off. Meanwhile, I will try to bear up under the yoke. I am not the only slave in the world. Why should I fret? I can bear as much as any of them. Besides, I am but a boy, and all boys are bound to someone. It may be that my misery in slavery will only increase my happiness when I get free. There is a better day coming."

Thus I used to think, and thus I used to speak to myself; goaded almost to madness at one moment, and at the next reconciling myself to my wretched lot.

I have already intimated that my condition was much worse, during the first six months of my stay at Mr. Covey's, than in the last six. The circumstances leading to the change in Mr. Covey's course toward me form an epoch in my humble history. You have seen how a man was made a slave; you shall see how a slave was made a man. On one of the hottest days of the month of August, 1833, Bill Smith, William Hughes, a slave named Eli, and myself, were engaged in fanning wheat.[2] Hughes was clearing the fanned wheat from before the fan.

---

1 *ague ... fever* The point here is that there is little difference between the two; "ague" was a term given to a range of infectious maladies for which a high fever was a key symptom.

2 *fanning wheat* Separating chaff from the wheat by means of a large fanning mill.

Eli was turning, Smith was feeding, and I was carrying wheat to the fan. The work was simple, requiring strength rather than intellect; yet, to one entirely unused to such work, it came very hard. About three o'clock of that day, I broke down; my strength failed me; I was seized with a violent aching of the head, attended with extreme dizziness; I trembled in every limb. Finding what was coming, I nerved myself up, feeling it would never do to stop work. I stood as long as I could stagger to the hopper with grain. When I could stand no longer, I fell, and felt as if held down by an immense weight. The fan of course stopped; every one had his own work to do; and no one could do the work of the other, and have his own go on at the same time.

Mr. Covey was at the house, about one hundred yards from the treading-yard where we were fanning. On hearing the fan stop, he left immediately, and came to the spot where we were. He hastily inquired what the matter was. Bill answered that I was sick, and there was no one to bring wheat to the fan. I had by this time crawled away under the side of the post and rail-fence by which the yard was enclosed, hoping to find relief by getting out of the sun. He then asked where I was. He was told by one of the hands. He came to the spot, and, after looking at me awhile, asked me what was the matter. I told him as well as I could, for I scarce had strength to speak. He then gave me a savage kick in the side, and told me to get up. I tried to do so, but fell back in the attempt. He gave me another kick, and again told me to rise. I again tried, and succeeded in gaining my feet; but, stooping to get the tub with which I was feeding the fan, I again staggered and fell. While down in this situation, Mr. Covey took up the hickory slat with which Hughes had been striking off the half-bushel measure, and with it gave me a heavy blow upon the head, making a large wound, and the blood ran freely; and with this again told me to get up. I made no effort to comply, having now made up my mind to let him do his worst. In a short time after receiving this blow, my head grew better. Mr. Covey had now left me to my fate. At this moment I resolved, for the first time, to go to my master, enter a complaint, and ask his protection. In order to [do] this, I must that afternoon walk seven miles; and this, under the circumstances, was truly a severe undertaking. I was exceedingly feeble; made so as much by the kicks and blows which I received, as by the severe fit of sickness to which I had been subjected. I, however, watched my chance, while Covey was looking in an opposite direction, and started for St. Michael's. I succeeded in getting a considerable distance on my way to the woods, when Covey discovered me, and called after me to come back, threatening what he would do if I did not come. I disregarded both his calls and his threats, and made my way to the woods as fast as my feeble state would allow; and thinking I might be overhauled by him if I kept the road, I walked through the woods, keeping far enough from the road to avoid detection, and near enough to prevent losing my way. I had not gone far before my little strength again failed me. I could go no farther. I fell down, and lay for a considerable time. The blood was yet oozing from the wound on my head. For a time I thought I should bleed to death; and think now that I should have done so, but that the blood so matted my hair as to stop the wound. After lying there about three quarters of an hour, I nerved myself up again, and started on my way, through bogs and briers, barefooted and bareheaded, tearing my feet sometimes at nearly every step; and after a journey of about seven miles, occupying some five hours to perform it, I arrived at master's store. I then presented an appearance enough to affect any but a heart of iron. From the crown of my head to my feet, I was covered with blood. My hair was all clotted with dust and blood; my shirt was stiff with blood. I suppose I looked like a man who had escaped a den of wild beasts, and barely escaped them. In this state I appeared before my master, humbly entreating him to interpose his authority for my protection. I told him all the circumstances as well as I could, and it seemed, as I spoke, at times to affect him. He would then walk the floor, and seek to justify Covey by saying he expected I deserved it. He asked me what I wanted. I told him, to let me get a new home; that as sure as I lived with Mr. Covey again, I should live with but to die with him; that Covey would surely kill me; he was in a fair way for it. Master Thomas ridiculed the idea that there was any danger of Mr. Covey's killing me, and said that he knew Mr. Covey; that he was a good man, and that he could not think of taking me from him; that, should he do so, he would lose the whole year's wages; that I belonged to Mr. Covey for one year, and that I must go back to him, come what might; and that I must not trouble him with any more stories, or that he would himself get hold of me. After threatening me thus, he gave me a very large dose of salts,[1] telling me that I might remain in St. Michael's that night (it being quite late), but that I must be off back to Mr. Covey's early in the morning; and that if I did not, he would get hold of me, which meant that he would whip me. I remained all night, and, according to his orders, I started off to Covey's in the morning (Saturday morning), wearied in body and broken in spirit. I got no supper that night, or breakfast that morning. I reached Covey's about nine o'clock; and just as I was getting over the fence that divided Mrs. Kemp's fields from ours, out ran Covey with his cowskin, to give me another whipping. Before he could reach me, I succeeded in getting to the cornfield; and as the corn was very high, it afforded me the means of hiding. He seemed very angry, and searched for me a long time. My behavior was altogether unaccountable. He finally gave up the chase, thinking, I suppose, that I must come home for something to eat; he would give himself no further trouble in looking for me. I spent that day mostly in the woods, having the alternative before me—to go home and be whipped to death, or stay in the woods and be starved to death. That night, I fell in with Sandy Jenkins, a slave with whom I was somewhat acquainted. Sandy had a free wife[2] who lived about four miles from Mr. Covey's; and it being Saturday, he was on his way to see her. I told him my circumstances, and he very kindly invited me to go home with him. I went home with him, and talked this whole matter over, and got his advice as to what course it was best for me to pursue. I found Sandy an old adviser. He told me, with great solemnity, I must go back to Covey; but that before I went, I must go with him into another part of the woods, where there was a certain root, which, if I would take some of it with me, carrying it always on my right side, would render it impossible for Mr. Covey, or any other white man, to whip me. He said he had carried it for years; and since he had done so, he had never received a blow, and never expected to while he carried it. I at first rejected the idea, that the simple carrying of a root in my pocket would have any such effect as he had said, and was not disposed to take it; but Sandy impressed the necessity with

1 *large dose of salts* I.e., smelling salts, comprising a mixture of carbonate of ammonia and other scented components, used to restore people from spells of fainting or dizziness.

2 *a free wife* Because slavery often resulted in spouses being sold to different enslavers, it sometimes occurred that one would be granted their freedom while the other remained enslaved.

much earnestness, telling me it could do no harm, if it did no good. To please him, I at length took the root, and, according to his direction, carried it upon my right side. This was Sunday morning. I immediately started for home; and upon entering the yard gate, out came Mr. Covey on his way to meeting. He spoke to me very kindly, bade me drive the pigs from a lot near by, and passed on towards the church. Now, this singular conduct of Mr. Covey really made me begin to think that there was something in the root which Sandy had given me; and had it been on any other day than Sunday, I could have attributed the conduct to no other cause than the influence of that root; and as it was, I was half inclined to think the root to be something more than I at first had taken it to be. All went well till Monday morning. On this morning, the virtue of the root was fully tested. Long before daylight, I was called to go and rub, curry,[1] and feed, the horses. I obeyed, and was glad to obey. But whilst thus engaged, whilst in the act of throwing down some blades from the loft, Mr. Covey entered the stable with a long rope; and just as I was half out of the loft, he caught hold of my legs, and was about tying me. As soon as I found what he was up to, I gave a sudden spring, and as I did so, he holding to my legs, I was brought sprawling on the stable floor. Mr. Covey seemed now to think he had me, and could do what he pleased; but at this moment—from whence came the spirit I don't know—I resolved to fight; and, suiting my action to the resolution, I seized Covey hard by the throat; and as I did so, I rose. He held on to me, and I to him. My resistance was so entirely unexpected that Covey seemed taken all aback. He trembled like a leaf. This gave me assurance, and I held him uneasy, causing the blood to run where I touched him with the ends of my fingers. Mr. Covey soon called out to Hughes for help. Hughes came, and, while Covey held me, attempted to tie my right hand. While he was in the act of doing so, I watched my chance, and gave him a heavy kick close under the ribs. This kick fairly sickened Hughes, so that he left me in the hands of Mr. Covey. This kick had the effect of not only weakening Hughes, but Covey also. When he saw Hughes bending over with pain, his courage quailed. He asked me if I meant to persist in my resistance. I told him I did, come what might; that he had used me like a brute for

---

1 *curry* Brush.

six months, and that I was determined to be used so no longer. With that, he strove to drag me to a stick that was lying just out of the stable door. He meant to knock me down. But just as he was leaning over to get the stick, I seized him with both hands by his collar, and brought him by a sudden snatch to the ground. By this time, Bill came. Covey called upon him for assistance. Bill wanted to know what he could do. Covey said, "Take hold of him, take hold of him!" Bill said his master hired him out to work, and not to help to whip me; so he left Covey and myself to fight our own battle out. We were at it for nearly two hours. Covey at length let me go, puffing and blowing at a great rate, saying that if I had not resisted, he would not have whipped me half so much. The truth was, that he had not whipped me at all. I considered him as getting entirely the worst end of the bargain; for he had drawn no blood from me, but I had from him. The whole six months afterwards, that I spent with Mr. Covey, he never laid the weight of his finger upon me in anger. He would occasionally say, he didn't want to get hold of me again. "No," thought I, "you need not; for you will come off worse than you did before."

This battle with Mr. Covey was the turning-point in my career as a slave. It rekindled the few expiring embers of freedom, and revived within me a sense of my own manhood. It recalled the departed self-confidence, and inspired me again with a determination to be free. The gratification afforded by the triumph was a full compensation for whatever else might follow, even death itself. He only can understand the deep satisfaction which I experienced, who has himself repelled by force the bloody arm of slavery. I felt as I never felt before. It was a glorious resurrection, from the tomb of slavery, to the heaven of freedom. My long-crushed spirit rose, cowardice departed, bold defiance took its place; and I now resolved that, however long I might remain a slave in form, the day had passed forever when I could be a slave in fact. I did not hesitate to let it be known of me, that the white man who expected to succeed in whipping, must also succeed in killing me.

From this time I was never again what might be called fairly whipped, though I remained a slave four years afterwards. I had several fights, but was never whipped.

It was for a long time a matter of surprise to me why Mr. Covey did not immediately have me taken by the constable to the whipping-post, and there regularly whipped for the crime of raising my hand against a white man in defence of myself. And the only explanation I can now think of does not entirely satisfy me; but such as it is, I will give it. Mr. Covey enjoyed the most unbounded reputation for being a first-rate overseer and negro-breaker. It was of considerable importance to him. That reputation was at stake; and had he sent me—a boy about sixteen years old—to the public whipping-post, his reputation would have been lost; so, to save his reputation, he suffered me to go unpunished.

My term of actual service to Mr. Edward Covey ended on Christmas day, 1833. The days between Christmas and New Year's Day are allowed as holidays; and, accordingly, we were not required to perform any labor, more than to feed and take care of the stock. This time we regarded as our own, by the grace of our masters; and we therefore used or abused it nearly as we pleased. Those of us who had families at a distance, were generally allowed to spend the whole six days in their society. This time, however, was spent in various ways. The staid, sober, thinking and industrious ones of our number would employ themselves in making corn-brooms, mats, horse-collars, and baskets; and another class of us would spend the time in hunting opossums, hares, and coons. But by far the larger part engaged in such sports and merriments as playing ball, wrestling, running foot-races, fiddling, dancing, and drinking whisky; and this latter mode of spending the time was by far the most agreeable to the feelings of our masters. A slave who would work during the holidays was considered by our masters as scarcely deserving them. He was regarded as one who rejected the favor of his master. It was deemed a disgrace not to get drunk at Christmas; and he was regarded as lazy indeed, who had not provided himself with the necessary means, during the year, to get whisky enough to last him through Christmas.

From what I know of the effect of these holidays upon the slave, I believe them to be among the most effective means in the hands of the slaveholder in keeping down the spirit of insurrection. Were the slaveholders at once to abandon this practice, I have not the slightest doubt it would lead to an immediate insurrection among the slaves. These holidays serve as conductors, or safety-valves, to carry off the rebellious spirit of enslaved humanity. But for these, the slave would be forced up to the wildest desperation; and woe betide the slaveholder, the day he ventures to remove or hinder the operation of those conductors! I warn him that, in such an event, a spirit will go forth in their midst, more to be dreaded than the most appalling earthquake.

The holidays are part and parcel of the gross fraud, wrong, and inhumanity of slavery. They are professedly a custom established by the benevolence of the slaveholders; but I undertake to say, it is the result of selfishness, and one of the grossest frauds committed upon the down-trodden slave. They do not give the slaves this time because they would not like to have their work during its continuance, but because they know it would be unsafe to deprive them of it. This will be seen by the fact, that the slaveholders like to have their slaves spend those days just in such a manner as to make them as glad of their ending as of their beginning. Their object seems to be, to disgust their slaves with freedom, by plunging them into the lowest depths of dissipation. For instance, the slaveholders not only like to see the slave drink of his own accord, but will adopt various plans to make him drunk. One plan is, to make bets on their slaves, as to who can drink the most whisky without getting drunk; and in this way they succeed in getting whole multitudes to drink to excess. Thus, when the slave asks for virtuous freedom, the cunning slaveholder, knowing his ignorance, cheats him with a dose of vicious dissipation, artfully labelled with the name of liberty. The most of us used to drink it down, and the result was just what might be supposed; many of us were led to think that there was little to choose between liberty and slavery. We felt, and very properly too, that we had almost as well be slaves to man as to rum. So, when the holidays ended, we staggered up from the filth of our wallowing, took a long breath, and marched to the field—feeling, upon the whole, rather glad to go, from what our master had deceived us into a belief was freedom, back to the arms of slavery.

I have said that this mode of treatment is a part of the whole system of fraud and inhumanity of slavery. It is so. The mode here adopted to disgust the slave with freedom, by allowing him to see only the abuse of it, is carried out in other things. For instance, a slave loves molasses; he steals some. His master, in many cases, goes off to town, and buys a large quantity; he returns, takes his whip, and commands the slave to eat the molasses, until the poor fellow is made sick at the very mention of it. The same mode is sometimes adopted to make the slaves refrain from asking for more food than their regular allowance. A slave runs through his allowance, and applies for more. His master is enraged at him; but, not willing to send him off without food, gives him more than is necessary, and compels him to eat it within a given time. Then, if he complains that he cannot eat it, he is said to be satisfied neither full nor fasting, and is whipped for being hard to please! I have an abundance of such illustrations of the same principle, drawn from my own observation, but think the cases I have cited sufficient. The practice is a very common one.

On the first of January, 1834, I left Mr. Covey, and went to live with Mr. William Freeland, who lived about three miles from St. Michael's. I soon found Mr. Freeland a very different man from Mr. Covey. Though not rich, he was what would be called an educated southern gentleman. Mr. Covey, as I have shown, was a well-trained negro-breaker and slave-driver. The former (slaveholder though he was) seemed to possess some regard for honor, some reverence for justice, and some respect for humanity. The latter seemed totally insensible to all such sentiments. Mr. Freeland had many of the faults peculiar to slaveholders, such as being very passionate and fretful; but I must do him the justice to say, that he was exceedingly free from those degrading vices to which Mr. Covey was constantly addicted. The one was open and frank, and we always knew where to find him. The other was a most artful deceiver, and could be understood only by such as were skilful enough to detect his cunningly-devised frauds. Another advantage I gained in my new master was, he made no pretensions to, or profession of, religion; and this, in my opinion, was truly a great advantage. I assert most unhesitatingly, that the religion of the south is a mere covering for the most horrid crimes—a justifier of the most appalling barbarity—a sanctifier of the most hateful frauds—and a dark shelter under, which the darkest, foulest, grossest, and most infernal deeds of slaveholders find the strongest protection. Were I to be again reduced to the chains of slavery, next to that enslavement, I should regard being the slave of a religious master the greatest calamity that could befall me. For of all slaveholders with whom I have ever met, religious slaveholders are the worst. I have ever found them the meanest and basest, the most cruel and cowardly, of all others. It was my unhappy lot not only to belong to a religious slaveholder, but to live in a community of such religionists. Very near Mr. Freeland lived the Rev. Daniel Weeden, and in the same neighborhood lived the Rev. Rigby Hopkins. These were members and ministers in the Reformed Methodist Church. Mr. Weeden owned, among others, a woman slave, whose name I have forgotten. This woman's back, for weeks, was kept literally raw, made so by the lash of this merciless, religious wretch. He used to hire hands. His maxim was, Behave well or behave ill, it is the duty of a master occasionally to whip a slave, to remind him of his master's authority. Such was his theory, and such his practice.

Mr. Hopkins was even worse than Mr. Weeden. His chief boast was his ability to manage slaves. The peculiar feature of his government was that of whipping slaves in advance of deserving it. He always managed to have one or more of his slaves to whip every Monday morning. He did this to alarm their fears, and strike terror into those who escaped. His plan was to whip for the smallest offences, to prevent the commission of large ones. Mr. Hopkins could always find some excuse for whipping a slave. It would astonish one, unaccustomed to a slaveholding life, to see with what wonderful ease a slaveholder can find things, of which to make occasion to whip a slave. A mere look, word, or motion—a mistake, accident, or want of power—are all matters for which a slave may be whipped at any time. Does a slave look dissatisfied? It is said, he has the devil in him, and it must be whipped out. Does he speak loudly when spoken to by his master? Then he is getting high-minded, and should be taken down a button-hole lower. Does he forget to pull off his hat at the approach of a white person? Then he is wanting in reverence, and should be whipped for it. Does he ever venture to vindicate his conduct, when censured for it? Then he is guilty of impudence—one of the greatest crimes of which a slave can be guilty. Does he ever venture to suggest a different mode of doing things from that pointed out by his master? He is indeed presumptuous, and getting above himself; and nothing less than a flogging will do for him. Does he, while ploughing, break a plough—or, while hoeing, break a hoe? It is owing to his carelessness, and for it a slave must always be whipped. Mr. Hopkins could always find something of this sort to justify the use of the lash, and he seldom failed to embrace such opportunities. There was not a man in the whole county, with whom the slaves who had the getting their own home, would not prefer to live, rather than with this Rev. Mr. Hopkins. And yet there was not a man anywhere round, who made higher professions of religion, or was more active in revivals—more attentive to the class, love-feast, prayer and preaching meetings, or more devotional in his family—that prayed earlier, later, louder, and longer—than this same reverend slave-driver, Rigby Hopkins.

But to return to Mr. Freeland, and to my experience while in his employment. He, like Mr. Covey, gave us enough to eat; but, unlike Mr. Covey, he also gave us sufficient time to take our meals. He worked us hard, but always between sunrise and sunset. He required a good deal of work to be done, but gave us good tools with which to work. His farm was large, but he employed hands enough to work it, and with ease, compared with many of his neighbors. My treatment, while in his employment, was heavenly, compared with what I experienced at the hands of Mr. Edward Covey.

Mr. Freeland was himself the owner of but two slaves. Their names were Henry Harris and John Harris. The rest of his hands he hired. These consisted of myself, Sandy Jenkins,[1] and Handy Caldwell. Henry and John were quite intelligent, and in a very little while after I went there, I succeeded in creating in them a strong desire to learn how to read. This desire soon sprang up in the others also. They very soon mustered up some old spelling-books, and nothing would do but that I must keep a Sabbath school. I agreed to do so, and accordingly devoted my Sundays to teaching these my loved fellow-slaves how to read. Neither of them knew his letters when I went there. Some of the slaves of the neighboring farms found what was going on, and also availed themselves of this little opportunity to learn to read. It was understood, among all who came, that there must be as little display about it as possible. It was necessary to keep our religious masters at St. Michael's unacquainted with the fact, that, instead of spending the Sabbath in wrestling, boxing, and drinking whisky, we were trying to learn how to read the will of God; for they had much rather see us engaged in those degrading sports, than to see us behav-

1 [Douglass's note] This is the same man who gave me the roots to prevent my being whipped by Mr. Covey. He was "a clever soul." We used frequently to talk about the fight with Covey, and as often as we did so, he would claim my success as the result of the roots which he gave me. This superstition is very common among the more ignorant slaves. A slave seldom dies but that his death is attributed to trickery.

ing like intellectual, moral, and accountable beings. My blood boils as I think of the bloody manner in which Messrs. Wright Fairbanks and Garrison West, both class-leaders, in connection with many others, rushed in upon us with sticks and stones, and broke up our virtuous little Sabbath school, at St. Michael's—all calling themselves Christians! humble followers of the Lord Jesus Christ! But I am again digressing.

I held my Sabbath school at the house of a free colored man, whose name I deem it imprudent to mention; for should it be known, it might embarrass him greatly, though the crime of holding the school was committed ten years ago. I had at one time over forty scholars, and those of the right sort, ardently desiring to learn. They were of all ages, though mostly men and women. I look back to those Sundays with an amount of pleasure not to be expressed. They were great days to my soul. The work of instructing my dear fellow-slaves was the sweetest engagement with which I was ever blessed. We loved each other, and to leave them at the close of the Sabbath was a severe cross indeed. When I think that these precious souls are today shut up in the prison-house of slavery, my feelings overcome me, and I am almost ready to ask, "Does a righteous God govern the universe? and for what does he hold the thunders in his right hand, if not to smite the oppressor, and deliver the spoiled out of the hand of the spoiler?"[1] These dear souls came not to Sabbath school because it was popular to do so, nor did I teach them because it was reputable to be thus engaged. Every moment they spent in that school, they were liable to be taken up, and given thirty-nine lashes. They came because they wished to learn. Their minds had been starved by their cruel masters. They had been shut up in mental darkness. I taught them, because it was the delight of my soul to be doing something that looked like bettering the condition of my race. I kept up my school nearly the whole year I lived with Mr. Freeland; and, beside my Sabbath school, I devoted three evenings in the week, during the winter, to teaching the slaves at home. And I have the happiness to know, that several of those who came to Sabbath school learned how to read; and that one, at least, is now free through my agency.

---

1 *Does a righteous … the spoiler* These lines contain allusions to several biblical passages, including Exodus 15 and Isaiah 33.1.

The year passed off smoothly. It seemed only about half as long as the year which preceded it. I went through it without receiving a single blow. I will give Mr. Freeland the credit of being the best master I ever had, till I became my own master. For the ease with which I passed the year, I was, however, somewhat indebted to the society of my fellow-slaves. They were noble souls; they not only possessed loving hearts, but brave ones. We were linked and interlinked with each other. I loved them with a love stronger than anything I have experienced since. It is sometimes said that we slaves do not love and confide in each other. In answer to this assertion, I can say, I never loved any or confided in any people more than my fellow-slaves, and especially those with whom I lived at Mr. Freeland's. I believe we would have died for each other. We never undertook to do anything, of any importance, without a mutual consultation. We never moved separately. We were one; and as much so by our tempers and dispositions, as by the mutual hardships to which we were necessarily subjected by our condition as slaves.

At the close of the year 1834, Mr. Freeland again hired me of my master, for the year 1835. But, by this time, I began to want to live upon free land as well as with Freeland; and I was no longer content, therefore, to live with him or any other slaveholder. I began, with the commencement of the year, to prepare myself for a final struggle, which should decide my fate one way or the other. My tendency was upward. I was fast approaching manhood, and year after year had passed, and I was still a slave. These thoughts roused me—I must do something. I therefore resolved that 1835 should not pass without witnessing an attempt, on my part, to secure my liberty. But I was not willing to cherish this determination alone. My fellow-slaves were dear to me. I was anxious to have them participate with me in this, my life-giving determination. I therefore, though with great prudence, commenced early to ascertain their views and feelings in regard to their condition, and to imbue their minds with thoughts of freedom. I bent myself to devising ways and means for our escape, and meanwhile strove, on all fitting occasions, to impress them with the gross fraud and inhumanity of slavery. I went first to Henry, next to John, then to the others. I found, in them all, warm hearts and noble spirits. They were ready to hear, and ready to act when a feasible plan should be proposed. This was what I wanted. I talked to them of our want of manhood, if we submitted to our enslavement without at least one noble effort to be free. We met often, and consulted frequently, and told our hopes and fears, recounted the difficulties, real and imagined, which we should be called on to meet. At times we were almost disposed to give up, and try to content ourselves with our wretched lot; at others, we were firm and unbending in our determination to go. Whenever we suggested any plan, there was shrinking—the odds were fearful. Our path was beset with the greatest obstacles; and if we succeeded in gaining the end of it, our right to be free was yet questionable—we were yet liable to be returned to bondage. We could see no spot, this side of the ocean, where we could be free. We knew nothing about Canada. Our knowledge of the north did not extend farther than New York; and to go there, and be forever harassed with the frightful liability of being returned to slavery—with the certainty of being treated tenfold worse than before—the thought was truly a horrible one, and one which it was not easy to overcome. The case sometimes stood thus: At every gate through which we were to pass, we saw a watchman—at every ferry a guard—on every bridge a sentinel—and in every wood a patrol. We were hemmed in upon every side. Here were the difficulties, real or imagined—the good to be sought, and the evil to be shunned. On the one hand, there stood slavery, a stern reality, glaring frightfully upon us—its robes already crimsoned with the blood of millions, and even now feasting itself greedily upon our own flesh. On the other hand, away back in the dim distance, under the flickering light of the north star, behind some craggy hill or snow-covered mountain, stood a doubtful freedom—half frozen—beckoning us to come and share its hospitality. This in itself was sometimes enough to stagger us; but when we permitted ourselves to survey the road, we were frequently appalled. Upon either side we saw grim death, assuming the most horrid shapes. Now it was starvation, causing us to eat our own flesh; now we were contending with the waves, and were drowned; now we were overtaken, and torn to pieces by the fangs of the terrible bloodhound. We were stung by scorpions, chased by wild beasts, bitten by snakes, and finally, after having nearly reached the desired spot—after swimming rivers, encountering wild beasts, sleeping in the woods, suffering hunger and nakedness—we were overtaken by our pursuers, and, in our resistance, we were shot dead upon the spot! I say, this picture sometimes appalled us, and made us

> rather bear those ills we had,
> Than fly to others, that we knew not of.[1]

In coming to a fixed determination to run away, we did more than Patrick Henry, when he resolved upon liberty or death. With us it was a doubtful liberty at most, and almost certain death if we failed. For my part, I should prefer death to hopeless bondage.

Sandy, one of our number, gave up the notion, but still encouraged us. Our company then consisted of Henry Harris, John Harris, Henry Bailey, Charles Roberts, and myself. Henry Bailey was my uncle, and belonged to my master. Charles married my aunt: he belonged to my master's father-in-law, Mr. William Hamilton.

The plan we finally concluded upon was, to get a large canoe belonging to Mr. Hamilton, and upon the Saturday night previous to Easter holidays, paddle directly up the Chesapeake Bay. On our arrival at the head of the bay, a distance of seventy or eighty miles from where we lived, it was our purpose to turn our canoe adrift, and follow the guidance of the north star till we got beyond the limits of Maryland. Our reason for taking the water route was, that we were less liable to be suspected as runaways; we hoped to be regarded as fishermen; whereas, if we should take the land route, we should be subjected to interruptions of almost every kind. Anyone having a white face, and being so disposed, could stop us, and subject us to examination.

The week before our intended start, I wrote several protections, one for each of us. As well as I can remember, they were in the following words, to wit:

> This is to certify that I, the undersigned, have given the bearer, my servant, full liberty to go to Baltimore, and spend the Easter holidays. Written with mine own hand, &c., 1835.
> WILLIAM HAMILTON,
> Near St. Michael's, in Talbot county, Maryland

---

1 *rather bear … knew not of* See Shakespeare's *Hamlet* 3.1.89–90.

We were not going to Baltimore; but, in going up the bay, we went toward Baltimore, and these protections were only intended to protect us while on the bay.

As the time drew near for our departure, our anxiety became more and more intense. It was truly a matter of life and death with us. The strength of our determination was about to be fully tested. At this time, I was very active in explaining every difficulty, removing every doubt, dispelling every fear, and inspiring all with the firmness indispensable to success in our undertaking; assuring them that half was gained the instant we made the move; we had talked long enough; we were now ready to move; if not now, we never should be; and if we did not intend to move now, we had as well fold our arms, sit down, and acknowledge ourselves fit only to be slaves. This, none of us were prepared to acknowledge. Every man stood firm; and at our last meeting, we pledged ourselves afresh, in the most solemn manner, that, at the time appointed, we would certainly start in pursuit of freedom. This was in the middle of the week, at the end of which we were to be off. We went, as usual, to our several fields of labor, but with bosoms highly agitated with thoughts of our truly hazardous undertaking. We tried to conceal our feelings as much as possible; and I think we succeeded very well.

After a painful waiting, the Saturday morning, whose night was to witness our departure, came. I hailed it with joy, bring what of sadness it might. Friday night was a sleepless one for me. I probably felt more anxious than the rest, because I was, by common consent, at the head of the whole affair. The responsibility of success or failure lay heavily upon me. The glory of the one, and the confusion of the other, were alike mine. The first two hours of that morning were such as I never experienced before, and hope never to again. Early in the morning, we went, as usual, to the field. We were spreading manure; and all at once, while thus engaged, I was overwhelmed with an indescribable feeling, in the fulness of which I turned to Sandy, who was near by, and said, "We are betrayed!" "Well," said he, "that thought has this moment struck me." We said no more. I was never more certain of anything.

The horn was blown as usual, and we went up from the field to the house for breakfast. I went for the form, more than for want of anything to eat that morning. Just as I got to the house, in looking out at the lane gate, I saw four white men, with two colored men. The white men were on horseback, and the colored ones were walking behind, as if tied. I watched them a few moments till they got up to our lane gate. Here they halted, and tied the colored men to the gate-post. I was not yet certain as to what the matter was. In a few moments, in rode Mr. Hamilton, with a speed betokening great excitement. He came to the door, and inquired if Master William was in. He was told he was at the barn. Mr. Hamilton, without dismounting, rode up to the barn with extraordinary speed. In a few moments, he and Mr. Freeland returned to the house. By this time, the three constables rode up, and in great haste dismounted, tied their horses, and met Master William and Mr. Hamilton returning from the barn; and after talking awhile, they all walked up to the kitchen door. There was no one in the kitchen but myself and John. Henry and Sandy were up at the barn. Mr. Freeland put his head in at the door, and called me by name, saying, there were some gentlemen at the door who wished to see me. I stepped to the door, and inquired what they wanted. They at once seized me, and, without giving me any satisfaction, tied me—lashing my hands closely together. I insisted upon knowing what the matter was. They at length said, that they had learned I had been in a "scrape," and that I was to be examined before my master; and if their information proved false, I should not be hurt.

In a few moments, they succeeded in tying John. They then turned to Henry, who had by this time returned, and commanded him to cross his hands. "I won't!" said Henry, in a firm tone, indicating his readiness to meet the consequences of his refusal. "Won't you?" said Tom Graham, the constable. "No, I won't!" said Henry, in a still stronger tone. With this, two of the constables pulled out their shining pistols, and swore, by their Creator, that they would make him cross his hands or kill him. Each cocked his pistol, and, with fingers on the trigger, walked up to Henry, saying, at the same time, if he did not cross his hands, they would blow his damned heart out. "Shoot me, shoot me!" said Henry; "you can't kill me but once. Shoot, shoot—and be damned! I won't be tied!" This he said in a tone of loud defiance; and at the same time, with a motion as quick as lightning, he with one single stroke dashed the pistols from the hand of each constable. As he did this, all hands fell upon him, and, after beating him some time, they finally overpowered him, and got him tied.

During the scuffle, I managed, I know not how, to get my pass out, and, without being discovered, put it into the fire. We were all now tied; and just as we were to leave for Easton jail, Betsy Freeland, mother of William Freeland, came to the door with her hands full of biscuits, and divided them between Henry and John. She then delivered herself of a speech, to the following effect: addressing herself to me, she said, "You devil! You yellow devil! it was you that put it into the heads of Henry and John to run away. But for you, you long-legged mulatto devil! Henry nor John would never have thought of such a thing." I made no reply, and was immediately hurried off towards St. Michael's. Just a moment previous to the scuffle with Henry, Mr. Hamilton suggested the propriety of making a search for the protections which he had understood Frederick had written for himself and the rest. But, just at the moment he was about carrying his proposal into effect, his aid was needed in helping to tie Henry; and the excitement attending the scuffle caused them either to forget, or to deem it unsafe, under the circumstances, to search. So we were not yet convicted of the intention to run away.

When we got about half way to St. Michael's, while the constables having us in charge were looking ahead, Henry inquired of me what he should do with his pass. I told him to eat it with his biscuit, and own nothing; and we passed the word around, "Own nothing"; and "Own nothing!" said we all. Our confidence in each other was unshaken. We were resolved to succeed or fail together, after the calamity had befallen us as much as before. We were now prepared for anything. We were to be dragged that morning fifteen miles behind horses, and then to be placed in the Easton jail. When we reached St. Michael's, we underwent a sort of examination. We all denied that we ever intended to run away. We did this more to bring out the evidence against us, than from any hope of getting clear of being sold; for, as I have said, we were ready for that. The fact was, we cared but little where we went, so we went together. Our greatest concern was about separation. We dreaded that more than anything this side of death. We found the evidence against us to be the testimony of one person; our master would not tell who it was; but we came to a unanimous decision among ourselves as to who their informant was. We were sent off to the jail at Easton. When we got there, we were delivered up to the sheriff, Mr. Joseph Graham, and by him placed in jail. Henry,

John, and myself, were placed in one room together—Charles, and Henry Bailey, in another. Their object in separating us was to hinder concert.

We had been in jail scarcely twenty minutes, when a swarm of slave traders, and agents for slave traders, flocked into jail to look at us, and to ascertain if we were for sale. Such a set of beings I never saw before! I felt myself surrounded by so many fiends from perdition.[1] A band of pirates never looked more like their father, the devil. They laughed and grinned over us, saying, "Ah, my boys! we have got you, haven't we?" And after taunting us in various ways, they one by one went into an examination of us, with intent to ascertain our value. They would impudently ask us if we would not like to have them for our masters. We would make them no answer, and leave them to find out as best they could. Then they would curse and swear at us, telling us that they could take the devil out of us in a very little while, if we were only in their hands.

While in jail, we found ourselves in much more comfortable quarters than we expected when we went there. We did not get much to eat, nor that which was very good; but we had a good clean room, from the windows of which we could see what was going on in the street, which was very much better than though we had been placed in one of the dark, damp cells. Upon the whole, we got along very well, so far as the jail and its keeper were concerned. Immediately after the holidays were over, contrary to all our expectations, Mr. Hamilton and Mr. Freeland came up to Easton, and took Charles, the two Henrys, and John, out of jail, and carried them home, leaving me alone. I regarded this separation as a final one. It caused me more pain than anything else in the whole transaction. I was ready for anything rather than separation. I supposed that they had consulted together, and had decided that, as I was the whole cause of the intention of the others to run away, it was hard to make the innocent suffer with the guilty; and that they had, therefore, concluded to take the others home, and sell me, as a warning to the others that remained. It is due to the noble Henry to say, he seemed almost as reluctant at leaving the prison as at leaving home to come to the prison. But we knew we should, in all probability, be separated, if

1 *perdition* Hell.

we were sold; and since he was in their hands, he concluded to go peaceably home.

I was now left to my fate. I was all alone, and within the walls of a stone prison. But a few days before, and I was full of hope. I expected to have been safe in a land of freedom; but now I was covered with gloom, sunk down to the utmost despair. I thought the possibility of freedom was gone. I was kept in this way about one week, at the end of which, Captain Auld, my master, to my surprise and utter astonishment, came up, and took me out, with the intention of sending me, with a gentleman of his acquaintance, into Alabama. But, from some cause or other, he did not send me to Alabama, but concluded to send me back to Baltimore, to live again with his brother Hugh, and to learn a trade.

Thus, after an absence of three years and one month, I was once more permitted to return to my old home at Baltimore. My master sent me away, because there existed against me a very great prejudice in the community, and he feared I might be killed.

In a few weeks after I went to Baltimore, Master Hugh hired me to Mr. William Gardner, an extensive ship-builder, on Fell's Point. I was put there to learn how to caulk.[1] It, however, proved a very unfavorable place for the accomplishment of this object. Mr. Gardner was engaged that spring in building two large man-of-war brigs, professedly for the Mexican government. The vessels were to be launched in the July of that year, and in failure thereof, Mr. Gardner was to lose a considerable sum; so that when I entered, all was hurry. There was no time to learn anything. Every man had to do that which he knew how to do. In entering the shipyard, my orders from Mr. Gardner were, to do whatever the carpenters commanded me to do. This was placing me at the beck and call of about seventy-five men. I was to regard all these as masters. Their word was to be my law. My situation was a most trying one. At times I needed a dozen pair of hands. I was called a dozen ways in the space of a single minute. Three or four voices would strike my ear at the same moment. It was—"Fred., come help me to cant[2] this timber here."—"Fred., come carry this timber yonder."—"Fred., bring that roller here."—"Fred., go get

---

1 *caulk* Seal the wooden seams of a boat against leakage with oakum and melted tar.

2 *cant* Smoothen a sharp angle.

a fresh can of water."—"Fred., come help saw off the end of this timber."—"Fred., go quick, and get the crowbar."—"Fred., hold on the end of this fall."[1]—"Fred., go to the blacksmith's shop, and get a new punch."—"Hurra, Fred! run and bring me a cold chisel."—"I say, Fred., bear a hand, and get up a fire as quick as lightning under that steam-box."—"Halloo, nigger! come, turn this grindstone."—"Come, come! move, move! and bowse[2] this timber forward."—"I say, darky, blast your eyes, why don't you heat up some pitch?"—"Halloo! halloo! halloo!" (Three voices at the same time.) "Come here!—Go there!—Hold on where you are! Damn you, if you move, I'll knock your brains out!"

This was my school for eight months; and I might have remained there longer, but for a most horrid fight I had with four of the white apprentices, in which my left eye was nearly knocked out, and I was horribly mangled in other respects. The facts in the case were these: Until a very little while after I went there, white and black ship-carpenters worked side by side, and no one seemed to see any impropriety in it. All hands seemed to be very well satisfied. Many of the black carpenters were freemen. Things seemed to be going on very well. All at once, the white carpenters knocked off, and said they would not work with free colored workmen. Their reason for this, as alleged, was, that if free colored carpenters were encouraged, they would soon take the trade into their own hands, and poor white men would be thrown out of employment. They therefore felt called upon at once to put a stop to it. And, taking advantage of Mr. Gardner's necessities, they broke off, swearing they would work no longer, unless he would discharge his black carpenters. Now, though this did not extend to me in form, it did reach me in fact. My fellow-apprentices very soon began to feel it degrading to them to work with me. They began to put on airs, and talk about the "niggers" taking the country, saying we all ought to be killed; and, being encouraged by the journeymen, they commenced making my condition as hard as they could, by hectoring me around, and sometimes striking me. I, of course, kept the vow I made after the fight with Mr. Covey, and struck back again, regardless of consequences; and while I kept them from combining, I succeeded

1 *fall* Free end of a rope used for hauling.
2 *bowse* Haul.

very well; for I could whip the whole of them, taking them separately. They, however, at length combined, and came upon me, armed with sticks, stones, and heavy handspikes. One came in front with a half brick. There was one at each side of me, and one behind me. While I was attending to those in front, and on either side, the one behind ran up with the handspike, and struck me a heavy blow upon the head. It stunned me. I fell, and with this they all ran upon me, and fell to beating me with their fists. I let them lay on for a while, gathering strength. In an instant, I gave a sudden surge, and rose to my hands and knees. Just as I did that, one of their number gave me, with his heavy boot, a powerful kick in the left eye. My eyeball seemed to have burst. When they saw my eye closed, and badly swollen, they left me. With this I seized the handspike, and for a time pursued them. But here the carpenters interfered, and I thought I might as well give it up. It was impossible to stand my hand against so many. All this took place in sight of not less than fifty white ship-carpenters, and not one interposed a friendly word; but some cried, "Kill the damned nigger! Kill him! kill him! He struck a white person." I found my only chance for life was in flight. I succeeded in getting away without an additional blow, and barely so; for to strike a white man is death by Lynch law[1]—and that was the law in Mr. Gardner's shipyard; nor is there much of any other out of Mr. Gardner's shipyard.

I went directly home, and told the story of my wrongs to Master Hugh; and I am happy to say of him, irreligious as he was, his conduct was heavenly, compared with that of his brother Thomas under similar circumstances. He listened attentively to my narration of the circumstances leading to the savage outrage, and gave many proofs of his strong indignation at it. The heart of my once overkind mistress was again melted into pity. My puffed-out eye and blood-covered face moved her to tears. She took a chair by me, washed the blood from my face, and, with a mother's tenderness, bound up my head, covering the wounded eye with a lean piece of fresh beef. It was almost

1 *is death by Lynch law* Will lead inevitably to being lynched (i.e., killed by a vigilante mob falsely claiming to be administering justice). Though some lynchings targeted Jews and other minorities, the vast majority were racially motivated murders of black persons by white mobs; the practice became increasingly widespread following the end of Reconstruction in 1877, and remained common throughout the early decades of the twentieth century, during the Jim Crow era of segregation.

compensation for my suffering to witness, once more, a manifestation of kindness from this, my once affectionate old mistress. Master Hugh was very much enraged. He gave expression to his feelings by pouring out curses upon the heads of those who did the deed. As soon as I got a little the better of my bruises, he took me with him to Esquire Watson's, on Bond Street, to see what could be done about the matter. Mr. Watson inquired who saw the assault committed. Master Hugh told him it was done in Mr. Gardner's ship-yard at midday, where there were a large company of men at work. "As to that," he said, "the deed was done, and there was no question as to who did it." His answer was, he could do nothing in the case, unless some white man would come forward and testify. He could issue no warrant on my word. If I had been killed in the presence of a thousand colored people, their testimony combined would have been insufficient to have arrested one of the murderers. Master Hugh, for once, was compelled to say this state of things was too bad. Of course, it was impossible to get any white man to volunteer his testimony in my behalf, and against the white young men. Even those who may have sympathized with me were not prepared to do this. It required a degree of courage unknown to them to do so; for just at that time, the slightest manifestation of humanity toward a colored person was denounced as abolitionism, and that name subjected its bearer to frightful liabilities. The watchwords of the bloody-minded in that region, and in those days, were, "Damn the abolitionists!" and "Damn the niggers!" There was nothing done, and probably nothing would have been done if I had been killed. Such was, and such remains, the state of things in the Christian city of Baltimore.

Master Hugh, finding he could get no redress, refused to let me go back again to Mr. Gardner. He kept me himself, and his wife dressed my wound till I was again restored to health. He then took me into the ship-yard of which he was foreman, in the employment of Mr. Walter Price. There I was immediately set to calking, and very soon learned the art of using my mallet and irons. In the course of one year from the time I left Mr. Gardner's, I was able to command the highest wages given to the most experienced caulkers. I was now of some importance to my master. I was bringing him from six to seven dollars per week. I sometimes brought him nine dollars per week: my wages were a dollar and a half a day. After learning how to caulk, I sought my own employment, made my own contracts, and collected the money which I earned. My pathway became much more smooth than before; my condition was now much more comfortable. When I could get no calking to do, I did nothing. During these leisure times, those old notions about freedom would steal over me again. When in Mr. Gardner's employment, I was kept in such a perpetual whirl of excitement, I could think of nothing, scarcely, but my life; and in thinking of my life, I almost forgot my liberty. I have observed this in my experience of slavery—that whenever my condition was improved, instead of its increasing my contentment, it only increased my desire to be free, and set me to thinking of plans to gain my freedom. I have found that, to make a contented slave, it is necessary to make a thoughtless one. It is necessary to darken his moral and mental vision, and, as far as possible, to annihilate the power of reason. He must be able to detect no inconsistencies in slavery; he must be made to feel that slavery is right; and he can be brought to that only when he ceases to be a man.

I was now getting, as I have said, one dollar and fifty cents per day. I contracted for it; I earned it; it was paid to me; it was rightfully my own; yet, upon each returning Saturday night, I was compelled to deliver every cent of that money to Master Hugh. And why? Not because he earned it—not because he had any hand in earning it—not because I owed it to him—nor because he possessed the slightest shadow of a right to it; but solely because he had the power to compel me to give it up. The right of the grim-visaged pirate upon the high seas is exactly the same.

Chapter II

I now come to that part of my life during which I planned, and finally succeeded in making, my escape from slavery. But before narrating any of the peculiar circumstances, I deem it proper to make known my intention not to state all the facts connected with the transaction. My reasons for pursuing this course may be understood from the following: First, were I to give a minute statement of all the facts, it is not only possible, but quite probable, that others would thereby be involved in the most embarrassing difficulties. Secondly, such a statement would most undoubtedly induce greater vigilance on the part of slaveholders than has existed heretofore among them; which would, of course, be the means of guarding a door whereby some dear brother bondsman might escape his galling chains. I deeply regret the necessity that impels me to suppress anything of importance connected with my experience in slavery. It would afford me great pleasure indeed, as well as materially add to the interest of my narrative, were I at liberty to gratify a curiosity, which I know exists in the minds of many, by an accurate statement of all the facts pertaining to my most fortunate escape. But I must deprive myself of this pleasure, and the curious of the gratification which such a statement would afford. I would allow myself to suffer under the greatest imputations which evil-minded men might suggest, rather than exculpate myself, and thereby run the hazard of closing the slightest avenue by which a brother slave might clear himself of the chains and fetters of slavery.

I have never approved of the very public manner in which some of our western friends have conducted what they call the underground railroad,[1] but which I think, by their open declarations, has been made most emphatically the upper-ground railroad. I honor those good men and women for their noble daring, and applaud them for willingly subjecting themselves to bloody persecution, by openly avowing their participation in the escape of slaves. I, however, can see very little good resulting from such a course, either to themselves or the slaves escaping; while, upon the other hand, I see and feel assured that those open declarations are a positive evil to the slaves remaining, who are seeking to escape. They do nothing towards enlightening the slave, whilst they do much towards enlightening the master. They stimulate him to greater watchfulness, and enhance his power to capture his slave. We owe something to the slave south of the line as well as to those north of it; and in aiding the latter on their way to freedom, we should be careful to do nothing which would be likely to hinder the former from escaping from slavery. I would keep the merciless slaveholder profoundly ignorant of the means of flight adopted by the slave. I would leave him to imagine himself surrounded by myriads of invisible tormentors, ever ready to snatch from his infernal grasp his

---

1 *underground railroad* Secret network of people and safe-houses whereby many enslaved persons escaped to the North.

trembling prey. Let him be left to feel his way in the dark; let darkness commensurate with his crime hover over him; and let him feel that at every step he takes, in pursuit of the flying bondman, he is running the frightful risk of having his hot brains dashed out by an invisible agency. Let us render the tyrant no aid; let us not hold the light by which he can trace the footprints of our flying brother. But enough of this. I will now proceed to the statement of those facts, connected with my escape, for which I am alone responsible, and for which no one can be made to suffer but myself.

In the early part of the year 1838, I became quite restless. I could see no reason why I should, at the end of each week, pour the reward of my toil into the purse of my master. When I carried to him my weekly wages, he would, after counting the money, look me in the face with a robber-like fierceness, and ask, "Is this all?" He was satisfied with nothing less than the last cent. He would, however, when I made him six dollars, sometimes give me six cents, to encourage me. It had the opposite effect. I regarded it as a sort of admission of my right to the whole. The fact that he gave me any part of my wages was proof, to my mind, that he believed me entitled to the whole of them. I always felt worse for having received anything; for I feared that the giving me a few cents would ease his conscience, and make him feel himself to be a pretty honorable sort of robber. My discontent grew upon me. I was ever on the look-out for means of escape; and, finding no direct means, I determined to try to hire my time, with a view of getting money with which to make my escape. In the spring of 1838, when Master Thomas came to Baltimore to purchase his spring goods, I got an opportunity, and applied to him to allow me to hire my time. He unhesitatingly refused my request, and told me this was another stratagem by which to escape. He told me I could go nowhere but that he could get me; and that, in the event of my running away, he should spare no pains in his efforts to catch me. He exhorted me to content myself, and be obedient. He told me, if I would be happy, I must lay out no plans for the future. He said, if I behaved myself properly, he would take care of me. Indeed, he advised me to complete thoughtlessness of the future, and taught me to depend solely upon him for happiness. He seemed to see fully the pressing necessity of setting aside my intellectual nature, in order to contentment in slavery. But in spite of him, and even in spite of myself, I continued to think, and to think about the injustice of my enslavement, and the means of escape.

About two months after this, I applied to Master Hugh for the privilege of hiring my time. He was not acquainted with the fact that I had applied to Master Thomas, and had been refused. He too, at first, seemed disposed to refuse; but, after some reflection, he granted me the privilege, and proposed the following terms: I was to be allowed all my time, make all contracts with those for whom I worked, and find my own employment; and, in return for this liberty, I was to pay him three dollars at the end of each week; find myself in calking tools, and in board and clothing. My board was two dollars and a half per week. This, with the wear and tear of clothing and calking tools, made my regular expenses about six dollars per week. This amount I was compelled to make up, or relinquish the privilege of hiring my time. Rain or shine, work or no work, at the end of each week the money must be forthcoming, or I must give up my privilege. This arrangement, it will be perceived, was decidedly in my master's favor. It relieved him of all need of looking after me. His money was sure. He received all the benefits of slaveholding without its evils; while I endured all the evils of a slave, and suffered all the care and anxiety of a freeman. I found it a hard bargain. But, hard as it was, I thought it better than the old mode of getting along. It was a step towards freedom to be allowed to bear the responsibilities of a freeman, and I was determined to hold on upon it. I bent myself to the work of making money. I was ready to work at night as well as day, and by the most untiring perseverance and industry, I made enough to meet my expenses, and lay up a little money every week. I went on thus from May till August. Master Hugh then refused to allow me to hire my time longer. The ground for his refusal was a failure on my part, one Saturday night, to pay him for my week's time. This failure was occasioned by my attending a camp meeting about ten miles from Baltimore. During the week, I had entered into an engagement with a number of young friends to start from Baltimore to the camp ground early Saturday evening; and being detained by my employer, I was unable to get down to Master Hugh's without disappointing the company. I knew that Master Hugh was in no special need of the money that night. I therefore decided to go to camp meeting, and upon my return pay him the three dollars. I stayed at the camp meeting one day longer than I intended when I left. But as soon as I returned, I called upon him to pay him what he considered his due. I found him very angry; he could scarce restrain his wrath. He said he had a great mind to give me a severe whipping. He wished to know how I dared to go out of the city without asking his permission. I told him I hired my time and while I paid him the price which he asked for it, I did not know that I was bound to ask him when and where I should go. This reply troubled him; and, after reflecting a few moments, he turned to me, and said I should hire my time no longer; that the next thing he should know of, I would be running away. Upon the same plea, he told me to bring my tools and clothing home forthwith. I did so; but instead of seeking work, as I had been accustomed to do previously to hiring my time, I spent the whole week without the performance of a single stroke of work. I did this in retaliation. Saturday night, he called upon me as usual for my week's wages. I told him I had no wages; I had done no work that week. Here we were upon the point of coming to blows. He raved, and swore his determination to get hold of me. I did not allow myself a single word; but was resolved, if he laid the weight of his hand upon me, it should be blow for blow. He did not strike me, but told me that he would find me in constant employment in future. I thought the matter over during the next day, Sunday, and finally resolved upon the third day of September, as the day upon which I would make a second attempt to secure my freedom. I now had three weeks during which to prepare for my journey. Early on Monday morning, before Master Hugh had time to make any engagement for me, I went out and got employment of Mr. Butler, at his ship-yard near the drawbridge, upon what is called the City Block, thus making it unnecessary for him to seek employment for me. At the end of the week, I brought him between eight and nine dollars. He seemed very well pleased, and asked why I did not do the same the week before. He little knew what my plans were. My object in working steadily was to remove any suspicion he might entertain of my intent to run away; and in this I succeeded admirably. I suppose he thought I was never better satisfied with my condition than at the very time during which I was planning my escape. The second week passed, and again I carried him my full wages; and so well pleased was he, that he gave me twenty-five cents (quite a large sum for a slaveholder to give a slave), and bade me to make a good use of it. I told him I would.

Things went on without very smoothly indeed, but within there was trouble.[1] It is impossible for me to describe my feelings as the time of my contemplated start drew near. I had a number of warm-hearted friends in Baltimore—friends that I loved almost as I did my life—and the thought of being separated from them forever was painful beyond expression. It is my opinion that thousands would escape from slavery, who now remain, but for the strong cords of affection that bind them to their friends. The thought of leaving my friends was decidedly the most painful thought with which I had to contend. The love of them was my tender point, and shook my decision more than all things else. Besides the pain of separation, the dread and apprehension of a failure exceeded what I had experienced at my first attempt. The appalling defeat I then sustained returned to torment me. I felt assured that, if I failed in this attempt, my case would be a hopeless one—it would seal my fate as a slave forever. I could not hope to get off with anything less than the severest punishment, and being placed beyond the means of escape. It required no very vivid imagination to depict the most frightful scenes through which I should have to pass, in case I failed. The wretchedness of slavery, and the blessedness of freedom, were perpetually before me. It was life and death with me. But I remained firm, and, according to my resolution, on the third day of September, 1838, I left my chains, and succeeded in reaching New York without the slightest interruption of any kind. How I did so—what means I adopted, what direction I travelled, and by what mode of conveyance—I must leave unexplained, for the reasons before mentioned.

I have been frequently asked how I felt when I found myself in a free State. I have never been able to answer the question with any satisfaction to myself. It was a moment of the highest excitement I ever experienced. I suppose I felt as one may imagine the unarmed mariner to feel when he is rescued by a friendly man-of-war[2] from the pursuit of a pirate. In writing to a dear friend, immediately after my arrival at New York, I said I felt like one who had escaped a den of hungry lions. This state of mind, however, very soon subsided; and I was again seized with a feeling of great insecurity and loneliness. I was yet liable to be

---

1 *within there was trouble* I felt troubled within myself.

2 *man-of-war* Large warship.

taken back, and subjected to all the tortures of slavery.[1] This in itself was enough to damp the ardor of my enthusiasm. But the loneliness overcame me. There I was in the midst of thousands, and yet a perfect stranger; without home and without friends, in the midst of thousands of my own brethren—children of a common Father, and yet I dared not to unfold to any one of them my sad condition. I was afraid to speak to anyone for fear of speaking to the wrong one, and thereby falling into the hands of money-loving kidnappers, whose business it was to lie in wait for the panting fugitive, as the ferocious beasts of the forest lie in wait for their prey. The motto which I adopted when I started from slavery was this—"Trust no man!" I saw in every white man an enemy, and in almost every colored man cause for distrust. It was a most painful situation; and, to understand it, one must needs experience it, or imagine himself in similar circumstances. Let him be a fugitive slave in a strange land—a land given up to be the hunting-ground for slaveholders—whose inhabitants are legalized kidnappers—where he is every moment subjected to the terrible liability of being seized upon by his fellowmen, as the hideous crocodile seizes upon his prey!—I say, let him place himself in my situation—without home or friends—without money or credit—wanting[2] shelter, and no one to give it—wanting bread, and no money to buy it—and at the same time let him feel that he is pursued by merciless men-hunters, and in total darkness as to what to do, where to go, or where to stay—perfectly helpless both as to the means of defence and means of escape—in the midst of plenty, yet suffering the terrible gnawings of hunger—in the midst of houses, yet having no home—among fellow-men, yet feeling as if in the midst of wild beasts, whose greediness to swallow up the trembling and half famished fugitive is only equalled by that with which the monsters of the deep swallow up the helpless fish upon which they subsist—I say, let him be placed in this most trying situation—the situation in which I was placed—then, and not till then, will he fully appreciate the hardships of, and know how to sympathize with, the toil-worn and whip-scarred fugitive slave.

---

1 *I was yet liable … tortures of slavery* When an enslaved person escaped, under the provisions of the Fugitive Slave Act of 1793 a slaveholder was guaranteed the right to seek out, capture, and return that person to enslavement. (Later, the Fugitive Slave Act of 1850 made these provisions even harsher.)

2 *wanting* Lacking.

Thank Heaven, I remained but a short time in this distressed situation. I was relieved from it by the humane hand of Mr. David Ruggles,[1] whose vigilance, kindness, and perseverance, I shall never forget. I am glad of an opportunity to express, as far as words can, the love and gratitude I bear him. Mr. Ruggles is now afflicted with blindness, and is himself in need of the same kind offices which he was once so forward in the performance of toward others. I had been in New York but a few days, when Mr. Ruggles sought me out, and very kindly took me to his boarding-house at the corner of Church and Lespenard Streets. Mr. Ruggles was then very deeply engaged in the memorable Darg case,[2] as well as attending to a number of other fugitive slaves, devising ways and means for their successful escape; and, though watched and hemmed in on almost every side, he seemed to be more than a match for his enemies.

Very soon after I went to Mr. Ruggles, he wished to know of me where I wanted to go; as he deemed it unsafe for me to remain in New York. I told him I was a caulker, and should like to go where I could get work. I thought of going to Canada; but he decided against it, and in favor of my going to New Bedford, thinking I should be able to get work there at my trade. At this time, Anna,[3] my intended wife, came on; for I wrote to her immediately after my arrival at New York (notwithstanding my homeless, houseless, and helpless condition), informing her of my successful flight, and wishing her to come on forthwith. In a few days after her arrival, Mr. Ruggles called in the Rev. J.W.C. Pennington,[4] who, in the presence of Mr. Ruggles, Mrs. Michaels, and two or three others, performed the marriage ceremony, and gave us a certificate, of which the following is an exact copy:

---

1 *Mr. David Ruggles* Free-born black abolitionist from Connecticut (1810–49), who aided fugitives via the Underground Railroad.

2 *Darg case* In 1838, Ruggles had been involved in assisting the enslaved man Thomas Hughes in escaping from the enslaver John P. Darg, for which involvement Ruggles was briefly imprisoned.

3 [Douglass's note] She was free.

4 *J.W.C. Pennington* Formerly enslaved abolitionist and minister (1807–70).

This may certify, that I joined together in holy matrimony Frederick Johnson[1] and Anna Murray, as man and wife, in the presence of Mr. David Ruggles and Mrs. Michaels.

JAMES W.C. PENNINGTON
New York, Sept. 15, 1838

Upon receiving this certificate, and a five-dollar bill from Mr. Ruggles, I shouldered one part of our baggage, and Anna took up the other, and we set out forthwith to take passage on board of the steamboat John W. Richmond for Newport, on our way to New Bedford. Mr. Ruggles gave me a letter to a Mr. Shaw in Newport, and told me, in case my money did not serve me to New Bedford, to stop in Newport and obtain further assistance; but upon our arrival at Newport, we were so anxious to get to a place of safety, that, notwithstanding we lacked the necessary money to pay our fare, we decided to take seats in the stage,[2] and promise to pay when we got to New Bedford. We were encouraged to do this by two excellent gentlemen, residents of New Bedford, whose names I afterward ascertained to be Joseph Ricketson and William C. Taber. They seemed at once to understand our circumstances, and gave us such assurance of their friendliness as put us fully at ease in their presence. It was good indeed to meet with such friends, at such a time. Upon reaching New Bedford, we were directed to the house of Mr. Nathan Johnson, by whom we were kindly received, and hospitably provided for. Both Mr. and Mrs. Johnson took a deep and lively interest in our welfare. They proved themselves quite worthy of the name of abolitionists. When the stage-driver found us unable to pay our fare, he held on upon our baggage as security for the debt. I had but to mention the fact to Mr. Johnson, and he forthwith advanced the money.

We now began to feel a degree of safety, and to prepare ourselves for the duties and responsibilities of a life of freedom. On the morning after our arrival at New Bedford, while at the breakfast-table, the question arose as to what name I should be called by. The name given me by my mother was, "Frederick Augustus Washington Bailey." I, however, had dispensed with the two middle names long before I left Maryland so that I was generally known by the name of "Frederick

1 [Douglass's note] I had changed my name from Frederick *Bailey* to that of *Johnson*.
2 *stage* Stagecoach.

Bailey." I started from Baltimore bearing the name of "Stanley." When I got to New York, I again changed my name to "Frederick Johnson," and thought that would be the last change. But when I got to New Bedford, I found it necessary again to change my name. The reason of this necessity was, that there were so many Johnsons in New Bedford, it was already quite difficult to distinguish between them. I gave Mr. Johnson the privilege of choosing me a name, but told him he must not take from me the name of "Frederick." I must hold on to that, to preserve a sense of my identity. Mr. Johnson had just been reading the "Lady of the Lake,"[1] and at once suggested that my name be "Douglass." From that time until now I have been called "Frederick Douglass"; and as I am more widely known by that name than by either of the others, I shall continue to use it as my own.

I was quite disappointed at the general appearance of things in New Bedford. The impression which I had received respecting the character and condition of the people of the north, I found to be singularly erroneous. I had very strangely supposed, while in slavery, that few of the comforts, and scarcely any of the luxuries, of life were enjoyed at the north, compared with what were enjoyed by the slaveholders of the south. I probably came to this conclusion from the fact that northern people owned no slaves. I supposed that they were about upon a level with the non-slaveholding population of the south. I knew they were exceedingly poor, and I had been accustomed to regard their poverty as the necessary consequence of their being non-slaveholders. I had somehow imbibed the opinion that, in the absence of slaves, there could be no wealth, and very little refinement. And upon coming to the north, I expected to meet with a rough, hard-handed, and uncultivated population, living in the most Spartan-like[2] simplicity, knowing nothing of the ease, luxury, pomp, and grandeur of southern slaveholders. Such being my conjectures, anyone acquainted with the appearance of New Bedford may very readily infer how palpably I must have seen my mistake.

In the afternoon of the day when I reached New Bedford, I visited

---

1 *Lady of the Lake* Narrative poem by Scottish author Sir Walter Scott (1771–1832). Two of the main characters are James Douglas, an exiled former mentor of King James V of Scotland, and Douglas's daughter Ellen Douglas.

2 *Spartan-like* Resembling the Spartans, who were known for their militaristic self-discipline and material plainness of living.

the wharves, to take a view of the shipping. Here I found myself surrounded with the strongest proofs of wealth. Lying at the wharves, and riding in the steam, I saw many ships of the finest model, in the best order, and of the largest size. Upon the right and left, I was walled in by granite warehouses of the widest dimensions, stowed to their utmost capacity with the necessaries and comforts of life. Added to this, almost every body seemed to be at work, but noiselessly so, compared with what I had been accustomed to in Baltimore. There were no loud songs heard from those engaged in loading and unloading ships. I heard no deep oaths or horrid curses on the laborer. I saw no whipping of men; but all seemed to go smoothly on. Every man appeared to understand his work, and went at it with a sober, yet cheerful earnestness, which betokened the deep interest which he felt in what he was doing, as well as a sense of his own dignity as a man. To me this looked exceedingly strange. From the wharves I strolled around and over the town, gazing with wonder and admiration at the splendid churches, beautiful dwellings, and finely-cultivated gardens; evincing an amount of wealth, comfort, taste, and refinement, such as I had never seen in any part of slaveholding Maryland.

Every thing looked clean, new, and beautiful. I saw few or no dilapidated houses, with poverty-stricken inmates; no half-naked children and barefooted women, such as I had been accustomed to see in Hillsborough, Easton, St. Michael's, and Baltimore. The people looked more able, stronger, healthier, and happier, than those of Maryland. I was for once made glad by a view of extreme wealth, without being saddened by seeing extreme poverty. But the most astonishing as well as the most interesting thing to me was the condition of the colored people, a great many of whom, like myself, had escaped thither as a refuge from the hunters of men. I found many, who had not been seven years out of their chains, living in finer houses, and evidently enjoying more of the comforts of life, than the average slaveholders in Maryland. I will venture to assert, that my friend Mr. Nathan Johnson (of whom I can say with a grateful heart, "I was hungry, and he gave me meat; I was thirsty, and he gave me drink; I was a stranger, and he took me in"[1]) lived in a neater house; dined at a better table; took, paid for, and read, more newspapers;

1 *I was hungry ... took me in* See Matthew 25.35.

better understood the moral, religious, and political character of the nation—than nine tenths of the slaveholders in Talbot county, Maryland. Yet Mr. Johnson was a working man. His hands were hardened by toil, and not his alone, but those also of Mrs. Johnson. I found the colored people much more spirited than I had supposed they would be. I found among them a determination to protect each other from the blood-thirsty kidnapper, at all hazards. Soon after my arrival, I was told of a circumstance which illustrated their spirit. A colored man and a fugitive slave were on unfriendly terms. The former was heard to threaten the latter with informing his master of his whereabouts. Straightway a meeting was called among the colored people, under the stereotyped[1] notice, "Business of importance!" The betrayer was invited to attend. The people came at the appointed hour, and organized the meeting by appointing a very religious old gentleman as president, who, I believe, made a prayer, after which he addressed the meeting as follows: "Friends, we have got him here, and I would recommend that you young men just take him outside the door, and kill him!" With this, a number of them bolted at him; but they were intercepted by some more timid than themselves, and the betrayer escaped their vengeance, and has not been seen in New Bedford since. I believe there have been no more such threats, and should there be hereafter, I doubt not that death would be the consequence.

I found employment, the third day after my arrival, in stowing a sloop with a load of oil.[2] It was new, dirty, and hard work for me; but I went at it with a glad heart and a willing hand. I was now my own master. It was a happy moment, the rapture of which can be understood only by those who have been slaves. It was the first work, the reward of which was to be entirely my own. There was no Master Hugh standing ready, the moment I earned the money, to rob me of it. I worked that day with a pleasure I had never before experienced. I was at work for myself and newly-married wife. It was to me the starting-point of a new existence. When I got through with that job, I went in pursuit of a job of calking; but such was the strength of prejudice against color, among the white caulkers, that they refused

1 *stereotyped* Printed. (Stereotyping was a then-new method of printing identical copies using metal plates.)

2 *stowing a sloop with a load of oil* Loading casks of [whale] oil onto a cargo sailing ship.

to work with me, and of course I could get no employment.[1] Finding my trade of no immediate benefit, I threw off my calking habiliments, and prepared myself to do any kind of work I could get to do. Mr. Johnson kindly let me have his wood-horse and saw, and I very soon found myself a plenty of work. There was no work too hard—none too dirty. I was ready to saw wood, shovel coal, carry wood, sweep the chimney, or roll oil casks—all of which I did for nearly three years in New Bedford, before I became known to the anti-slavery world.

In about four months after I went to New Bedford, there came a young man to me, and inquired if I did not wish to take the "Liberator."[2] I told him I did; but, just having made my escape from slavery, I remarked that I was unable to pay for it then. I, however, finally became a subscriber to it. The paper came, and I read it from week to week with such feelings as it would be quite idle for me to attempt to describe. The paper became my meat and my drink. My soul was set all on fire. Its sympathy for my brethren in bonds—its scathing denunciations of slaveholders—its faithful exposures of slavery—and its powerful attacks upon the upholders of the institution—sent a thrill of joy through my soul, such as I had never felt before!

I had not long been a reader of the "Liberator" before I got a pretty correct idea of the principles, measures, and spirit of the anti-slavery reform. I took right hold of the cause. I could do but little; but what I could, I did with a joyful heart, and never felt happier than when in an anti-slavery meeting. I seldom had much to say at the meetings, because what I wanted to say was said so much better by others. But, while attending an anti-slavery convention at Nantucket, on the 11th of August, 1841, I felt strongly moved to speak, and was at the same time much urged to do so by Mr. William C. Coffin, a gentleman who had heard me speak in the colored people's meeting at New Bedford.[3] It was a severe cross, and I took it up reluctantly. The truth was, I felt myself a slave, and the idea of speaking to white people weighed me

---

1 [Douglass's note] I am told that colored persons can now get employment at caulking in New Bedford—a result of anti-slavery effort.

2 *take* Subscribe to; *the "Liberator"* Radical abolitionist newspaper established in 1831 and published by William Lloyd Garrison.

3 *colored people's ... New Bedford* I.e., at the meeting of the African Methodist Episcopal Zion Church, where Douglass had begun preaching in 1839.

down. I spoke but a few moments, when I felt a degree of freedom, and said what I desired with considerable ease. From that time until now, I have been engaged in pleading the cause of my brethren—with what success, and with what devotion, I leave those acquainted with my labors to decide.

Appendix

I find, since reading over the foregoing Narrative, that I have, in several instances, spoken in such a tone and manner, respecting religion, as may possibly lead those unacquainted with my religious views to suppose me an opponent of all religion. To remove the liability of such misapprehension, I deem it proper to append the following brief explanation. What I have said respecting and against religion, I mean strictly to apply to the slaveholding religion of this land, and with no possible reference to Christianity proper; for, between the Christianity of this land, and the Christianity of Christ, I recognize the widest possible difference—so wide, that to receive the one as good, pure, and holy, is of necessity to reject the other as bad, corrupt, and wicked. To be the friend of the one, is of necessity to be the enemy of the other. I love the pure, peaceable, and impartial Christianity of Christ: I therefore hate the corrupt, slaveholding, women-whipping, cradle-plundering, partial and hypocritical Christianity of this land. Indeed, I can see no reason, but the most deceitful one, for calling the religion of this land Christianity. I look upon it as the climax of all misnomers, the boldest of all frauds, and the grossest of all libels. Never was there a clearer case of "stealing the livery of the court of heaven to serve the devil in."[1] I am filled with unutterable loathing when I contemplate the religious pomp and show, together with the horrible inconsistencies, which everywhere surround me. We have men-stealers for ministers, women-whippers for missionaries, and cradle-plunderers for church members. The man who wields the blood-clotted cowskin during the week fills the pulpit on Sunday, and claims to be a minister of the meek and lowly Jesus. The man who robs me of my earnings at the end of each week meets me as a class-leader on Sunday morning, to show

---

1 *stealing the livery ... devil in* From Book 8 of Scottish poet Robert Pollok's popular poem *The Course of Time* (1827).

me the way of life, and the path of salvation. He who sells my sister, for purposes of prostitution, stands forth as the pious advocate of purity. He who proclaims it a religious duty to read the Bible denies me the right of learning to read the name of the God who made me. He who is the religious advocate of marriage robs whole millions of its sacred influence, and leaves them to the ravages of wholesale pollution. The warm defender of the sacredness of the family relation is the same that scatters whole families—sundering husbands and wives, parents and children, sisters and brothers—leaving the hut vacant, and the hearth desolate. We see the thief preaching against theft, and the adulterer against adultery. We have men sold to build churches, women sold to support the gospel, and babes sold to purchase Bibles for the Poor Heathen! All For The Glory Of God And The Good Of Souls! The slave auctioneer's bell and the church-going bell chime in with each other, and the bitter cries of the heart-broken slave are drowned in the religious shouts of his pious master. Revivals of religion and revivals in the slave-trade go hand in hand together. The slave prison and the church stand near each other. The clanking of fetters and the rattling of chains in the prison, and the pious psalm and solemn prayer in the church, may be heard at the same time. The dealers in the bodies and souls of men erect their stand in the presence of the pulpit, and they mutually help each other. The dealer gives his blood-stained gold to support the pulpit, and the pulpit, in return, covers his infernal business with the garb of Christianity. Here we have religion and robbery the allies of each other—devils dressed in angels' robes, and hell presenting the semblance of paradise.

Just God! and these are they,
        Who minister at thine altar, God of right!
Men who their hands, with prayer and blessing, lay
        On Israel's ark of light.[1]

What! preach, and kidnap men?
        Give thanks, and rob thy own afflicted poor?
Talk of thy glorious liberty, and then
        Bolt hard the captive's door?

---

1 *Israel's ark of light* I.e., the Ark of the Covenant, containing the two stone tablets upon which the Ten Commandments were written, and thus symbolizing religious law as a whole.

What! servants of thy own
    Merciful Son, who came to seek and save
The homeless and the outcast, fettering down
    The tasked and plundered slave!

Pilate and Herod[1] friends!
    Chief priests and rulers, as of old, combine!
Just God and holy! is that church which lends
    Strength to the spoiler thine?[2]

The Christianity of America is a Christianity, of whose votaries it may be as truly said, as it was of the ancient scribes and Pharisees,[3] "They bind heavy burdens, and grievous to be borne, and lay them on men's shoulders, but they themselves will not move them with one of their fingers. All their works they do for to be seen of men. They love the uppermost rooms at feasts, and the chief seats in the synagogues, ... and to be called of men, Rabbi, Rabbi. But woe unto you, scribes and Pharisees, hypocrites! for ye shut up the kingdom of heaven against men; for ye neither go in yourselves, neither suffer ye them that are entering to go in. Ye devour widows' houses, and for a pretence make long prayers; therefore ye shall receive the greater damnation. Ye compass sea and land to make one proselyte, and when he is made, ye make him twofold more the child of hell than yourselves. Woe unto you, scribes and Pharisees, hypocrites! for ye pay tithe of mint, and anise, and cumin, and have omitted the weightier matters of the law, judgment, mercy, and faith; these ought ye to have done, and not to leave the other undone. Ye blind guides! which strain at a gnat, and swallow a camel. Woe unto you, scribes and Pharisees, hypocrites! for ye make clean the outside of the cup and of the platter; but within, they are full of extortion and excess. Woe unto you, scribes and Pharisees, hypocrites! for ye are like unto whited sepulchres, which indeed

---

1 *Pilate and Herod* Pontius Pilate, the Roman ruler who approved Jesus' crucifixion, and the Galilean ruler Herod Antipas, who was involved in the executions both of John the Baptist and Jesus.

2 *Just God … spoiler thine?* The above comprises the first four stanzas of John Greenleaf Whittier's poem "Clerical Oppressors" (1835).

3 *ancient scribes and Pharisees* The scribes were professional scholars of religious law, while the Pharisees were a sect whose members insisted on strict adherence to oral and written religious laws; the lines that follow are taken from Matthew 23.4–28, wherein Jesus denounces the scribes and Pharisees for hypocrisy.

appear beautiful outward, but are within full of dead men's bones, and of all uncleanness. Even so ye also outwardly appear righteous unto men, but within ye are full of hypocrisy and iniquity."

Dark and terrible as is this picture, I hold it to be strictly true of the overwhelming mass of professed Christians in America. They strain at a gnat, and swallow a camel. Could anything be more true of our churches? They would be shocked at the proposition of fellowshipping a sheep-stealer; and at the same time they hug to their communion a man-stealer, and brand me with being an infidel, if I find fault with them for it. They attend with Pharisaical strictness to the outward forms of religion, and at the same time neglect the weightier matters of the law, judgment, mercy, and faith. They are always ready to sacrifice, but seldom to show mercy. They are they who are represented as professing to love God whom they have not seen, whilst they hate their brother whom they have seen. They love the heathen on the other side of the globe. They can pray for him, pay money to have the Bible put into his hand, and missionaries to instruct him; while they despise and totally neglect the heathen at their own doors.

Such is, very briefly, my view of the religion of this land; and to avoid any misunderstanding, growing out of the use of general terms, I mean by the religion of this land, that which is revealed in the words, deeds, and actions, of those bodies, north and south, calling themselves Christian churches, and yet in union with slaveholders. It is against religion, as presented by these bodies, that I have felt it my duty to testify.

I conclude these remarks by copying the following portrait of the religion of the south (which is, by communion and fellowship, the religion of the north), which I soberly affirm is "true to the life," and without caricature or the slightest exaggeration. It is said to have been drawn, several years before the present anti-slavery agitation began, by a northern Methodist preacher, who, while residing at the south, had an opportunity to see slaveholding morals, manners, and piety, with his own eyes. "Shall I not visit for these things? saith the Lord. Shall not my soul be avenged on such a nation as this?"[1]

---

1 *Shall I not … as this?* See Jeremiah 5.9. The identity of the preacher to whom Douglass refers is unknown; the following poem, which parodies the popular Southern hymn "Heavenly Union," seems to have been written by Douglass himself.

A Parody

Come, saints and sinners, hear me tell
How pious priests whip Jack and Nell,
And women buy and children sell,
And preach all sinners down to hell,
    And sing of heavenly union.

They'll bleat and baa, dona like goats,
Gorge down black sheep, and strain at motes,
Array their backs in fine black coats,
Then seize their negroes by their throats,
    And choke, for heavenly union.

They'll church you if you sip a dram,
And damn you if you steal a lamb;
Yet rob old Tony, Doll, and Sam,
Of human rights, and bread and ham;
    Kidnapper's heavenly union.

They'll talk loudly of Christ's reward,
And bind his image with a cord,
And scold, and swing the lash abhorred,
And sell their brother in the Lord
    To handcuffed heavenly union.

They'll read and sing a sacred song,
And make a prayer both loud and long,
And teach the right and do the wrong,
Hailing the brother, sister throng,
    With words of heavenly union.

We wonder how such saints can sing,
Or praise the Lord upon the wing,
Who roar, and scold, and whip, and sting,
And to their slaves and mammon cling,
    In guilty conscience union.

They'll raise tobacco, corn, and rye,
And drive, and thieve, and cheat, and lie,
And lay up treasures in the sky,

By making switch and cowskin fly,
        In hope of heavenly union.

They'll crack old Tony on the skull,
And preach and roar like Bashan bull,[1]
Or braying ass, of mischief full,
Then seize old Jacob by the wool,
        And pull for heavenly union.

A roaring, ranting, sleek man-thief,
Who lived on mutton, veal, and beef,
Yet never would afford relief
To needy, sable sons of grief,
        Was big with heavenly union.

"Love not the world," the preacher said,
And winked his eye, and shook his head;
He seized on Tom, and Dick, and Ned,
Cut short their meat, and clothes, and bread,
        Yet still loved heavenly union.

Another preacher whining spoke
Of One whose heart for sinners broke:
He tied old Nanny to an oak,
And drew the blood at every stroke,
        And prayed for heavenly union.

Two others oped their iron jaws,
And waved their children-stealing paws;
There sat the children in gewgaws;[2]
By stinting negroes' backs and maws,
        They kept up heavenly union.

All good from Jack another takes,
And entertains their flirts and rakes[3]
Who dress as sleek as glossy snakes,
And cram their mouths with sweetened cakes;
        And this goes down for union.

---

1 *Bashan bull* Strong bull mentioned in Psalm 22.12–13.

2 *gewgaws* Ornamental or showy clothing.

3 *rakes* Licentious or immoral men.

Sincerely and earnestly hoping that this little book may do something toward throwing light on the American slave system, and hastening the glad day of deliverance to the millions of my brethren in bonds—faithfully relying upon the power of truth, love, and justice, for my success in my humble efforts—and solemnly pledging my self anew to the sacred cause—I subscribe myself,

FREDERICK DOUGLASS
LYNN, Mass., April 28, 1845

—1845

In Context

Responses to Frederick Douglass's *Narrative*

Margaret Fuller, Review of *Narrative of the Life of Frederick Douglass, an American Slave*, from *The New York Tribune* (10 June 1845)

Douglass's *Narrative* was welcomed with enthusiasm in the abolitionist press; most notably, the *New York Tribune* on 10 June 1845 printed on its front page a long and highly favorable review written by prominent feminist and Transcendentalist Margaret Fuller. Like many of her contemporaries, Fuller saw parallels between the fight for women's rights and the fight for racial equality, which she saw as linked by a "natural following out of principles." Yet the extent of Fuller's support for abolitionism as a movement has also been the source of substantial disagreement among readers, even among her contemporaries. According to English sociologist Harriet Martineau, Fuller regarded "the anti-slavery subject as simply a low and disagreeable one, which should be left to unrefined persons to manage, while others were occupied with higher things" (*Harriet Martineau's Autobiography*, 1877). Martineau continued: "The difference between us was that while [Fuller] was living and moving in an ideal world ... she looked down upon persons who acted instead of talking finely, and devoted their fortunes, their peace, their repose, and their very lives to the preservation of the principles of the republic." Whether entirely fair or not, the same criticism could have been made of numerous Transcendentalists in the 1830s and 40s, including Ralph Waldo Emerson and Henry David Thoreau—both of whom became ardent abolitionists in the years leading up to the Civil War. Fuller herself died in a shipwreck in 1850, leaving forever unanswered the question of whether or not she would have immersed herself deeper into the antislavery movement later in life.

Frederick Douglass has been for some time a prominent member of the Abolition party. He is said to be an excellent speaker—can speak from a thorough personal experience—and has upon the audience, beside, the influence of a strong character and uncommon talents. In the book before us he has put into the story of his life the thoughts, the feelings and the adventures that have been so affecting through the living voice; nor are they less so from the printed page. He has had the courage to name the persons, times and places, thus exposing himself to obvious danger, and setting the seal on his deep convictions as to the religious need of speaking the whole truth. Considered merely as a narrative, we have never read one more simple, true, coherent, and warm with genuine feeling. It is an excellent piece of writing, and on that score to be prized as a specimen of the powers of the Black Race, which Prejudice persists in disputing. We prize highly all evidence of this kind, and it is becoming more abundant. The Cross of the Legion of Honor has just been conferred in France on Dumas and Soulié,[1] both celebrated in the paths of light literature. Dumas, whose father was a General in the French Army, is a Mulatto; Soulié, a Quadroon.[2] He went from New-Orleans, where, though to the eye a white man, yet, as known to have African blood in his veins, he could never have enjoyed the privileges due to a human being. Leaving the Land of Freedom, he found himself free to develop the powers that God had given.

Two wise and candid thinkers—the Scotchman, Kinment,[3] prematurely lost to this country, of which he was so faithful and generous a

---

1 *Dumas and Soulié* Alexandre Dumas (1802–70) and Frédéric Soulié (1800–47), widely read French novelists; Dumas's paternal grandmother, Marie-Cessette Dumas, was an enslaved woman of African descent who lived in the French colony of Saint-Domingue (present-day Haiti).

2 *Mulatto ... Quadroon* Terms commonly used in the nineteenth century to classify individuals of mixed racial background; while "mulatto" generally meant a person with one white parent and one parent of African descent, and "quadroon" a person with one grandparent of African descent, the terms were often used rather loosely and might refer more to a person's physical appearance than to his or her actual known ancestry. Persons who were known to have African ancestry or who appeared mixed-race often had more limited social and legal opportunities than those who could "pass" for white.

3 *Kinment* Alexander Kinmont (1799–1838), Scottish philosopher and educator who taught in Cincinnati for several years.

student, and the late Dr. Channing[1]—both thought that the African Race had in them a peculiar element, which, if it could be assimilated with those imported among us from Europe, would give to genius a development, and to the energies of character a balance and harmony beyond what has been seen heretofore in the history of the world. Such an element is indicated in their lowest estate by a talent for melody, a ready skill at imitation and adaptation, an almost indestructible elasticity of nature. It is to be remarked in the writings both of Soulié and Dumas, full of faults but glowing with plastic life and fertile in invention. The same torrid energy and saccharine fulness may be felt in the writings of this Douglass, though his life being one of action or resistance, was less favorable to *such* powers than one of a more joyous flow might have been.

The book is prefaced by two communications—one from Garrison, and one from Wendell Phillips[.] That from the former is in his usual over emphatic style. His motives and his course have been noble and generous. We look upon him with high respect, but he has indulged in violent invective and denunciation till he has spoiled the temper of his mind. Like a man who has been in the habit of screaming himself hoarse to make the deaf hear, he can no longer pitch his voice on a key agreeable to common ears. Mr. Phillips's remarks are equally decided, without this exaggeration in the tone. Douglass himself seems very just and temperate[.] We feel that his view, even of those who have injured him most, may be relied upon. He knows how to allow for motives and influences. Upon the subject of Religion, he speaks with great force, and not more than our own sympathies can respond to. The inconsistencies of Slaveholding professors of religion[2] cry to Heaven. We are not disposed to detest, or refuse communion with them. Their blindness is but one form of that prevalent fallacy which substitutes a creed for a faith, a ritual for a life. We have seen too much of this system of atonement not to know that those who adopt it often began with good intentions, and are, at any rate, in their mistakes worthy of the deepest pity. But that is no reason why the truth should not be uttered, trumpet-tongued, about the thing.

1 *Dr. Channing* William Ellery Channing (1780–1842), American Unitarian preacher who became an abolitionist late in life (but nevertheless maintained a rather paternalistic form of racism in his writings).

2 *professors of religion* I.e., those who profess, or pretend, to embrace religious values.

"Bring no more vain oblations"; sermons must daily be preached anew on that text. Kings, five hundred years ago, built churches with the spoils of war; clergymen today command slaves to obey a Gospel which they will not allow them to read, and call themselves Christians amid the curses of their fellow men. The world ought to get on a little faster than that, if there be really any principle of improvement in it. The Kingdom of Heaven may not at the beginning have dropped seed larger than a mustard-seed, but even from that we had a right to expect a fuller growth than can be believed to exist,[1] when we read such a book as this of Douglass. Unspeakably affecting is the fact that he never saw his mother at all by daylight....

Copies of the work may be had of W.H. Graham, Tribune Buildings. Price, 50 cents.

A.C.C. Thompson, "TO THE PUBLIC. FALSEHOOD REFUTED," *The Liberator* (12 December 1845)

It was common practice for antislavery publications to reprint in their pages articles in support of slavery—in order to refute their claims. Thus was this piece, originally from *The Delaware Republican*, reprinted in *The Liberator*, the abolitionist paper run by Douglass's friend and supporter, William Lloyd Garrison.

It is with considerable regret that I find myself measurably compelled to appear before the public; but my attention has lately been arrested by a pamphlet which has been freely circulated in Wilmington and elsewhere, with the following superscription: *Extract from a Narrative of Frederick Douglass, an American Slave, written by himself.*

And although I am aware that no sensible, unprejudiced person will credit such a ridiculous publication, which bears the glaring impress of falsehood on every page, yet I deem it expedient that I should give the public some information respecting the validity of this narrative, because I was for many years a citizen of the section of country where the scenes of the above mentioned narrative are laid;

1 *The Kingdom of Heaven ... to exist* See Matthew 13.31–32: "The kingdom of heaven is like to a grain of mustard seed, which a man took, and sowed in his field: Which indeed is the least of all seeds: but when it is grown, it is the greatest among herbs, and becometh a tree, so that the birds of the air come and lodge in the branches thereof."

and am intimately acquainted with most of the gentlemen whose characters are so shamefully traduced; and I am also aware, that the Narrative was not written by the professed author, but from statements of this runaway slave, some evil designed[1] person or persons have composed this catalogue of lies to excite the indignation of the public opinion against the slaveholders of the South; and have even attempted to plunge their venomous fangs in the vitals of the church.

I shall, therefore, briefly notice some of the most glaring falsehoods contained in the aforesaid Narrative, and give a true representation of the character of those gentlemen, who have been censured in such an uncharitable manner, as murderers, hypocrites, and everything else that is vile.

I indulge no animosity against the fabricators and circulators of the Narrative, neither do I know them; but I positively declare the whole to be a bucket of falsehoods, from beginning to end.

1st. The identity of the author. About eight years ago, I knew this recreant[2] slave by the name of Frederick Bailey (instead of Douglass). He then lived with Mr. Edward Covy, and was an unlearned, and rather an ordinary negro, and [I] am confident he was not capable of writing the Narrative alluded to; for none but an educated man, and one who had some knowledge of the rules of grammar, could write so correctly. Although, to make the imposition at all creditable, the composer has labored to write it in as plain a style as possible: consequently, the detection of this first falsehood proves the whole production to be notoriously untrue.

Again. "It is a common custom in the part of Maryland from which I ran away, to separate children from their mothers at a very early age."[3]

This also I know to be false. There is no such custom prevalent in that section of the country; but, on the contrary, the children are raised with their mothers, and generally live with them in the same house, except in some few instances where the mother is hired out as a cook or laborer in some other family.

The gentlemen whose names are so prominently set forth in the said Narrative are Col. Edward Lloyd, Capt. Anthony, Austin Gore,

---

1 *evil designed* I.e., with evil intentions.

2 *recreant* Disobedient.

3 *It is … early age* Quotation from Douglass's *Narrative*.

Thomas Lamdin (not Lanman), Giles Hicks, Thomas Auld, and Edward Covy. Most of these persons I am intimately acquainted with and shall give a brief sketch of their characters as follows:

Col. Edward Lloyd was one of the most wealthy and respectable planters in the State of Maryland. He was at one time the Governor of the State, and for several years, a member of the Legislature. He owned several thousand acres of land, and between 4 and 500 slaves. He died before I had much knowledge of him; but I know that he was a kind and charitable man, and in every respect an honorable and worthy citizen.

Most of the same slaves are now owned by his three sons, and they manage their servants in the same manner as did their father; and I know there are no such barbarities committed on their plantations.

Could it be possible that charitable feeling men could murder human beings, with as little remorse of conscience, as the narrative of this infamous libel wishes to make us believe; and that the laws of Maryland, which operate *alike upon black and white*, bond or free, could permit such foul murders to pass unnoticed? No! it is impossible; and every sensible man knows that these false accusations are the ebullition of an unchristian prejudice.

Captain Anthony and Giles Hicks, I know but little of. The accused murderer, Mr. Gore, is a respectable citizen, living near St. Michaels, and I believe a worthy member of the Methodist Episcopal Church; he was formerly an overseer for Col. Lloyd, and at this time, all who know him, think him anything but a murderer.

Thomas Lamdin, who, it is said (in the Narrative), boasted so frequently of his murders, is at this time an honest school teacher in the District where I formerly lived; and all the harm that can be said of him is, that he is too good-natured and harmless to injure any person but himself.

Capt. Thomas Auld, whose hypocritical meanness is so strongly depicted in the aforesaid Narrative, was for many years a respectable merchant in the town of St. Michaels, and an honorable and worthy member of the Methodist E. Church, and only notable for his integrity and irreproachable Christian character. He is now retired from the turmoil of a mercantile life, and engaged in the worthy occupation of tilling the soil, little dreaming of the foul accusations that are circulated against him.

Edward Covy, the renowned "negro breaker," is also a plain, honest farmer, and a tried and faithful member of the Methodist E. Church. Mr. Covy lived for several years on a farm adjoining my father's, at which time this runaway negro lived with him, and I am well aware that no such bloody tragedy as is recorded in that lying Narrative ever occurred on Mr. Covy's farm. All that can be said of Mr. Covy is that he is a good Christian, and a hard working man, and makes every one around him work and treats them well. By his honest industry, he has purchased a fine farm, and is now reaping the reward of his labor.

Such are the characters of the men whom the imposers of this dirty Narrative have so uncharitably traduced, and by blending these false accusations with the Methodist religion of the South, they wish to lacerate her already bleeding wounds.

I was raised among slaves, and have also owned them, and am well aware that the slaves live better and fare better in many respects than the free blacks.

Yet, I am positively opposed to slavery, for I know it is a great evil; but *the evil falls not upon the slave*, but on the owner.

Intrigue and false accusations will never liberate the slave of the South; but, on the contrary, every such attempt will only forge for them new and stronger fetters.

Let the tender-hearted philanthropists of the North speak truth and love towards their southern brethren, and make a liberal application of their gold for the removing the blacks from the country, and their chance of success will be more flattering.

I have given a true representation of the persons connected with the aforesaid Narrative, and I respectfully submit the facts to the judgment of an impartial public.

A.C.C. THOMPSON
No. 101 Market-st. Wilmington, Del.

☞ This attempt to invalidate the Narrative of Frederick Douglass, only confirms its correctness, as Mr. Thompson admits everything but the cruelty described by Douglass—and on that point the latter speaks from experience and knowledge.

Frederick Douglass, "Reply to Mr. A.C.C. Thompson," *The Liberator* (27 February 1846)

To the Editor of the Liberator

DEAR FRIEND—For the sake of our righteous cause, I was delighted to see, by an extract copied into the *Liberator* of 12th Dec. 1845, from *The Delaware Republican*, that Mr. A.C.C. Thompson, No. 101, Market-street, Wilmington, has undertaken to invalidate my testimony against the slaveholders, whose names I have made prominent in the narrative of my experience while in slavery.

Slaveholders and slave-traders never betray greater indiscretion, than when they venture to defend themselves, or their system of plunder, in any other community than a slaveholding one. Slavery has its own standard of morality, humanity, justice, and Christianity. Tried by that standard, it is a system of the greatest kindness to the slave—sanctioned by the purest morality—in perfect agreement with justice—and, of course, not inconsistent with Christianity. But, tried by any other, it is doomed to condemnation. The naked relation of master and slave is one of those monsters of darkness, to whom the light of truth is death! The wise ones among the slaveholders know this, and they studiously avoid doing anything, which, in their judgment, tends to elicit truth. They seem fully to understand, that their safety is in their silence. They may have learned this wisdom from Junius, who counselled his opponent, Sir William Draper, when defending Lord Granby,[1] never to attract attention to a character, which would only pass without condemnation, when it passed without observation.

I am now almost too far away[2] to answer this attempted refutation by Mr. Thompson. I fear his article will be forgotten, before you get my reply. I, however, think the whole thing worth reviving, as it is

---

1 *Junius ... Lord Granby* "Junius" was the pseudonym of a writer of anonymous letters to the London newspaper *Public Advertiser* in 1769–72, which aimed to publicly expose various failures of the British government at that time. In particular, Douglass refers to an instance in which military officer William Draper attempted to defend Member of Parliament John Manners, Lord Granby, from accusations of heavy drinking and unscrupulousness leveled by Junius, only to inadvertently confirm those accusations through his defense.

2 *I am ... far away* Douglass was living in the United Kingdom (which then included both Britain and all of Ireland) at this time, in part to avoid capture by people who hunted fugitives from slavery.

seldom we have so good a case for dissection. In any country but the United States, I might hope to get a hearing[1] through the columns of the paper in which I was attacked. But this would be inconsistent with American usage and magnanimity. It would be folly to expect such a hearing. They might possibly advertise me as a runaway slave, and share the reward of my apprehension; but on no other conditions would they allow my reply a place in their columns.

In this, however, I may judge the "Republican" harshly. It may be that, having admitted Mr. Thompson's article, the editor will think it but fair—negro though I am—to allow my reply an insertion.

In replying to Mr. Thompson, I shall proceed as I usually do in preaching the slaveholder's sermon,—dividing the subject under two general heads, as follows:

1st. The statement of Mr. Thompson, in confirmation of the truth of my narrative.

2ndly. His denials of its truthfulness.

Under the first, I beg Mr. Thompson to accept my thanks for his full, free and unsolicited testimony, in regard to my identity. There now need be no doubt on that point, however much there might have been before. Your testimony, Mr. Thompson, has settled the question forever. I give you the fullest credit for the deed, saying nothing of the motive. But for you, sir, the pro-slavery people in the North might have persisted, with some show of reason, in representing me as being an imposter—a free negro who had never been south of Mason & Dixon's line—one whom the abolitionists, acting on the jesuitical principle, that the end justifies the means, had educated and sent forth to attract attention to their faltering cause. I am greatly indebted to you, sir, for silencing those truly prejudicial insinuations. I wish I could make you understand the amount of service you have done me. You have completely tripped up the heels of your pro-slavery friends, and laid them flat at my feet. You have done a piece of anti-slavery work, which no anti-slavery man could do. Our cautious and truth-loving people in New England would never have believed this testimony, in proof of my identity, had it been borne by an abolitionist. Not that they really think an abolitionist capable of bearing false witness intentionally; but such persons are thought fanatical, and to

1 *get a hearing* I.e., take Thompson to court for libel.

look at everything through a distorted medium. They will believe you—they will believe a slaveholder. They have, somehow or other, imbibed (and, I confess, strangely enough) the idea that persons such as yourself are dispassionate, impartial and disinterested, and therefore capable of giving a fair representation of things connected with slavery. Now, under these circumstances, your testimony is of the utmost importance. It will serve to give effect to my exposures of slavery, both at home and abroad. I hope I shall not administer to your vanity when I tell you that you seem to have been raised up for this purpose! I came to this land with the highest testimonials from some of the most intelligent and distinguished abolitionists in the United States; yet some here have entertained and expressed doubt as to whether I have ever been a slave. You may easily imagine the perplexing and embarrassing nature of my situation, and how anxious I must have been to be relieved from it. You, sir, have relieved me. I now stand before both the American and British public, endorsed by you as being just what I have ever represented myself to be—to wit, an *American slave.*

You say, "I knew this recreant slave by the name of Frederick Bailey (instead of Douglass)." Yes, that was my name; and, leaving out the term recreant, which savors a little of bitterness, your testimony is direct and perfect—just what I have long wanted. But you are not yet satisfied. You seem determined to bear the most ample testimony in my favor. You say you knew me when I lived with Mr. Covey. "And with most of the persons" mentioned in my narrative, "you are intimately acquainted." This is excellent. Then Mr. Edward Covey is not a creature of my imagination, but really did, and may yet exist.

You thus brush away the miserable insinuation of my northern pro-slavery enemies, that I have used fictitious not real names. You say—"Col. Lloyd was a wealthy planter. Mr. Gore was once an overseer for Col. Lloyd, but is now living near St. Michael's, is respected and [you] believe he is a member of the Methodist Episcopal Church. Mr. Thomas Auld is an honorable and worthy member of the Methodist Episcopal Church. Mr. Covey, too, is a member of the Methodist church, and all that can be said of him is, that he is a good Christian," &c. &c. Do allow me, once more, to thank you for this triumphant vindication of the truth of my statements; and to show you how highly I value your testimony, I will inform you that I am now publishing a second edition of my narrative in this country,[1] having already disposed of the first. I will insert your article with my reply as an appendix to the edition now in progress. If you find any fault with my frequent thanks, you may find some excuse for me in the fact, that I have serious fears that you will be but poorly thanked by those whose characters you have felt it your duty to defend. I am almost certain they will regard you as running before you were sent, and as having spoken when you should have been silent. Under these trying circumstances, it is evidently the duty of those interested in your welfare to extend to you such words of consolation as may ease, if not remove, the pain of your sad disappointment! But enough of this.

Now, then, to the second part—or your denials. You are confident I did not write the book; and the reason of your confidence is, that when you knew me, I was an unlearned and rather an ordinary negro. Well, I have to admit I was rather an ordinary negro when you knew me, and I do not claim to be a very extraordinary one now. But you knew me under very unfavorable circumstances. It was when I lived with Mr. Covey, the negro-breaker, *and member of the Methodist Church*. I had just been living with master Thomas Auld, where I had been reduced by hunger. Master Thomas did not allow me enough to eat. Well, when I lived with Mr. Covey, I was driven so hard, and whipped so often, that my soul was crushed and my spirits broken. I was a mere wreck. The degradation to which I was then subjected, as I now look back to it, seems more like a dream than a horrible reality. I can scarcely realize how I ever passed through it, without quite losing all my moral and intellectual energies. I can easily understand that you sincerely doubt if I wrote the narrative; for if any one had told me, seven years ago, I should ever be able to write such an one, I should have doubted as strongly as you now do. You must not judge me now by what I then was—a change of circumstances has made a surprising change in age. Frederick Douglass, the *freeman*, is a very different person from Frederick Bailey,[2] the *slave*. I feel myself almost a new man—freedom has given me new life. I fancy you would scarcely know me. I think I have altered very much in my general appearance, and know I have in my manners. You remember when I used to meet you on the road to St.

---

1 *this country* I.e., the United Kingdom.

2 [Douglass's note] My former name.

Michael's, or near Mr. Covey's lane gate, I hardly dared to lift my head, and look up at you. If I should meet you now, amid the free hills of old Scotland, where the ancient "black Douglass"[1] once met his foes, I presume I might summon sufficient fortitude to look you full in the face; and were you to attempt to make a slave of me, it is possible you might find me almost as disagreeable a subject, as was the Douglass to whom I have just referred. Of one thing, I am certain—you would see *a great change* in me!

I trust I have now explained away your reason for thinking I did not write the narrative in question.

You next deny the existence of such cruelty in Maryland as I reveal in my narrative; and ask, with truly marvellous simplicity, "could it be possible that charitable, feeling men could murder human beings with as little remorse as the narrative of this infamous libeller would make us believe; and that the laws of Maryland, which operate alike upon black and white, bond and free, could permit such foul murders to pass unnoticed?" "No," you say, "it is impossible." I am not to determine what charitable, feeling men can do; but, to show what Maryland slaveholders actually do, their charitable feeling is to be determined by their deeds, and not their deeds by their charitable feelings. The cowskin[2] makes as deep a gash in my flesh, when wielded by a professed saint, as it does when wielded by an open sinner. The deadly musket does as fatal execution when its trigger is pulled by Austin Gore, the Christian, as when the same is done by Beal Bondly,[3] the infidel. The best way to ascertain what those charitable, feeling men can do, will be to point you to the laws made by them, and which you say operate alike upon the white and the black, the bond and the free. By consulting the statute laws of Maryland, you will find the following: "Any slave for rambling in the night, or riding horses in the day time without leave, or running away, may be punished by whipping, cropping,[4] branding in the cheek, or otherwise—not rendering him unfit for labor."—p. 337.

---

1 *black Douglass* Douglass's chosen namesake, a character from Walter Scott's loosely historical poem "The Lady of the Lake" (1810). The historical "black Douglas" was James Douglas, Lord of Douglas (c. 1286–1330), an important leader in the fight for Scottish independence.

2 *cowskin* Whip made of cowhide.

3 *Austin Gore ... Beal Bondly* Cruel enslavers mentioned in Douglass's *Narrative*.

4 *cropping* Cutting off one's ears.

Then another: "Any slave convicted of petty treason, murder, or wilful burning of dwelling-houses, may be sentenced to have the right hand cut off, to be hanged in the usual way—his head severed from his body—the body divided into four quarters, and the head and quarters set up in the most public place where such act was committed."—Page 190.

Now, Mr. Thompson, when you consider with what ease a slave may be convicted of any one or all of these crimes, how bloody and atrocious do those laws appear! Yet, sir, they are but the breath of those pious and charitable feeling men, whom you would defend. I am sure I have recorded in my narrative, nothing so revoltingly cruel, murderous, and infernal, as may be found in your own statute book.

You say that the laws of Maryland operate alike upon the white and black, the bond and free. If you mean by this, that the parties named are all equally protected by law, you perpetrate a falsehood as big as that told by President Polk in his inaugural address.[1] It is a notorious fact, even on this side the Atlantic, that a black man cannot testify against a white in any court in Maryland, or any other slave State. If you do not know this, you are more than ordinarily ignorant, and are to be pitied rather than censured. I will not say "that the detection of this falsehood proves all you have said to be false"—for I wish to avail myself of your testimony, in regard to my identity—but I will say, you have made yourself very liable to suspicion.

I will close these remarks by saying, your positive opposition to slavery is fully explained, and will be well understood by anti-slavery men, when you say the evil of the system does not fall upon the slave, but the slaveholder. This is like saying that the evil of being burnt is not felt by the person burnt, but by him who kindles up the fire about him.

FREDERICK DOUGLASS
Perth, (Scotland,) 27th Jan. 1846

---

1 *President Polk ... inaugural address* Douglass is likely referring to the following statement made by President James Polk in his inaugural address of March 1845: "All distinctions of birth or rank have been abolished. All citizens, whether native or adopted, are placed upon terms of precise equality. All are entitled to equal rights and equal protection." Polk was a slaveholder throughout most of his adult life.

from *To My Old Master*

Douglass published this as an open letter in the 8 September 1848 issue of the *North Star*; the letter was reprinted in William Lloyd Garrison's abolitionist newspaper *The Liberator* two weeks later, and Douglass also included it, with minor revisions, in the appendices to his second autobiography, *My Bondage and My Freedom* (1855).

THOMAS AULD—SIR:

… I have often thought I should like to explain to you the grounds upon which I have justified myself in running away from you. I am almost ashamed to do so now, for by this time you may have discovered them yourself. I will, however, glance at them. When yet but a child about six years old, I imbibed the determination to run away. The very first mental effort that I now remember on my part, was an attempt to solve the mystery, Why am I a slave? and with this question my youthful mind was troubled for many days, pressing upon me more heavily at times than others. When I saw the slave-driver whip a slave-woman, cut the blood out of her neck, and heard her piteous cries, I went away into the corner of the fence, wept and pondered over this mystery. I had, through some medium, I know not what, got some idea of God, the Creator of all mankind, the black and the white, and that he had made the blacks to serve the whites as slaves. How he could do this and be *good*, I could not tell. I was not satisfied with this theory, which made God responsible for slavery, for it pained me greatly, and I have wept over it long and often. At one time, your first wife, Mrs. Lucretia, heard me singing and saw me shedding tears, and asked of me the matter, but I was afraid to tell her. I was puzzled with this question, till one night, while sitting in the kitchen, I heard some of the old slaves talking of their parents having been stolen from Africa by white men, and were sold here as slaves. The whole mystery was solved at once. Very soon after this, my aunt Jinny and uncle Noah ran away, and the great noise made about it by your father-in-law, made me for the first time acquainted with the fact, that there were free States as well as slave

States. From that time, I resolved that I would someday run away. The morality of the act, I dispose of as follows: I am myself; you are yourself; we are two distinct persons, equal persons. What you are I am. You are a man, so am I. God created both, and made us separate beings. I am not by nature bound to you, or you to me. Nature does not make your existence depend upon me, or mine to depend upon yours. I cannot walk upon your legs, or you upon mine. I cannot breathe for you, or you for me; I must breathe for myself, and you for yourself. We are distinct persons, and are each equally provided with faculties necessary to our individual existence. In leaving you, I took nothing but what belonged to me, and in no way lessened your means of obtaining an *honest* living. Your faculties remained yours, and mine became useful to their rightful owner. I therefore see no wrong in any part of the transaction. It is true, I went off secretly, but that was more your fault than mine. Had I let you into the secret, you would have defeated the enterprise entirely; but for this, I should have been really glad to have made you acquainted with my intention to leave.

You may perhaps want to know how I like my present condition. I am free to say, I greatly prefer it to that which I occupied in Maryland. I am, however, by no means prejudiced against that State as such. Its geography, climate, fertility, and products, are such as to make it a very desirable abode for any man; and but for the existence of slavery there, it is not impossible that I might again take up my abode in that State. It is not that I love Maryland less, but freedom more.[1] You will be surprised to learn that people at the North labor under the strange delusion that if the slaves were emancipated at the South, they would all flock to the North. So far from this being the case, in that event, you would see many old and familiar faces back again at the South. The fact is, there are few here who would not return to the South in the event of emancipation. We want to live in the land of our birth, and to lay our bones by the side of our fathers'; and nothing short of an intense love of personal freedom keeps us from the South. For the sake of this, most of us would live on a crust of bread and a cup of cold water.

---

1 *not that … freedom more* See Shakespeare's *Julius Caesar* 3.2.21–24: "If then that friend demand why Brutus rose against Caesar, this is my answer: not that I loved Caesar less, but that I loved Rome more."

Since I left you, I have had a rich experience. I have occupied stations which I never dreamed of when a slave. Three out of the ten years since I left you, I spent as a common laborer on the wharves of New Bedford, Massachusetts. It was there I earned my first free dollar. It was mine. I could spend it as I pleased. I could buy hams or herring with it, without asking any odds of anybody. That was a precious dollar to me. You remember when I used to make seven or eight, and even nine dollars a week in Baltimore, you would take every cent of it from me every Saturday night, saying that I belonged to you, and my earnings also. I never liked this conduct on your part—to say the best, I thought it a little mean.[1] I would not have served you so. But let that pass. I was a little awkward about counting money in New Bedford. I like to have betrayed myself several times. I caught myself saying phip,[2] for four pence; and one time a man actually charged me with being a runaway, whereupon I was silly enough to become one by running away from him, for I was greatly afraid he might adopt measures to get me again into slavery, a condition I then dreaded more than death.

I soon, however, learned to count money as well as to make it, and got on swimmingly. I married soon after leaving you:[3] in fact, I was engaged to be married before I left you; and instead of finding my companion a burden, she was truly a helpmeet. She went to live—at service, and I to work on the wharf, and though we toiled hard the first winter, we never lived more happily. After remaining in New Bedford for three years, I met with Wm. Lloyd Garrison,[4] a person of whom you have *possibly* heard, as he is pretty generally known among slaveholders. He put it into my head that I might make myself serviceable to the cause of the slave by devoting a portion of my time to telling my own sorrows, and those of other slaves which had come under my observation. This was the commencement of a higher state of existence than any to which I had ever aspired. I was thrown into

---

1 *mean* Ungenerous; ignoble.

2 *phip* Maryland slang for a four-pence coin.

3 *I married ... leaving you* Douglass's first wife, Anna Murray-Douglass (1813–82), was born free in Maryland and provided Douglass with crucial aid in his self-emancipation.

4 *Wm. Lloyd Garrison* Among the most prominent white abolitionists of the era, William Lloyd Garrison (1805–79) founded the abolitionist newspaper *The Liberator* as well as the American Anti-Slavery Society.

society the most pure, enlightened and benevolent that the country affords. Among these, I have never forgotten you, but have invariably made you the topic of conversation—thus giving you all the notoriety I could do. I need not tell you that the opinion formed of you in these circles, is far from being favorable. They have little respect for your honesty, and less for your religion.

But I was going on to relate to you something of my interesting experience. I had not long enjoyed the excellent society to which I have referred, before the light of its excellence exerted a beneficial influence on my mind and heart. Much of my early dislike of white persons was removed, and their manners, habits and customs, so entirely unlike what I have been used to in the kitchen-quarters on the plantations of the South, fairly charmed me, and gave me a strong disrelish for the coarse and degrading customs of my former condition. I therefore made an effort so to improve my mind and deportment, as to be somewhat fitted to the station to which I seemed almost Providentially called. The transition from degradation to respectability was indeed great, and to get from one to the other without carrying some marks of one's former condition, is truly a difficult matter. I would not have you think that I am now entirely clear of all plantation peculiarities, but my friends here, while they entertain the strongest dislike to them, regard me with that charity to which my past life somewhat entitles me, so that my condition in this respect is exceedingly pleasant. So far as my domestic affairs are concerned, I can boast of as comfortable a dwelling as your own. I have an industrious and neat companion, and four dear children—the oldest a girl of nine years, and three fine boys, the oldest eight, the next six, and the youngest four years old. The three oldest are now going regularly to school—two can read and write, and the other can spell with tolerable correctness words of two syllables. Dear fellows! they are all in comfortable beds, and are sound asleep, perfectly secure under my own roof. There are no slaveholders here to rend my heart by snatching them from my arms, or blast a proud mother's dearest hopes by tearing them from her bosom. These dear children are ours—not to work up into rice, sugar, and tobacco, but to watch over, regard, and protect, and to rear them up in the nurture and admonition of the gospel—to train them up in the paths of wisdom and virtue, and, as far as we can, to make them useful to the world and to themselves. Oh! sir, a slaveholder never appears to me so completely an agent of hell, as when I think of and look upon my dear children. It is then that my feelings rise above my control. I meant to have said more with respect to my own prosperity and happiness, but thoughts and feelings which this recital has quickened, unfits me to proceed further in that direction. The grim horrors of slavery rise in all their ghastly terror before me, the wails of millions pierce my heart, and chill my blood. I remember the chain, the gag, the bloody whip, the deathlike gloom overshadowing the broke spirit of the fettered bondman, the appalling liability of his being torn away from wife and children and sold like a beast in the market. Say not this is a picture of fancy.[1] You well know that I wear stripes[2] on my back inflicted by your direction; and that you, while we were brothers in the same church, caused this right hand, with which I am now penning this letter, to be closely tied to my left, and my person dragged at the pistol's mouth, fifteen miles, from the Bay side to Easton, to be sold like a beast in the market, for the alleged crime of intending to escape from your possession. All this and more you remember, and know to be perfectly true, not only of yourself, but of nearly all of the slaveholders around you.

At this moment, you are probably the guilty holder of at least three of my own dear sisters, and my only brother in bondage. These you regard as your property. They are recorded on your ledger, or perhaps have been sold to human flesh mongers, with a view to filling your own ever-hungry purse. Sir, I desire to know how and where these dear sisters are. Have you sold them? or are they still in your possession? What has become of them? are they living or dead? And my dear old grandmother, whom you turned out like an old horse, to die in the woods—is she still alive? Write and let me know all about them. If my grandmother be still alive, she is of no service to you, for by this time she must be nearly eighty years old—too old to be cared for by one to whom she has ceased to be of service; send her to me at Rochester,[3] or

1 *fancy* Imagination; a fiction.
2 *stripes* I.e., scars from having been whipped.
3 *Rochester* The home of Douglass and his family, in New York.

bring her to Philadelphia,[1] and it shall be the crowning happiness of my life to take care of her in her old age. Oh! she was to me a mother, and a father, so far as hard toil for my comfort could make her such. Send me my grandmother! that I may watch over and take care of her in her old age. And my sisters, let me know all about them. I would write to them, and learn all I want to know of them, without disturbing you in any way, but that, through your unrighteous conduct, they have been entirely deprived of the power to read and write. You have kept them in utter ignorance, and have therefore robbed them of the sweet enjoyments of writing or receiving letters from absent friends and relatives. Your wickedness and cruelty committed in this respect on your fellow-creatures, are greater than all the stripes you have laid upon my back, or theirs. It is an outrage upon the soul—a war upon the immortal spirit, and one for which you must give account at the bar of our common Father and Creator.

The responsibility which you have assumed in this regard is truly awful—and how you could stagger under it these many years is marvellous. Your mind must have become darkened, your heart hardened, your conscience seared and petrified, or you would have long since thrown off the accursed load and sought relief at the hands of a sin-forgiving God. How, let me ask, would you look upon me, were I some dark night in company with a band of hardened villains, to enter the precincts of your own elegant dwelling and seize the person of your own lovely daughter Amanda, and carry her off from your family, friends, and all the loved ones of her youth—make her my slave—compel her to work, and I take her wages—place her name on my ledger as property—disregard her personal rights—fetter the powers of her immortal soul by denying her the right and privilege of learning to read and write—feed her coarsely—clothe her scantily, and whip her on the naked back occasionally; more and still more horrible, leave her unprotected—a degraded victim to the brutal lust of fiendish overseers who would pollute, blight, and blast her fair soul—rob her of all dignity—destroy her virtue, and annihilate all in her person the graces that adorn the character of virtuous woman-

1 *Philadelphia* One of Douglass's first stops on his way to freedom, Philadelphia was largely populated by Quakers, who generally opposed slavery. (Though Pennsylvania was the first state to pass an act abolishing slavery in 1780, its gradual nature meant that there were still people living enslaved in the state well into the early nineteenth century.)

hood? I ask how would you regard me, if such were my conduct? Oh! the vocabulary of the damned would not afford a word sufficiently infernal, to express your idea of my God-provoking wickedness. Yet sir, your treatment of my beloved sisters is in all essential points, precisely like the case I have now supposed. Damning as would be such a deed on my part, it would be no more so than that which you have committed against me and my sisters.

I will now bring this letter to a close; you shall hear from me again unless you let me hear from you. I intend to make use of you as a weapon with which to assail the system of slavery—as a means of concentrating public attention on the system, and deepening the horror of trafficking in the souls and bodies of men. I shall make use of you as a means of exposing the character of the American church and clergy—and as a means of bringing this guilty nation with yourself to repentance. In doing this I entertain no malice towards you personally. There is no roof under which you would be more safe than mine, and there is nothing in my house which you might need for your comfort, which I would not readily grant. Indeed, I should esteem it a privilege, to set you an example as to how mankind ought to treat each other.

I am your fellow man but not your slave,

FREDERICK DOUGLASS

P.S. I send a copy of the paper containing this letter, to save postage.—F.D.

—1848

What to the Slave Is the Fourth of July?

In 1852, Douglass was invited by the Rochester Ladies' Anti-Slavery Society to deliver an oration before the citizenry of Rochester, as part of the local Independence Day celebrations. He did not give the resulting speech a title; it is often referred to as "What to the Slave Is the Fourth of July?" and often, in excerpted form, given the title "The Hypocrisy of American Slavery." The full speech was issued in pamphlet form later in 1852, titled simply "Oration, Delivered in Corinthian Hall, Rochester." In 1855 Douglass published an extract from the speech in the appendices to *My Bondage and My Freedom*. That extract omits some of the speech's more inflammatory passages.

Mr. President, Friends and Fellow Citizens:

He who could address this audience without a quailing sensation has stronger nerves than I have. I do not remember ever to have appeared as a speaker before any assembly more shrinkingly, nor with greater distrust of my ability, than I do this day. A feeling has crept over me, quite unfavorable to the exercise of my limited powers of speech. The task before me is one which requires much previous thought and study for its proper performance. I know that apologies of this sort are generally considered flat and unmeaning. I trust, however, that mine will not be so considered. Should I seem at ease, my appearance would much misrepresent me. The little experience I have had in addressing public meetings, in country schoolhouses, avails me nothing on the present occasion.

The papers and placards say that I am to deliver a 4th of July oration. This certainly sounds large and out of the common way for me. It is true that I have often had the privilege to speak in this beautiful Hall, and to address many who now honor me with their presence. But neither their familiar faces, nor the perfect gage I think I have of Corinthian Hall, seems to free me from embarrassment.

The fact is, ladies and gentlemen, the distance between this platform and the slave plantation, from which I escaped, is considerable—and the difficulties to be overcome in getting from the latter to the former, are by no means slight. That I am here today is, to me, a matter of astonishment as well as of gratitude. You will not, therefore, be surprised, if in what I have to say I evince no elaborate preparation, nor grace my speech with any high sounding exordium.[1] With little experience and with less learning, I have been able to throw my thoughts hastily and imperfectly together; and trusting to your patient and generous indulgence, I will proceed to lay them before you.

This, for the purpose of this celebration, is the 4th of July.[2] It is the birthday of your National Independence, and of your political freedom. This, to you, is what the Passover[3] was to the emancipated people of God. It carries your minds back to the day, and to the act of your great deliverance, and to the signs, and to the wonders, associated with that act, and that day. This celebration also marks the beginning of another year of your national life, and reminds you that the Republic of America is now 76 years old. I am glad, fellow-citizens, that your nation is so young. Seventy-six years, though a good old age for a man, is but a mere speck in the life of a nation. Three score years and ten is the allotted time for individual men; but nations number their years by thousands. According to this fact, you are, even now, only in the beginning of your national career, still lingering in the period of childhood. I repeat, I am glad this is so. There is hope in the thought, and hope is much needed, under the dark clouds which lower above the horizon. The eye of the reformer is met with angry flashes, portending disastrous times; but his heart may well beat lighter at the thought that America is young, and that she is still in the impressible stage of her existence. May he not hope that high lessons of wisdom, of justice and of truth, will yet give direction to her destiny? Were the nation older, the patriot's heart might be sadder, and the reformer's brow heavier. Its future might be shrouded in gloom, and the hope of its prophets go out in sorrow. There is consolation in the thought that America is young. Great streams are not easily

---

1 *exordium* Introduction.

2 *This … 4th of July* Though the address was part of the Independence Day festivities, it was delivered on the 5th of July rather than the 4th.

3 *Passover* Event described in the Book of Exodus in which God frees the Israelites from slavery in Egypt by punishing the Egyptians with ten plagues, the last of which is the death of all the first-born children. God passes over the homes of the Israelites when he brings this final plague.

turned from channels, worn deep in the course of ages. They may sometimes rise in quiet and stately majesty, and inundate the land, refreshing and fertilizing the earth with their mysterious properties. They may also rise in wrath and fury, and bear away, on their angry waves, the accumulated wealth of years of toil and hardship. They, however, gradually flow back to the same old channel, and flow on as serenely as ever. But, while the river may not be turned aside, it may dry up, and leave nothing behind but the withered branch, and the unsightly rock, to howl in the abyss-sweeping wind, the sad tale of departed glory. As with rivers so with nations.

Fellow citizens, I shall not presume to dwell at length on the associations that cluster about this day. The simple story of it is that, 76 years ago, the people of this country were British subjects. The style and title of your "sovereign people" (in which you now glory) was not then born. You were under the British Crown. Your fathers esteemed the English Government as the home government, and England as the fatherland. This home government, you know, although a considerable distance from your home, did, in the exercise of its parental prerogatives, impose upon its colonial children such restraints, burdens and limitations as, in its mature judgment, it deemed wise, right and proper.

But your fathers, who had not adopted the fashionable idea of this day of the infallibility of government, and the absolute character of its acts, presumed to differ from the home government in respect to the wisdom and the justice of some of those burdens and restraints. They went so far in their excitement as to pronounce the measures of government unjust, unreasonable, and oppressive, and altogether such as ought not to be quietly submitted to. I scarcely need say, fellow citizens, that my opinion of those measures fully accords with that of your fathers. Such a declaration of agreement on my part would not be worth much to anybody. It would, certainly, prove nothing, as to what part I might have taken, had I lived during the great controversy of 1776. To say *now* that America was right, and England wrong, is exceedingly easy. Everybody can say it; the dastard, not less than the noble brave, can flippantly descant on[1] the tyranny of England towards the American Colonies. It is fashionable to do

1 *descant on* Discuss.

so; but there was a time when to pronounce against England, and in favor of the cause of the colonies, tried men's souls. They who did so were accounted in their day plotters of mischief, agitators and rebels, dangerous men. To side with the right against the wrong, with the weak against the strong, and with the oppressed against the oppressor! *here* lies the merit, and the one which, of all others, seems unfashionable in our day. The cause of liberty may be stabbed by the men who glory in the deeds of your fathers. But, to proceed.

Feeling themselves harshly and unjustly treated by the home government, your fathers, like men of honesty, and men of spirit, earnestly sought redress. They petitioned and remonstrated; they did so in a decorous, respectful, and loyal manner. Their conduct was wholly unexceptionable. This, however, did not answer the purpose. They saw themselves treated with sovereign indifference, coldness and scorn. Yet they persevered. They were not the men to look back.

As the sheet anchor takes a firmer hold, when the ship is tossed by the storm, so did the cause of your fathers grow stronger, as it breasted the chilling blasts of kingly displeasure. The greatest and best of British statesmen admitted its justice, and the loftiest eloquence of the British Senate came to its support. But, with that blindness which seems to be the unvarying characteristic of tyrants, since Pharaoh and his hosts were drowned in the Red Sea,[1] the British Government persisted in the exactions complained of.

The madness of this course, we believe, is admitted now, even by England; but we fear the lesson is wholly lost on our present rulers.

Oppression makes a wise man mad.[2] Your fathers were wise men, and if they did not go mad, they became restive under this treatment. They felt themselves the victims of grievous wrongs, wholly incurable in their colonial capacity. With brave men there is always a remedy for oppression. Just here, the idea of a total separation of the colonies from the crown was born! It was a startling idea, much more so, than we, at this distance of time, regard it. The timid and the prudent (as has been intimated) of that day, were, of course, shocked and alarmed by it.

---

1 *since Pharaoh … Red Sea* Douglass refers to the crossing of the Red Sea in the Book of Exodus, when God parts the sea to allow the Israelites to pass through and then drowns the pursuing Egyptian army.

2 *Oppression … mad* See Ecclesiastes 7.7: "Surely oppression maketh a wise man mad."

Such people lived then, had lived before, and will, probably, ever have a place on this planet; and their course, in respect to any great change (no matter how great the good to be attained, or the wrong to be redressed by it), may be calculated with as much precision as can be the course of the stars. They hate all changes, but silver, gold and copper change! Of this sort of change they are always strongly in favor.

These people were called Tories[1] in the days of your fathers; and the appellation probably conveyed the same idea that is meant by a more modern, though a somewhat less euphonious term,[2] which we often find in our papers, applied to some of our old politicians.

Their opposition to the then dangerous thought was earnest and powerful; but, amid all their terror and affrighted vociferations against it, the alarming and revolutionary idea moved on, and the country with it.

On the 2d of July, 1776, the old Continental Congress, to the dismay of the lovers of ease, and the worshipers of property, clothed that dreadful idea with all the authority of national sanction.[3] They did so in the form of a resolution; and as we seldom hit upon resolutions, drawn up in our day, whose transparency is at all equal to this, it may refresh your minds and help my story if I read it.

> Resolved, That these united colonies are, and of right, ought to be free and Independent States; that they are absolved from all allegiance to the British Crown; and that all political connection between them and the State of Great Britain is, and ought to be, dissolved.

Citizens, your fathers made good that resolution. They succeeded; and today you reap the fruits of their success. The freedom gained is yours; and you, therefore, may properly celebrate this anniversary. The 4th of July is the first great fact in your nation's history—the very ringbolt in the chain of your yet undeveloped destiny.

---

1 *Tories* Term used in Britain and elsewhere to refer to Conservative politicians and their supporters; it came during the American Revolutionary War to refer to Loyalists to the British cause.

2 *somewhat … term* Douglass is likely alluding to the term "hunker," which was often applied to conservative politicians in the United States in the mid-nineteenth century; *euphonious* Pleasant-sounding.

3 *On the 2d … sanction* The Declaration of Independence was passed by the Second Continental Congress on the 2nd of July, and ratified on the 4th.

Pride and patriotism, not less than gratitude, prompt you to celebrate and to hold it in perpetual remembrance. I have said that the Declaration of Independence is the ringbolt to the chain of your nation's destiny; so, indeed, I regard it. The principles contained in that instrument are saving principles. Stand by those principles, be true to them on all occasions, in all places, against all foes, and at whatever cost.

From the round top of your ship of state, dark and threatening clouds may be seen. Heavy billows, like mountains in the distance, disclose to the leeward[1] huge forms of flinty rocks! That *bolt* drawn, that *chain* broken, and all is lost. *Cling to this day—cling to it*, and to its principles, with the grasp of a storm-tossed mariner to a spar[2] at midnight.

The coming into being of a nation, in any circumstances, is an interesting event. But, besides general considerations, there were peculiar circumstances which make the advent of this republic an event of special attractiveness.

The whole scene, as I look back to it, was simple, dignified and sublime.

The population of the country, at the time, stood at the insignificant number of three millions. The country was poor in the munitions of war. The population was weak and scattered, and the country a wilderness unsubdued. There were then no means of concert[3] and combination such as exist now. Neither steam nor lightning[4] had then been reduced to order and discipline. From the Potomac to the Delaware was a journey of many days. Under these, and innumerable other disadvantages, your fathers declared for liberty and independence and triumphed.

Fellow Citizens, I am not wanting[5] in respect for the fathers of this republic. The signers of the Declaration of Independence were brave men. They were great men too—great enough to give fame to a great age. It does not often happen to a nation to raise, at one time, such a number of truly great men. The point from which I am compelled

1 *leeward* Side facing away from the wind.

2 *spar* Mast or other pole used to support a ship's sails.

3 *concert* Coming together.

4 *steam nor lightning* I.e., neither steam power nor electricity.

5 *wanting* Lacking.

to view them is not, certainly, the most favorable; and yet I cannot contemplate their great deeds with less than admiration. They were statesmen, patriots and heroes, and for the good they did, and the principles they contended for, I will unite with you to honor their memory.

They loved their country better than their own private interests; and, though this is not the highest form of human excellence, all will concede that it is a rare virtue, and that when it is exhibited, it ought to command respect. He who will, intelligently, lay down his life for his country, is a man whom it is not in human nature to despise. Your fathers staked their lives, their fortunes, and their sacred honor, on the cause of their country. In their admiration of liberty, they lost sight of all other interests.

They were peace men; but they preferred revolution to peaceful submission to bondage. They were quiet men; but they did not shrink from agitating against oppression. They showed forbearance; but that they knew its limits. They believed in order; but not in the order of tyranny. With them, nothing was "*settled*" that was not right. With them, justice, liberty and humanity were "*final*"; not slavery and oppression. You may well cherish the memory of such men. They were great in their day and generation. Their solid manhood stands out the more as we contrast it with these degenerate times.

How circumspect, exact and proportionate were all their movements! How unlike the politicians of an hour! Their statesmanship looked beyond the passing moment, and stretched away in strength into the distant future. They seized upon eternal principles, and set a glorious example in their defense. Mark them!

Fully appreciating the hardship to be encountered, firmly believing in the right of their cause, honorably inviting the scrutiny of an onlooking world, reverently appealing to heaven to attest their sincerity, soundly comprehending the solemn responsibility they were about to assume, wisely measuring the terrible odds against them, your fathers, the fathers of this republic, did, most deliberately, under the inspiration of a glorious patriotism, and with a sublime faith in the great principles of justice and freedom, lay deep the corner-stone of the national superstructure, which has risen and still rises in grandeur around you.

Of this fundamental work, this day is the anniversary. Our eyes are met with demonstrations of joyous enthusiasm. Banners and pennants[1] wave exultingly on the breeze. The din of business, too, is hushed. Even mammon[2] seems to have quitted his grasp on this day. The ear-piercing fife and the stirring drum unite their accents with the ascending peal of a thousand church bells. Prayers are made, hymns are sung, and sermons are preached in honor of this day; while the quick martial tramp of a great and multitudinous nation, echoed back by all the hills, valleys and mountains of a vast continent, bespeak the occasion one of thrilling and universal interest—a nation's jubilee.

Friends and citizens, I need not enter further into the causes which led to this anniversary. Many of you understand them better than I do. You could instruct me in regard to them. That is a branch of knowledge in which you feel, perhaps, a much deeper interest than your speaker. The causes which led to the separation of the colonies from the British crown have never lacked for a tongue. They have all been taught in your common schools, narrated at your firesides, unfolded from your pulpits, and thundered from your legislative halls, and are as familiar to you as household words. They form the staple of your national poetry and eloquence.

I remember, also, that, as a people, Americans are remarkably familiar with all facts which make in their own favor. This is esteemed by some as a national trait—perhaps a national weakness. It is a fact that whatever makes for the wealth or for the reputation of Americans—and can be had *cheap*!—will be found by Americans. I shall not be charged with slandering Americans, if I say I think the American side of any question may be safely left in American hands.

I leave, therefore, the great deeds of your fathers to other gentlemen whose claim to have been regularly descended will be less likely to be disputed than mine!

The Present

My business, if I have any here today, is with the present. The accepted time with God and his cause is the ever-living now.

---

1 *pennants* Narrow, triangular flags.

2 *mammon* Wealth and profit (regarded as a false god).

Trust no future, however pleasant,
    Let the dead past bury its dead;
Act, act in the living present,
    Heart within, and God overhead.[1]

We have to do with the past only as we can make it useful to the present and to the future. To all inspiring motives, to noble deeds which can be gained from the past, we are welcome. But now is the time, the important time. Your fathers have lived, died, and have done their work, and have done much of it well. You live and must die, and you must do your work. You have no right to enjoy a child's share in the labor of your fathers, unless your children are to be blessed by your labors. You have no right to wear out and waste the hard-earned fame of your fathers to cover your indolence. Sydney Smith[2] tells us that men seldom eulogize the wisdom and virtues of their fathers, but to excuse some folly or wickedness of their own. This truth is not a doubtful one. There are illustrations of it near and remote, ancient and modern. It was fashionable, hundreds of years ago, for the children of Jacob to boast, we have "Abraham to our father," when they had long lost Abraham's faith and spirit.[3] That people contented themselves under the shadow of Abraham's great name, while they repudiated the deeds which made his name great. Need I remind you that a similar thing is being done all over this country today? Need I tell you that the Jews are not the only people who built the tombs of the prophets, and garnished the sepulchres of the righteous? Washington could not die till he had broken the chains of his slaves. Yet his monument is built up by the price of human blood,[4] and the traders in the bodies and souls of men, shout—"We have Washington to '*our father.*'" Alas! that it should be so; yet so it is.

---

1 *Trust no … God overhead* See Henry Wadsworth Longfellow's "A Psalm of Life" (1838).

2 *Sydney Smith* English humorist and Anglican minister (1771–1845).

3 *children of Jacob … spirit* See Matthew 3.9; Jacob, a biblical patriarch and grandson of Abraham, appears in the Book of Genesis.

4 *Washington … human blood* At the time of his death in 1799, George Washington owned 124 enslaved people, all of whom were freed under the terms of his will. The monument to which Douglass refers is the Washington Monument, construction of which had begun in 1848 (though it was not completed until 1884); given that slavery in Washington, D.C. did not end until 1862, it is highly likely that enslaved people played a large role in the early stages of the monument's construction.

The evil that men do, lives after them,
The good is oft' interred with their bones.[1]

Fellow citizens, pardon me, allow me to ask, why am I called upon to speak here today?[2] What have I, or those I represent, to do with your national independence? Are the great principles of political freedom and of natural justice, embodied in that Declaration of Independence, extended to us? and am I, therefore, called upon to bring our humble offering to the national altar, and to confess the benefits and express devout gratitude for the blessings resulting from your independence to us?

Would to God, both for your sakes and ours, that an affirmative answer could be truthfully returned to these questions! Then would my task be light, and my burden easy and delightful. For *who* is there so cold that a nation's sympathy could not warm him? Who so obdurate and dead to the claims of gratitude, that would not thankfully acknowledge such priceless benefits? Who so stolid and selfish, that would not give his voice to swell the hallelujahs of a nation's jubilee, when the chains of servitude had been torn from his limbs? I am not that man. In a case like that, the dumb[3] might eloquently speak, and the "lame man leap as an hart."[4]

But such is not the state of the case. I say it with a sad sense of the disparity between us. I am not included within the pale of this glorious anniversary! Your high independence only reveals the immeasurable distance between us. The blessings in which you, this day, rejoice, are not enjoyed in common. The rich inheritance of justice, liberty, prosperity and independence, bequeathed by your fathers, is shared by you, not by me. The sunlight that brought life and healing to you, has brought stripes[5] and death to me. This Fourth July is *yours*, not *mine*. *You* may rejoice, *I* must mourn. To drag a man in fetters into the grand illuminated temple of liberty, and call upon him to join you in joyous anthems, were inhuman mockery and sacrilegious irony.

---

1 *The evil ... their bones* See Shakespeare's *Julius Caesar* 3.2.84–85.

2 *Fellow citizens ... today?* Douglass begins his 1855 "Extract" here.

3 *dumb* Mute.

4 *lame man ... hart* See Isaiah 35.6: "Then shall the lame man leap as an hart, and the tongue of the dumb sing: for in the wilderness shall waters break out, and streams in the desert"; *hart* Stag.

5 *stripes* I.e., scars from having been whipped.

Do you mean, citizens, to mock me, by asking me to speak today? If so, there is a parallel to your conduct.[1] And let me warn you that it is dangerous to copy the example of a nation whose crimes, towering up to heaven, were thrown down by the breath of the Almighty, burying that nation in irrecoverable ruin![2] I can today take up the plaintive lament of a peeled[3] and woe-smitten people!

> By the rivers of Babylon, there we sat down. Yea! we wept when we remembered Zion. We hanged our harps upon the willows in the midst thereof. For there, they that carried us away captive, required of us a song; and they who wasted us required of us mirth, saying, Sing us one of the songs of Zion. How can we sing the Lord's song in a strange land? If I forget thee, O Jerusalem, let my right hand forget her cunning. If I do not remember thee, let my tongue cleave to the roof of my mouth.

Fellow citizens; above your national, tumultuous joy, I hear the mournful wail of millions! whose chains, heavy and grievous yesterday, are today rendered more intolerable by the jubilee shouts that reach them. If I do forget, if I do not faithfully remember those bleeding children of sorrow this day, "may my right hand forget her cunning, and may my tongue cleave to the roof of my mouth"! To forget them, to pass lightly over their wrongs, and to chime in with the popular theme, would be treason most scandalous and shocking, and would make me a reproach before God and the world. My subject, then, fellow citizens, is American Slavery. I shall see this day, and its popular characteristics, from the slave's point of view. Standing, there, identified with the American bondman, making his wrongs mine, I do not hesitate to declare, with all my soul, that the character and conduct of this nation never looked blacker to me than on this 4th of July! Whether we turn to the declarations of the past, or to the professions

---

1 *there is … your conduct* Douglass alludes to the treatment of the Israelites during their period as captives of the Babylonian King Nebuchadnezzar. Psalm 137 (quoted from below) describes how the Israelites refuse their captor's demand that they "sing the Lord's song in a strange land."

2 *a nation … irrevocable ruin* The destruction of the kingdom of Babylon is prophesied in the Old Testament, and described in the Book of Revelations, where the kingdom's sinful history is symbolized by the figure of the "Whore of Babylon."

3 *peeled* Wretched.

of the present, the conduct of the nation seems equally hideous and revolting. America is false to the past, false to the present, and solemnly binds herself to be false to the future. Standing with God and the crushed and bleeding slave on this occasion, I will, in the name of humanity which is outraged, in the name of liberty which is fettered, in the name of the constitution and the Bible, which are disregarded and trampled upon, dare to call in question and to denounce, with all the emphasis I can command, everything that serves to perpetuate slavery—the great sin and shame of America! "I will not equivocate; I will not excuse";[1] I will use the severest language I can command; and yet not one word shall escape me that any man, whose judgment is not blinded by prejudice, or who is not at heart a slaveholder, shall not confess to be right and just.

But I fancy I hear some one of my audience say, it is just in this circumstance that you and your brother abolitionists fail to make a favorable impression on the public mind. Would you argue more, and denounce less,[2] would you persuade more, and rebuke less, your cause would be much more likely to succeed. But, I submit, where all is plain, there is nothing to be argued. What point in the anti-slavery creed would you have me argue? On what branch of the subject do the people of this country need light? Must I undertake to prove that the slave is a man? That point is conceded already. Nobody doubts it. The slaveholders themselves acknowledge it in the enactment of laws for their government. They acknowledge it when they punish disobedience on the part of the slave. There are seventy-two crimes in the State of Virginia, which, if committed by a black man (no matter how ignorant he be), subject him to the punishment of death; while only two of the same crimes will subject a white man to the like punishment. What is this but the acknowledgement that the slave is a moral, intellectual and responsible being? The manhood of the slave is conceded. It is admitted in the fact that Southern statute books are covered with enactments forbidding, under severe fines and penalties, the teaching of the slave to read or to write. When you can point to any such laws, in reference to the beasts of the field, then I

1 *I will ... not excuse* Douglass here quotes from William Lloyd Garrison's opening article in the first issue of *The Liberator* (1831), an influential antislavery newspaper.

2 *argue ... less* I.e., present more arguments in favor of your goals, and make fewer denunciations of the present state.

may consent to argue the manhood of the slave. When the dogs in your streets, when the fowls of the air, when the cattle on your hills, when the fish of the sea, and the reptiles that crawl, shall be unable to distinguish the slave from a brute, *then* will I argue with you that the slave is a man!

For the present, it is enough to affirm the equal manhood of the negro race. Is it not astonishing that, while we are ploughing, planting and reaping, using all kinds of mechanical tools, erecting houses, constructing bridges, building ships, working in metals of brass, iron, copper, silver and gold; that, while we are reading, writing and cyphering,[1] acting as clerks, merchants and secretaries, having among us lawyers, doctors, ministers, poets, authors, editors, orators and teachers; that, while we are engaged in all manner of enterprises common to other men, digging gold in California, capturing the whale in the Pacific, feeding sheep and cattle on the hill-side, living, moving, acting, thinking, planning, living in families as husbands, wives and children, and, above all, confessing and worshipping the Christian's God, and looking hopefully for life and immortality beyond the grave, we are called upon to prove that we are men!

Would you have me argue that man is entitled to liberty? that he is the rightful owner of his own body? You have already declared it. Must I argue the wrongfulness of slavery? Is that a question for republicans?[2] Is it to be settled by the rules of logic and argumentation, as a matter beset with great difficulty, involving a doubtful application of the principle of justice, hard to be understood? How should I look today, in the presence of Americans, dividing and subdividing a discourse, to show that men have a natural right to freedom? speaking of it relatively, and positively, negatively, and affirmatively? To do so would be to make myself ridiculous, and to offer an insult to your understanding. There is not a man beneath the canopy of heaven, that does not know that slavery is wrong *for him*.

What, am I to argue that it is wrong to make men brutes, to rob them of their liberty, to work them without wages, to keep them ignorant of their relations to their fellow men, to beat them with sticks, to flay their flesh with the lash, to load their limbs with irons,

1 *cyphering* Doing calculations.
2 *republicans* I.e., citizens of a republic.

to hunt them with dogs, to sell them at auction, to sunder their families, to knock out their teeth, to burn their flesh, to starve them into obedience and submission to their masters? Must I argue that a system thus marked with blood, and stained with pollution, is *wrong*? No I will not. I have better employment for my time and strength than such arguments would imply.

What, then, remains to be argued? Is it that slavery is not divine; that God did not establish it; that our doctors of divinity are mistaken? There is blasphemy in the thought. That which is inhuman, cannot be divine! *Who* can reason on such a proposition? They that can, may; I cannot. The time for such argument is past.

At a time like this, scorching irony, not convincing argument, is needed. O! had I the ability, and could I reach the nation's ear, I would, today, pour out a fiery stream of biting ridicule, blasting reproach, withering sarcasm, and stern rebuke. For it is not light that is needed, but fire; it is not the gentle shower, but thunder. We need the storm, the whirlwind, and the earthquake. The feeling of the nation must be quickened; the conscience of the nation must be roused; the propriety of the nation must be startled; the hypocrisy of the nation must be exposed; and its crimes against God and man must be proclaimed and denounced.

What, to the American slave, is your 4th of July? I answer: a day that reveals to him, more than all other days in the year, the gross injustice and cruelty to which he is the constant victim. To him, your celebration is a sham; your boasted liberty, an unholy license; your national greatness, swelling vanity; your sounds of rejoicing are empty and heartless; your denunciations of tyrants, brass fronted impudence; your shouts of liberty and equality, hollow mockery; your prayers and hymns, your sermons and thanksgivings, with all your religious parade, and solemnity, are, to him, mere bombast, fraud, deception, impiety, and hypocrisy—a thin veil to cover up crimes which would disgrace a nation of savages. There is not a nation on the earth guilty of practices more shocking and bloody than are the people of these United States, at this very hour.

Go where you may, search where you will, roam through all the monarchies and despotisms of the old world, travel through South America, search out every abuse, and when you have found the last, lay your facts by the side of the everyday practices of this nation, and you will say with me, that, for revolting barbarity and shameless hypocrisy, America reigns without a rival.[1]

The Internal Slave Trade

Take the American slave-trade, which, we are told by the papers, is especially prosperous just now. Ex-Senator Benton[2] tells us that the price of men was never higher than now. He mentions the fact to show that slavery is in no danger. This trade is one of the peculiarities of American institutions. It is carried on in all the large towns and cities in one-half of this confederacy; and millions are pocketed every year by dealers in this horrid traffic. In several states, this trade is a chief source of wealth. It is called (in contradistinction to the foreign slave-trade) "*the internal slave-trade*." It is, probably, called so, too, in order to divert from it the horror with which the foreign slave-trade is contemplated. That trade has long since been denounced by this government, as piracy.[3] It has been denounced with burning words, from the high places of the nation, as an execrable traffic. To arrest it, to put an end to it, this nation keeps a squadron, at immense cost, on the coast of Africa. Everywhere, in this country, it is safe to speak of this foreign slave-trade as a most inhuman traffic, opposed alike to the laws of God and of man. The duty to extirpate and destroy it, is admitted even by our Doctors of Divinity. In order to put an end to it, some of these last have consented that their colored brethren (nominally free) should leave this country, and establish themselves on the western coast of Africa![4] It is, however, a notable fact that, while so much execration is poured out by Americans upon those engaged in the foreign slave-trade, the men engaged in the slave-trade between the states pass without condemnation, and their business is deemed honorable.

---

1 *without a rival* The "Extract" in Douglass's *My Bondage and My Freedom* ends here.

2 *Ex-Senator Benton* Thomas Hart Benton (1782–1858), Democratic senator who, though he owned enslaved people for much of his life, came to oppose the institution.

3 *That trade … as piracy* The Atlantic slave trade was abolished by the United States in 1808.

4 *In order … of Africa* Douglass alludes to the colonization movement, led chiefly by the American Colonization Society, whose members (many of whom belonged to the clergy, and all of whom were white men) advocated for the relocation of free African Americans to the African continent. This movement was widely condemned by many—though not all—abolitionists in the nineteenth century.

Behold the practical operation of this internal slave-trade, the American slave-trade, sustained by American politics and American religion. Here you will see men and women, reared like swine for the market. You know what is a swine-drover? I will show you a man-drover.[1] They inhabit all our Southern States. They perambulate the country, and crowd the highways of the nation, with droves of human stock. You will see one of these human flesh jobbers,[2] armed with pistol, whip and bowie-knife,[3] driving a company of a hundred men, women, and children, from the Potomac to the slave market at New Orleans. These wretched people are to be sold singly, or in lots, to suit purchasers. They are food for the cotton-field, and the deadly sugar-mill. Mark the sad procession, as it moves wearily along, and the inhuman wretch who drives them. Hear his savage yells and his blood-chilling oaths, as he hurries on his affrighted captives! There, see the old man, with locks thinned and gray. Cast one glance, if you please, upon that young mother, whose shoulders are bare to the scorching sun, her briny tears falling on the brow of the babe in her arms. See, too, that girl of thirteen, weeping, *yes*! weeping, as she thinks of the mother from whom she has been torn! The drove moves tardily. Heat and sorrow have nearly consumed their strength; suddenly you hear a quick snap, like the discharge of a rifle; the fetters clank, and the chain rattles simultaneously; your ears are saluted with a scream, that seems to have torn its way to the centre of your soul! The crack you heard, was the sound of the slave-whip; the scream you heard, was from the woman you saw with the babe. Her speed had faltered under the weight of her child and her chains! that gash on her shoulder tells her to move on. Follow the drove to New Orleans. Attend the auction; see men examined like horses; see the forms of women rudely and brutally exposed to the shocking gaze of American slave-buyers. See this drove sold and separated forever; and never forget the deep, sad sobs that arose from that scattered multitude. Tell me citizens, where, under the sun, you can witness a spectacle more fiendish and shocking. Yet this is but a glance at the American slave-trade, as it exists, at this moment, in the ruling part of the United States.

---

1 *drover* Herder; one who is in charge of moving a herd (or "drove") of animals from place to place.

2 *jobbers* Dealers.

3 *bowie-knife* Short fighting-knife often associated with the American South.

I was born amid such sights and scenes. To me the American slave-trade is a terrible reality. When a child, my soul was often pierced with a sense of its horrors. I lived on Philpot Street, Fell's Point, Baltimore, and have watched from the wharves, the slave ships in the Basin, anchored from the shore, with their cargoes of human flesh, waiting for favorable winds to waft them down the Chesapeake. There was, at that time, a grand slave mart kept at the head of Pratt Street, by Austin Woldfolk. His agents were sent into every town and county in Maryland, announcing their arrival, through the papers, and on flaming "*hand-bills*," headed CASH FOR NEGROES. These men were generally well dressed men, and very captivating in their manners. Ever ready to drink, to treat, and to gamble. The fate of many a slave has depended upon the turn of a single card; and many a child has been snatched from the arms of its mother, by bargains arranged in a state of brutal drunkenness.

The flesh-mongers gather up their victims by dozens, and drive them, chained, to the general depot at Baltimore. When a sufficient number have been collected here, a ship is chartered, for the purpose of conveying the forlorn crew to Mobile, or to New Orleans. From the slave prison to the ship, they are usually driven in the darkness of night; for since the antislavery agitation, a certain caution is observed.

In the deep still darkness of midnight, I have been often aroused by the dead heavy footsteps, and the piteous cries of the chained gangs that passed our door. The anguish of my boyish heart was intense; and I was often consoled, when speaking to my mistress in the morning, to hear her say that the custom was very wicked; that she hated to hear the rattle of the chains, and the heart-rending cries. I was glad to find one who sympathized with me in my horror.

Fellow citizens, this murderous traffic is, today, in active operation in this boasted republic. In the solitude of my spirit, I see clouds of dust raised on the highways of the South; I see the bleeding footsteps; I hear the doleful wail of fettered humanity, on the way to the slave-markets, where the victims are to be sold like *horses*, *sheep*, and *swine*, knocked off to the highest bidder. There I see the tenderest ties ruthlessly broken, to gratify the lust, caprice and rapacity of the buyers and sellers of men. My soul sickens at the sight.

Is this the land your Fathers loved,
    The freedom which they toiled to win?
Is this the earth whereon they moved?
    Are these the graves they slumber in?[1]

But a still more inhuman, disgraceful, and scandalous state of things remains to be presented.

By an act of the American Congress, not yet two years old, slavery has been nationalized in its most horrible and revolting form. By that act, Mason & Dixon's line has been obliterated; New York has become as Virginia; and the power to hold, hunt, and sell men, women, and children as slaves remains no longer a mere state institution, but is now an institution of the whole United States.[2] The power is co-extensive with the star-spangled banner, and American Christianity. Where these go, may also go the merciless slave-hunter. Where these are, man is not sacred. He is a bird for the sportsman's gun. By that most foul and fiendish of all human decrees, the liberty and person of every man are put in peril. Your broad republican domain is hunting ground for *men. Not* for thieves and robbers, enemies of society, merely, but for men guilty of no crime. Your lawmakers have commanded all good citizens to engage in this hellish sport. Your President, your Secretary of State, your *lords, nobles,* and ecclesiastics, enforce, as a duty you owe to your free and glorious country, and to your God, that you do this accursed thing. Not fewer than forty Americans have, within the past two years, been hunted down, and, without a moment's warning, hurried away in chains, and consigned to slavery and excruciating torture. Some of these have had wives and children, dependent on them for bread; but of this, no account was made. The right of the hunter to his prey stands superior to the

1 *Is this … slumber in?* See "Stanzas for the Times" by antislavery poet John Greenleaf Whittier.

2 *By an act … United States* Douglass refers to the Fugitive Slave Act of 1850 (a part of the Compromise of 1850), under the terms of which it became illegal for anyone, whether in the North or the South, to give aid to people escaping slavery; citizens throughout the country were expected to actively participate in the apprehension and return of such fugitives. Given that the testimony of captured African Americans was not accepted in court, the Act inevitably resulted in the capture and enslavement of many free African Americans, as well as of many who had been previously enslaved; *Mason & Dixon's line* Line separating parts of Pennsylvania and Delaware from parts of Maryland and Virginia; the phrase was used as shorthand for the boundary between the Northern free states and the Southern slave states.

right of marriage, and to *all* rights in this republic, the rights of God included! For black men there are neither law, justice, humanity, nor religion. The Fugitive Slave *Law* makes mercy to them, a crime; and bribes the judge who tries them. An American Judge gets ten dollars for every victim he consigns to slavery, and five, when he fails to do so. The oath of any two villains is sufficient, under this hell-black enactment, to send the most pious and exemplary black man into the remorseless jaws of slavery! His own testimony is nothing. He can bring no witnesses for himself. The minister of American justice is bound, by the law, to hear but *one* side; and *that* side, is the side of the oppressor. Let this damning fact be perpetually told. Let it be thundered around the world, that, in tyrant-killing, king-hating, people-loving, democratic, Christian America, the seats of justice are filled with judges, who hold their offices under an open and palpable *bribe*, and are bound, in deciding in the case of a man's liberty, *to hear only his accusers*!

In glaring violation of justice, in shameless disregard of the forms of administering law, in cunning arrangement to entrap the defenseless, and in diabolical intent, this Fugitive Slave Law stands alone in the annals of tyrannical legislation. I doubt if there be another nation on the globe, having the brass and the baseness to put such a law on the statute-book. If any man in this assembly thinks differently from me in this matter, and feels able to disprove my statements, I will gladly confront him at any suitable time and place he may select.

Religious Liberty

I take this law to be one of the grossest infringements of Christian Liberty, and, if the churches and ministers of our country were not stupidly blind, or most wickedly indifferent, they, too, would so regard it.

At the very moment that they are thanking God for the enjoyment of civil and religious liberty, and for the right to worship God according to the dictates of their own consciences, they are utterly silent in respect to a law which robs religion of its chief significance, and makes it utterly worthless to a world lying in wickedness. Did this law concern the "*mint*, *anise* and *cumin*"[1]—abridge the right to sing psalms, to partake of the sacrament, or to engage in any of the ceremonies of religion, it would be smitten by the thunder of a thousand pulpits. A general shout would go up from the church, demanding *repeal*, *repeal*, *instant repeal*! And it would go hard with that politician who presumed to solicit the votes of the people without inscribing this motto on his banner. Further, if this demand were not complied with, another Scotland would be added to the history of religious liberty, and the stern old covenanters[2] would be thrown into the shade. A John Knox would be seen at every church door, and heard from every pulpit, and Fillmore would have no more quarter than was shown by Knox to the beautiful but treacherous queen Mary of Scotland.[3] The fact that the church of our country (with fractional exceptions) does not esteem "the Fugitive Slave Law" as a declaration of war against religious liberty, implies that that church regards religion simply as a form of worship, an empty ceremony, and *not* a vital principle, requiring active benevolence, justice, love and good will towards man. It esteems sacrifice above mercy; psalm-singing above right doing; solemn meetings above practical righteousness. A worship that can be conducted by persons who refuse to give shelter to the houseless, to give bread to the hungry, clothing to the naked, and who enjoin obedience to a law forbidding these acts of mercy, is a curse, not a blessing to mankind. The Bible addresses all such persons as "scribes, pharisees, hypocrites, who pay tithe of *mint*, *anise*, and *cumin*, and have omitted the weightier matters of the law, judgment, mercy and faith."

---

1 *mint, anise and cumin* See Matthew 23.23: "Woe unto you, scribes and Pharisees, hypocrites! for ye pay tithe of mint and anise and cumin, and have omitted the weightier matters of the law, judgment, mercy, and faith: these ought ye to have done, and not to leave the other undone."

2 *covenanters* Name given to the Scottish Presbyterians who signed the National Covenant in 1638, seeking to uphold the Presbyterian Church in Scotland in the face of persecution by King Charles I.

3 *A John Knox … Scotland* John Knox (1514–72), religious dissenter and founder of the Scottish Presbyterian Church, was an ardent opponent of the Catholic Mary Queen of Scots, who was executed for treason in 1587. Millard Fillmore, who was President of the United States at the time of Douglass's speech, was instrumental in the passage of the Fugitive Slave Act.

The Church Responsible

But the church of this country is not only indifferent to the wrongs of the slave, it actually takes sides with the oppressors. It has made itself the bulwark of American slavery, and the shield of American slave-hunters. Many of its most eloquent Divines, who stand as the very lights of the church, have shamelessly given the sanction of religion, and the Bible, to the whole slave system. They have taught that man may, properly, be a slave; that the relation of master and slave is ordained of God; that to send back an escaped bondman to his master is clearly the duty of all the followers of the Lord Jesus Christ; and this horrible blasphemy is palmed off upon the world for Christianity.

For my part, I would say, welcome infidelity! welcome atheism! welcome anything! in preference to the gospel, *as preached by those Divines*! They convert the very name of religion into an engine of tyranny, and barbarous cruelty, and serve to confirm more infidels, in this age, than all the infidel writings of Thomas Paine, Voltaire, and Bolingbroke,[1] put together, have done! These ministers make religion a cold and flinty-hearted thing, having neither principles of right action, nor bowels of compassion. They strip the love of God of its beauty, and leave the throng of religion a huge, horrible, repulsive form. It is a religion for oppressors, tyrants, man-stealers, and *thugs*. It is not that "*pure and undefiled religion*"[2] which is from above, and which is "*first pure, then peaceable, easy to be entreated*, full of mercy and good fruits, *without partiality, and without hypocrisy*." But a religion which favors the rich against the poor; which exalts the proud above the humble; which divides mankind into two classes, tyrants and slaves; which says to the man in chains, *stay there*; and to the oppressor, *oppress on*; it is a religion which may be professed and enjoyed by all the robbers and enslavers of mankind; it makes God a respecter of

---

1 *Thomas Paine* English-born political theorist whose *Common Sense* (1776) was profoundly influential during the time of the American Revolution, and whose *The Age of Reason* (1794–1807) was highly critical of organized religion; *Voltaire* French Enlightenment philosopher (1694–1778) who advocated freedom of speech and the separation of church and state, and was often accused of atheism; *Bolingbroke* Henry St. John, 1st Viscount Bolingbroke (1678–1751), English political philosopher whose antireligious views influenced Voltaire as well as numerous key figures of the American Revolution.

2 *pure and undefiled religion* See James 1.27.

persons,[1] denies his fatherhood of the race, and tramples in the dust the great truth of the brotherhood of man. All this we affirm to be true of the popular church, and the popular worship of our land and nation—a religion, a church, and a worship which, on the authority of inspired wisdom, we pronounce to be an abomination in the sight of God. In the language of Isaiah, the American church might be well addressed, "Bring no more vain oblations; incense is an abomination unto me: the new moons and Sabbaths, the calling of assemblies, I cannot away with; it is iniquity, even the solemn meeting. Your new moons, and your appointed feasts my soul hateth. They are a trouble to me; I am weary to bear them; and when ye spread forth your hands I will hide mine eyes from you. Yea! when ye make many prayers, I will not hear. YOUR HANDS ARE FULL OF BLOOD; cease to do evil, learn to do well; seek judgment; relieve the oppressed; judge for the fatherless; plead for the widow."[2]

The American church is guilty, when viewed in connection with what it is doing to uphold slavery; but it is superlatively guilty when viewed in connection with its ability to abolish slavery.

The sin of which it is guilty is one of omission as well as of commission. Albert Barnes[3] but uttered what the common sense of every man at all observant of the actual state of the case will receive as truth, when he declared that "There is no power out of the church that could sustain slavery an hour, if it were not sustained in it."

Let the religious press, the pulpit, the Sunday school, the conference meeting, the great ecclesiastical, missionary, Bible and tract associations of the land array their immense powers against slavery, and slave-holding; and the whole system of crime and blood would be scattered to the winds; and that they do not do this involves them in the most awful responsibility of which the mind can conceive.

In prosecuting the anti-slavery enterprise, we have been asked to spare the church, to spare the ministry; but *how*, we ask, could such a thing be done? We are met on the threshold of our efforts for the redemption of the slave, by the church and ministry of the country, in

1 *respecter of persons* In Acts 10.34, Peter claims that "God is no respecter of persons"; i.e., that he does not favor people of higher status.

2 *In the language ... the widow* See Isaiah 1.13–17.

3 *Albert Barnes* American antislavery theologian (1798–1870) who wrote numerous books on the subject of slavery and religion.

battle arrayed against us; and we are compelled to fight or flee. From *what* quarter, I beg to know, has proceeded a fire so deadly upon our ranks, during the last two years, as from the Northern pulpit? As the champions of oppressors, the chosen men of American theology have appeared—men, honored for their so-called piety, and their real learning. The Lords of Buffalo, the Springs of New York, the Lathrops of Auburn, the Coxes and Spencers of Brooklyn, the Gannets and Sharps of Boston, the Deweys of Washington,[1] and other great religious lights of the land, have, in utter denial of the authority of *Him*, by whom they professed to be called to the ministry, deliberately taught us, against the example of the Hebrews, and against the remonstrance of the Apostles, they teach *that we ought to obey man's law before the law of God.*[2]

My spirit wearies of such blasphemy; and how such men can be supported, as the "standing types and representatives of Jesus Christ," is a mystery which I leave others to penetrate. In speaking of the American church, however, let it be distinctly understood that I mean the *great mass* of the religious organizations of our land. There are exceptions, and I thank God that there are. Noble men may be found, scattered all over these Northern States, of whom Henry Ward Beecher of Brooklyn, Samuel J. May[3] of Syracuse, and my esteemed friend[4] on the platform, are shining examples; and let me say further, that, upon these men lies the duty to inspire our ranks with high religious faith and zeal, and to cheer us on in the great mission of the slave's redemption from his chains.

Religion in England and Religion in America

One is struck with the difference between the attitude of the American church towards the anti-slavery movement, and that occupied by

1 *The Lords ... of Washington* Douglass alludes to a number of religious leaders who were either explicitly proslavery or who were morally opposed to slavery but favored not interfering with the institution.

2 *that we ... of God* See Acts 5.29: "Then Peter and the other apostles answered and said, We ought to obey God rather than men."

3 *Henry Ward Beecher* American Congregationalist minister (1813–87) and antislavery activist; *Samuel J. May* American Unitarian minister (1797–1871) and abolitionist.

4 [Douglass's note] Rev. R.R. Raymond. [Baptist minister and abolitionist who contributed to Julia Griffiths's 1853 abolitionist collection *Autographs for Freedom*.]

the churches in England towards a similar movement in that country. There, the church, true to its mission of ameliorating, elevating, and improving the condition of mankind, came forward promptly, bound up the wounds of the West Indian slave, and restored him to his liberty. There, the question of emancipation was a high religious question. It was demanded, in the name of humanity, and according to the law of the living God. The Sharps, the Clarksons, the Wilberforces, the Buxtons, and Burchells and the Knibbs,[1] were alike famous for their piety, and for their philanthropy. The anti-slavery movement *there* was not an anti-church movement, for the reason that the church took its full share in prosecuting that movement: and the anti-slavery movement in this country will cease to be an anti-church movement, when the church of this country shall assume a favorable, instead of a hostile position towards that movement.

Americans! your republican politics, not less than your republican religion, are flagrantly inconsistent. You boast of your love of liberty, your superior civilization, and your pure Christianity, while the whole political power of the nation, as embodied in the two great political parties, is solemnly pledged to support and perpetuate the enslavement of three millions of your countrymen. You hurl your anathemas at the crowned headed tyrants of Russia and Austria, and pride yourselves on your Democratic institutions, while you yourselves consent to be the mere *tools* and *bodyguards* of the tyrants of Virginia and Carolina. You invite to your shores fugitives of oppression from abroad, honor them with banquets, greet them with ovations, cheer them, toast them, salute them, protect them, and pour out your money to them like water; but the fugitives from your own land, you advertise, hunt, arrest, shoot and kill. You glory in your refinement, and your universal education; yet you maintain a system as barbarous and dreadful, as ever stained the character of a nation—a system begun in avarice, supported in pride, and perpetuated in cruelty. You shed tears over fallen Hungary,[2] and make the sad story of her wrongs the theme of your poets, statesmen and orators, till your

1 *The Sharps ... the Knibbs* Douglass alludes to numerous English abolitionists active in the eighteenth and early nineteenth centuries, among them the influential politician William Wilberforce (1759–1833).

2 *fallen Hungary* The Hungarian Revolution, which many Americans supported, took place in 1848; it was violently suppressed by the Austrian Empire.

gallant sons are ready to fly to arms to vindicate her cause against her oppressors; but, in regard to the ten thousand wrongs of the American slave, you would enforce the strictest silence, and would hail him as an enemy of the nation who dares to make those wrongs the subject of public discourse! You are all on fire at the mention of liberty for France or for Ireland; but are as cold as an iceberg at the thought of liberty for the enslaved of America. You discourse eloquently on the dignity of labor; yet you sustain a system which, in its very essence, casts a stigma upon labor. You can bare your bosom to the storm of British artillery, to throw off a three-penny tax on tea;[1] and yet wring the last hard-earned farthing from the grasp of the black laborers of your country. You profess to believe "that, of one blood, God made all nations of men to dwell on the face of all the earth,"[2] and hath commanded all men, everywhere to love one another; yet you notoriously hate (and glory in your hatred) all men whose skins are not colored like your own. You declare, before the world, and are understood by the world to declare, that you "*hold these truths to be self evident, that all men are created equal; and are endowed by their Creator with certain inalienable rights; and that, among these are, life, liberty, and the pursuit of happiness*";[3] and yet, you hold securely, in a bondage which, according to your own Thomas Jefferson, "*is worse than ages of that which your fathers rose in rebellion to oppose*,"[4] a *seventh part* of the inhabitants of your country.

Fellow-citizens! I will not enlarge further on your national inconsistencies. The existence of slavery in this country brands your republicanism as a sham, your humanity as a base pretence, and your Christianity as a lie. It destroys your moral power abroad; it corrupts your politicians at home. It saps the foundation of religion; it makes your name a hissing, and a by word to a mocking earth. It is the antagonistic force in your government, the only thing that seriously disturbs and endangers your *Union*. It fetters your progress; it is the

1 *throw off … on tea* Douglass alludes to the Boston Tea Party of 1773, in which colonists protested the British Tea Act on the grounds that they would not tolerate taxation without representation.

2 *that … the earth* See Acts 17.26.

3 *hold these truths … of happiness* From the Declaration of Independence.

4 *Thomas Jefferson … to oppose* Douglass paraphrases text included in a letter sent by Thomas Jefferson to Jean-Nicolas Démeunier in 1786, in which he decried the hypocrisy of American slavery. (Jefferson was himself a slaveholder.)

enemy of improvement, the deadly foe of education; it fosters pride; it breeds insolence; it promotes vice; it shelters crime; it is a curse to the earth that supports it; and yet, you cling to it, as if it were the sheet anchor of all your hopes. Oh! be warned! be warned! a horrible reptile is coiled up in your nation's bosom; the venomous creature is nursing at the tender breast of your youthful republic; *for the love of God, tear away*, and fling from you the hideous monster, and *let the weight of twenty millions crush and destroy it forever*!

The Constitution

But it is answered in reply to all this, that precisely what I have now denounced is, in fact, guaranteed and sanctioned by the Constitution of the United States; that the right to hold, and to hunt slaves is a part of that Constitution framed by the illustrious Fathers of this Republic.

Then, I dare to affirm, notwithstanding all I have said before, your fathers stooped, basely stooped.

> To palter with us in a double sense:
> And keep the word of promise to the ear,
> But break it to the heart.[1]

And instead of being the honest men I have before declared them to be, they were the veriest imposters that ever practiced on mankind. *This* is the inevitable conclusion, and from it there is no escape; but I differ from those who charge this baseness on the framers of the Constitution of the United States.[2] *It is a slander upon their memory*, at least, so I believe. There is not time now to argue the constitutional question at length; nor have I the ability to discuss it as it ought to be discussed. The subject has been handled with masterly power by Lysander Spooner, Esq., by William Goodell, by Samuel E. Sewall, Esq., and last, though not least, by Gerritt Smith, Esq.[3] These gentle-

1 *To palter ... heart* Paraphrase from Shakespeare's *Macbeth* 5.8.24–26.

2 *but I differ ... United States* This disagreement was among the factors that led to Douglass's falling-out with his former colleague William Lloyd Garrison, who strongly believed the Constitution to be an inherently proslavery document.

3 *Lysander ... Esq.* Douglass names several abolitionists who argued that slavery was unconstitutional.

men have, as I think, fully and clearly vindicated the Constitution from any design to support slavery for an hour.

Fellow citizens! there is no matter in respect to which the people of the North have allowed themselves to be so ruinously imposed upon, as that of the pro-slavery character of the Constitution. In *that* instrument I hold there is neither warrant, license, nor sanction of the hateful thing; but, interpreted as it *ought* to be interpreted, the Constitution is a Glorious Liberty Document. Read its preamble, consider its purposes. Is slavery among them? Is it at the gateway? or is it in the temple? It is neither. While I do not intend to argue this question on the present occasion, let me ask, if it be not somewhat singular that, if the Constitution were intended to be, by its framers and adopters, a slave-holding instrument, why neither *slavery*, *slaveholding*, nor *slave* can anywhere be found in it. What would be thought of an instrument, drawn up, *legally* drawn up, for the purpose of entitling the city of Rochester to a track of land, in which no mention of land was made? Now, there are certain rules of interpretation, for the proper understanding of all legal instruments. These rules are well established. They are plain, common-sense rules, such as you and I, and all of us, can understand and apply, without having passed years in the study of law. I scout the idea that the question of the constitutionality, or unconstitutionality of slavery, is not a question for the people. I hold that every American citizen has a right to form an opinion of the constitution, and to propagate that opinion, and to use all honorable means to make his opinion the prevailing one. Without this right, the liberty of an American citizen would be as insecure as that of a Frenchman. Ex-Vice-President Dallas[1] tells us that the constitution is an object to which no American mind can be too attentive, and no American heart too devoted. He further says, the constitution, in its words, is plain and intelligible, and is meant for the home-bred, unsophisticated understandings of our fellow-citizens. Senator Berrien[2] tells us that the Constitution is the fundamental law, that which controls all others. The charter of our liberties, which every citizen has a personal interest in understanding thoroughly. The testimony of

1 *Ex-Vice-President Dallas* George Dallas (1792–1864), Vice President to James K. Polk.

2 *Senator Berrien* John Berrien (1781–1856), Georgia Senator who argued that slavery was fundamental to the Constitution.

Senator Breese, Lewis Cass,[1] and many others that might be named, who are everywhere esteemed as sound lawyers, so regard the constitution. I take it, therefore, that it is not presumption in a private citizen to form an opinion of that instrument.

Now, take the constitution according to its plain reading, and I defy the presentation of a single pro-slavery clause in it. On the other hand it will be found to contain principles and purposes, entirely hostile to the existence of slavery.

I have detained my audience entirely too long already. At some future period I will gladly avail myself of an opportunity to give this subject a full and fair discussion.

Allow me to say, in conclusion, notwithstanding the dark picture I have this day presented of the state of the nation, I do not despair of this country. There are forces in operation, which must inevitably work the downfall of slavery. "*The arm of the Lord is not shortened*,"[2] and the doom of slavery is certain. I, therefore, leave off where I began, with *hope*. While drawing encouragement from the "Declaration of Independence," the great principles it contains, and the genius of American Institutions, my spirit is also cheered by the obvious tendencies of the age. Nations do not now stand in the same relation to each other that they did ages ago. No nation can now shut itself up, from the surrounding world, and trot round in the same old path of its fathers without interference. The time *was* when such could be done. Long established customs of hurtful character could formerly fence themselves in, and do their evil work with social impunity. Knowledge was then confined and enjoyed by the privileged few, and the multitude walked on in mental darkness. But a change has now come over the affairs of mankind. Walled cities and empires have become unfashionable. The arm of commerce has borne away the gates of the strong city. Intelligence is penetrating the darkest corners of the globe. It makes its pathway over and under the sea, as well as on the earth. Wind, steam, and lightning are its chartered agents. Oceans no longer divide, but link nations together. From Boston to London is now a holiday excursion. Space

1 *Senator Breese* Sidney Breese (1800–78), Illinois Senator who favored the rule of popular sovereignty on the question of slavery; *Lewis Cass* Michigan Senator who campaigned for the presidency in 1848 and was opposed to limiting the spread of slavery.

2 *The arm … not shortened* See Isaiah 59.1.

is comparatively annihilated. Thoughts expressed on one side of the Atlantic, are distinctly heard on the other.

The far off and almost fabulous[1] Pacific rolls in grandeur at our feet. The Celestial Empire, the mystery of ages, is being solved. The fiat of the Almighty, "*Let there be Light*,"[2] has not yet spent its force. No abuse, no outrage whether in taste, sport or avarice, can now hide itself from the all-pervading light. The iron shoe, and crippled foot of China must be seen, in contrast with nature. *Afric must rise and put on her yet unwoven garment.* "*Ethiopia shall stretch out her hand unto God.*"[3] In the fervent aspirations of William Lloyd Garrison, I say, and let every heart join in saying it:

God speed the year of jubilee
  The wide world o'er!
When from their galling chains set free,
Th' oppressed shall vilely bend the knee,
And wear the yoke of tyranny
  Like brutes no more.
That year will come, and freedom's reign,
To man his plundered rights again
  Restore.

God speed the day when human blood
  Shall cease to flow!
In every clime be understood,
The claims of human brotherhood,
And each return for evil, good,
  Not blow for blow;
That day will come all feuds to end,
And change into a faithful friend
  Each foe.

God speed the hour, the glorious hour,
  When none on earth
Shall exercise a lordly power,
Nor in a tyrant's presence cower;

1 *fabulous* I.e., fabled; of mythological reputation.

2 *Let there be Light* See Genesis 1.3.

3 *Ethiopia ... unto God* See Psalms 68.31; in the nineteenth century, Ethiopia was often thought of as symbolizing all Africa and all people of African descent.

But all to manhood's stature tower,
    By equal birth!
THAT HOUR WILL COME, to each, to all,
And from his prison-house, the thrall
    Go forth.

Until that year, day, hour, arrive,
With head, and heart, and hand I'll strive,
To break the rod, and rend the gyve,[1]
The spoiler of his prey deprive—
    So witness Heaven!
And never from my chosen post,
Whate'er the peril or the cost,
    Be driven.[2]

—1852

1 *gyve* Shackle.
2 *God speed … Be driven* See William Lloyd Garrison's "The Triumph of Freedom" (1852).

The Heroic Slave

Frederick Douglass's only work of fiction, *The Heroic Slave*, was first published as part of the 1853 abolitionist fundraising anthology *Autographs for Freedom*, edited primarily by Douglass's friend Julia Griffiths; it was serialized in *Frederick Douglass' Paper* shortly thereafter. At its center is Madison Washington, a historical figure who had in 1841 led a rebellion aboard the slave ship *Creole*, subduing its white crew, sailing to the British-occupied Bahamas, and thereby bringing about the emancipation of the ship's 128 surviving captives. The events had brought about a period of tense relations between the U.S. and Britain, as many white Americans felt that Britain had unjustifiably violated the property rights of the American enslavers who claimed to own the *Creole*'s human cargo. Douglass, however, focuses not on the rebellion's results or political ramifications but on the life of its leader in the few years preceding it. Little is known about the historical Washington, but the basics of Douglass's fictionalized account are accurate: Washington was enslaved in Virginia and fled to Canada, subsequently returned to his former plantation to rescue his enslaved wife, and was re-captured during this failed mission and placed aboard the *Creole* in order to be conveyed to the market at New Orleans.

Part I

Oh! child of grief, why weepest thou?
Why droops thy sad and mournful brow?
Why is thy look so like despair?
What deep, sad sorrow lingers there?[1]

The State of Virginia is famous in American annals for the multitudinous array of her statesmen and heroes. She has been dignified by some the mother of statesmen. History has not been sparing in recording their names, or in blazoning their deeds. Her high position in this respect, has given her an enviable distinction among her sister States. With Virginia for his birthplace, even a man

1 *Oh! ... lingers there?* Opening lines of a popular hymn appearing in books of Christian poetry at least as early as 1828.

of ordinary parts,[1] on account of the general partiality for her sons, easily rises to eminent stations. Men, not great enough to attract special attention in their native states, have, like a certain distinguished citizen in the state of New York, sighed and repined that they were not born in Virginia.[2] Yet not all the great ones of the Old Dominion[3] have, by the fact of their birthplace, escaped undeserved obscurity. By some strange neglect, *one* of the truest, manliest, and bravest of her children—one who, in after years, will, I think, command the pen of genius to set his merits forth—holds now no higher place in the records of that grand old Commonwealth than is held by a horse or an ox. Let those account for it who can, but there stands the fact, that a man who loved liberty as well as did Patrick Henry—who deserved it as much as Thomas Jefferson[4]—and who fought for it with a valor as high, an arm as strong, and against odds as great, as he who led all the armies of the American colonies through the great war for freedom and independence,[5] lives now only in the chattel records of his native State.

Glimpses of this great character are all that can now be presented. He is brought to view only by a few transient incidents, and these afford but partial satisfaction. Like a guiding star on a stormy night, he is seen through the parted clouds and the howling tempests; or, like the gray peak of a menacing rock on a perilous coast, he is seen by the quivering flash of angry lightning, and he again disappears covered with mystery.

Curiously, earnestly, anxiously we peer into the dark, and wish even for the blinding flash, or the light of northern skies to reveal him. But alas! he is still enveloped in darkness, and we return from the pursuit like a wearied and disheartened mother (after a tedious and unsuccessful search for a lost child), who returns weighed down with

---

1 *parts* Abilities.

2 *certain distinguished citizen … Virginia* Possibly a reference to Martin Van Buren (President from 1837 to 1841), who—although born and resident in New York—assiduously courted the votes of white Southerners.

3 *Old Dominion* Common nickname for Virginia.

4 *Patrick Henry … Thomas Jefferson* Virginia-born politicians who served as governors of Virginia, Henry from 1776 to 1779 and 1784 to 1786 and Jefferson from 1779 to 1781. Henry is famous for declaring "Give me liberty, or give me death!" before the Second Virginia Convention in 1775.

5 *he who … and independence* I.e., George Washington.

disappointment and sorrow. Speaking of marks, traces, possibles, and probabilities, we come before our readers.

In the spring of 1835, on a Sabbath morning, within hearing of the solemn peals of the church bells at a distant village, a Northern traveller through the State of Virginia drew up his horse to drink at a sparkling brook, near the edge of a dark pine forest. While his weary and thirsty steed drew in the grateful water, the rider caught the sound of a human voice, apparently engaged in earnest conversation.

Following the direction of the sound, he descried, among the tall pines, the man whose voice had arrested his attention. "To whom can he be speaking?" thought the traveller. "He seems to be alone." The circumstance interested him much, and he became intensely curious to know what thoughts and feelings, or, it might be, high aspirations, guided those rich and mellow accents. Tying his horse at a short distance from the brook, he stealthily drew near the solitary speaker; and, concealing himself by the side of a huge fallen tree, he distinctly heard the following soliloquy:

"What, then, is life to me? it is aimless and worthless, and worse than worthless. Those birds, perched on yon swinging boughs, in friendly conclave, sounding forth their merry notes in seeming worship of the rising sun, though liable to the sportsman's fowling-piece,[1] are still my superiors. They *live free*, though they may die slaves. They fly where they list[2] by day, and retire in freedom at night. But what is freedom to me, or I to it? I am a *slave*—born a slave, an abject slave—even before I made part of this breathing world, the scourge was platted[3] for my back; the fetters were forged for my limbs. How mean[4] a thing am I. That accursed and crawling snake, that miserable reptile, that has just glided into its slimy home, is freer and better off than I. He escaped my blow, and is safe. But here am I, a man—yes, *a man*!—with thoughts and wishes, with powers and faculties as far as angel's flight above that hated reptile—yet he is my superior, and

1 *sportsman's fowling-piece* Hunter's gun.

2 *list* Wish.

3 *platted* I.e., plaited, or braided; a reference to the braided whips used by enslavers and overseers.

4 *mean* Lowly.

scorns to own[1] me as his master, or to stop to take my blows. When he saw my uplifted arm, he darted beyond my reach, and turned to give me battle. I dare not do as much as that. I neither run nor fight, but do meanly stand, answering each heavy blow of a cruel master with doleful wails and piteous cries. I am galled with irons; but even these are more tolerable than the consciousness, the *galling* consciousness of cowardice and indecision. Can it be that I *dare* not run away? *Perish the thought*, I *dare* do anything which may be done by another. When that young man struggled with the waves *for life*, and others stood back appalled in helpless horror, did I not plunge in, forgetful of life, to save his? The raging bull from whom all others fled, pale with fright, did I not keep at bay with a single pitchfork? Could a coward do that? *No—no*—I wrong myself—I am no coward. *Liberty* I will have, or die in the attempt to gain it. This working that others may live in idleness! This cringing submission to insolence and curses! This living under the constant dread and apprehension of being sold and transferred, like a mere brute, is *too* much for me. I will stand it no longer. What others have done, I will do. These trusty legs, or these sinewy arms shall place me among the free. Tom escaped; so can I. The North Star will not be less kind to me than to him. I will follow it. I will at least make the trial. I have nothing to lose. If I am caught, I shall only be a slave. If I am shot, I shall only lose a life which is a burden and a curse. If I get clear (as something tells me I shall), liberty, the inalienable birthright of every man, precious and priceless, will be mine. My resolution is fixed. *I shall be free*."

At these words the traveller raised his head cautiously and noiselessly, and caught, from his hiding-place, a full view of the unsuspecting speaker. Madison (for that was the name of our hero) was standing erect, a smile of satisfaction rippled upon his expressive countenance, like that which plays upon the face of one who has but just solved a difficult problem, or vanquished a malignant foe; for at that moment he was free, at least in spirit. The future gleamed brightly before him, and his fetters lay broken at his feet. His air was triumphant.

Madison was of manly form. Tall, symmetrical, round, and strong. In his movements he seemed to combine, with the strength of the

1 *own* Admit.

lion, a lion's elasticity. His torn sleeves disclosed arms like polished iron. His face was "black, but comely."[1] His eye, lit with emotion, kept guard under a brow as dark and as glossy as the raven's wing. His whole appearance betokened Herculean strength; yet there was nothing savage or forbidding in his aspect. A child might play in his arms, or dance on his shoulders. A giant's strength, but not a giant's heart was in him. His broad mouth and nose spoke only of good nature and kindness. But his voice, that unfailing index of the soul, though full and melodious, had that in it which could terrify as well as charm. He was just the man you would choose when hardships were to be endured, or danger to be encountered—intelligent and brave. He had the head to conceive, and the hand to execute. In a word, he was one to be sought as a friend, but to be dreaded as an enemy.

As our traveller gazed upon him, he almost trembled at the thought of his dangerous intrusion. Still he could not quit the place. He had long desired to sound the mysterious depths of the thoughts and feelings of a slave. He was not, therefore, disposed to allow so providential an opportunity to pass unimproved. He resolved to hear more; so he listened again for those mellow and mournful accents which, he says, made such an impression upon him as can never be erased. He did not have to wait long. There came another gush from the same full fountain; now bitter, and now sweet. Scathing denunciations of the cruelty and injustice of slavery; heart-touching narrations of his own personal suffering, intermingled with prayers to the God of the oppressed for help and deliverance, were followed by presentations of the dangers and difficulties of escape, and formed the burden of his eloquent utterances; but his high resolution clung to him—for he ended each speech by an emphatic declaration of his purpose to be free. It seemed that the very repetition of this imparted a glow to his countenance. The hope of freedom seemed to sweeten, for a season, the bitter cup of slavery, and to make it, for a time, tolerable; for when in the very whirlwind of anguish—when his heart's cord seemed screwed up to snapping tension, hope sprung up and soothed his troubled spirit. Fitfully he would exclaim, "How can I leave her? Poor thing! what can she do when I am gone? Oh! oh! 'tis impossible that I can leave poor Susan!"

---

1 *black, but comely* See Song of Solomon 1.5: "I am black, but comely."

A brief pause intervened. Our traveller raised his head, and saw again the sorrow-smitten slave. His eye was fixed upon the ground. The strong man staggered under a heavy load. Recovering himself, he argued thus aloud: "All is uncertain here. Tomorrow's sun may not rise before I am sold, and separated from her I love. What, then, could I do for her? I should be in more hopeless slavery, and she no nearer to liberty—whereas if I were free—my arms my own—I might devise the means to rescue her."

This said, Madison cast around a searching glance, as if the thought of being overheard had flashed across his mind. He said no more, but, with measured steps, walked away, and was lost to the eye of our traveller amidst the wildering woods.

Long after Madison had left the ground, Mr. Listwell (our traveller) remained in motionless silence, meditating on the extraordinary revelations to which he had listened. He seemed fastened to the spot, and stood half hoping, half fearing the return of the sable[1] preacher to his solitary temple. The speech of Madison rung through the chambers of his soul, and vibrated through his entire frame. "Here is indeed a man," thought he, "of rare endowments—a child of God—guilty of no crime but the colour of his skin—hiding away from the face of humanity, and pouring out his thoughts and feelings, his hopes and resolutions to the lonely woods; to him those distant church bells have no grateful music. He shuns the church, the altar, and the great congregation of Christian worshippers, and wanders away to the gloomy forest, to utter in the vacant air complaints and griefs, which the religion of his times and his country can neither console nor relieve. Goaded almost to madness by the sense of the injustice done him, he resorts hither to give vent to his pent up feelings, and to debate with himself the feasibility of plans, plans of his own invention, for his own deliverance. From this hour I am an abolitionist. I have seen enough and heard enough, and I shall go to my home in Ohio resolved to atone for my past indifference to this ill-starred race, by making such exertions as I shall be able to do, for the speedy emancipation of every slave in the land."

1 *sable* Dark.

Part 2

The gaudy, blabbing and remorseful day
Is crept into the bosom of the sea;
And now loud-howling wolves arouse the jades° *horses*
That drag the tragic melancholy night;
Who with their drowsy, slow, and flagging wings
Clip dead men's graves, and from their misty jaws
Breathe foul contagions, darkness in the air.[1]

Shakespeare

Five years after the foregoing singular occurrence, in the winter of 1840, Mr. and Mrs. Listwell sat together by the fireside of their own happy home, in the State of Ohio. The children were all gone to bed. A single lamp burnt brightly on the centre-table. All was still and comfortable within; but the night was cold and dark; a heavy wind sighed and moaned sorrowfully around the house and barn, occasionally bringing against the clattering windows a stray leaf from the large oak trees that embowered their dwelling. It was a night for strange noises and for strange fancies. A whole wilderness of thought might pass through one's mind during such an evening. The smouldering embers, partaking of the spirit of the restless night, became fruitful of varied and fantastic pictures, and revived many bygone scenes and old impressions. The happy pair seemed to sit in silent fascination, gazing on the fire. Suddenly this *reverie* was interrupted by a heavy growl. Ordinarily such an occurrence would have scarcely provoked a single word, or excited the least apprehension. But there are certain seasons when the slightest sound sends a jar through all the subtle chambers of the mind; and such a season was this. The happy pair started up, as if some sudden danger had come upon them. The growl was from their trusty watch-dog.

"What can it mean? certainly no one can be out on such a night as this," said Mrs. Listwell.

"The wind has deceived the dog, my dear; he has mistaken the noise of falling branches, brought down by the wind, for that of the footsteps of persons coming to the house. I have several times tonight thought that I heard the sound of footsteps. I am sure, however, that

---

1 *The gaudy ... the air* Quotation from Shakespeare's *2 Henry VI* 4.1.1–7.

it was but the wind. Friends would not be likely to come out at such an hour, or such a night; and thieves are too lazy and self-indulgent to expose themselves to this biting frost; but should there be anyone about, our brave old Monte, who is on the lookout, will not be slow in sounding the alarm."

Saying this they quietly left the window, whither they had gone to learn the cause of the menacing growl, and re-seated themselves by the fire, as if reluctant to leave the slowly expiring embers, although the hour was late. A few minutes only intervened after resuming their seats, when again their sober meditations were disturbed. Their faithful dog now growled and barked furiously, as if assailed by an advancing foe. Simultaneously the good couple arose, and stood in mute expectation. The contest without[1] seemed fierce and violent. It was, however, soon over—the barking ceased, for, with true canine instinct, Monte quickly discovered that a friend, not an enemy of the family, was coming to the house, and instead of rushing to repel the supposed intruder, he was now at the door, whimpering and dancing for the admission of himself and his newly made friend.

Mr. Listwell knew by this movement that all was well; he advanced and opened the door, and saw by the light that streamed out into the darkness, a tall man advancing slowly towards the house, with a stick in one hand, and a small bundle in the other. "It is a traveller," thought he, "who has missed his way, and is coming to inquire the road. I am glad we did not go to bed earlier—I have felt all the evening as if somebody would be here tonight."

The man had now halted a short distance from the door, and looked prepared alike for flight or battle. "Come in, sir, don't be alarmed, you have probably lost your way."

Slightly hesitating, the traveller walked in; not, however, without regarding his host with a scrutinizing glance. "No, sir," said he, "I have come to ask you a greater favor."

Instantly Mr. Listwell exclaimed (as the recollection of the Virginia forest scene flashed upon him), "Oh, sir, I know not your name, but I have seen your face, and heard your voice before. I am glad to see you. *I know all*. You are flying for your liberty—be seated—be seated—banish all fear. You are safe under my roof."

---

1 *without* Outside.

This recognition, so unexpected, rather disconcerted and disquieted the noble fugitive. The timidity and suspicion of persons escaping from slavery are easily awakened, and often what is intended to dispel the one, and to allay the other, has precisely the opposite effect. It was so in this case. Quickly observing the unhappy impression made by his words and action, Mr. Listwell assumed a more quiet and inquiring aspect, and finally succeeded in removing the apprehensions which his very natural and generous salutation had aroused.

Thus assured, the stranger said, "Sir, you have rightly guessed, I am, indeed, a fugitive from slavery. My name is Madison—Madison Washington my mother used to call me. I am on my way to Canada, where I learn that persons of my color are protected in all the rights of men; and my object in calling upon you was to beg the privilege of resting my weary limbs for the night in your barn. It was my purpose to have continued my journey till morning; but the piercing cold and the frowning darkness compelled me to seek shelter; and, seeing a light through the lattice of your window, I was encouraged to come here to beg the privilege named. You will do me a great favor by affording me shelter for the night."

"A resting-place, indeed, sir, you shall have; not, however, in my barn, but in the best room of my house. Consider yourself, if you please, under the roof of a friend; for such I am to you, and to all your deeply injured race."

While this introductory conversation was going on, the kind lady had revived the fire, and was diligently preparing supper; for she, not less than her husband, felt for the sorrows of the oppressed and hunted ones of earth, and was always glad of an opportunity to do them a service. A bountiful repast[1] was quickly prepared, and the hungry and toil-worn bondman was cordially invited to partake thereof. Gratefully he acknowledged the favor of his benevolent benefactress; but appeared scarcely to understand what such hospitality could mean. It was the first time in his life that he had met so humane and friendly a greeting at the hands of persons whose color was unlike his own; yet it was impossible for him to doubt the charitableness of his new friends, or the genuineness of the welcome so freely given; and he therefore, with many thanks, took his seat at the table with Mr. and

1 *repast* Meal.

Mrs. Listwell, who, desirous to make him feel at home, took a cup of tea themselves, while urging upon Madison the best that the house could afford.

Supper over, all doubts and apprehensions banished, the three drew around the blazing fire, and a conversation commenced which lasted till long after midnight.

"Now," said Madison to Mr. Listwell, "I was a little surprised and alarmed when I came in, by what you said; do tell me, sir, *why* you thought you had seen my face before, and by what you knew me to be a fugitive from slavery; for I am sure that I never was before in this neighborhood, and I certainly sought to conceal what I supposed to be the manner of a fugitive slave."

Mr. Listwell at once frankly disclosed the secret; describing the place where he first saw him; rehearsing the language which he (Madison) had used; referring to the effect which his manner and speech had made upon him; declaring the resolution he there formed to be an abolitionist; telling how often he had spoken of the circumstance, and the deep concern he had ever since felt to know what had become of him; and whether he had carried out the purpose to make his escape, as in the woods he declared he would do.

"Ever since that morning," said Mr. Listwell, "you have seldom been absent from my mind, and though now I did not dare to hope that I should ever see you again, I have often wished that such might be my fortune; for, from that hour, your face seemed to be daguerreotyped[1] on my memory."

Madison looked quite astonished, and felt amazed at the narration to which he had listened. After recovering himself he said, "I well remember that morning, and the bitter anguish that wrung my heart; I will state the occasion of it. I had, on the previous Saturday, suffered a cruel lashing; had been tied up to the limb of a tree, with my feet chained together, and a heavy iron bar placed between my ankles. Thus suspended, I received on my naked back forty stripes, and was kept in this distressing position three or four hours, and was then let down, only to have my torture increased; for my bleeding back, gashed by the cow-skin,[2] was washed by the overseer with old brine,

1 *daguerreotyped* The daguerreotype was an early form of photography, widely popular in the 1840s and 1850s.

2 *cow-skin* Material commonly used for whips.

partly to augment my suffering, and partly, as he said, to prevent inflammation. My crime was that I had stayed longer at the mill, the day previous, than it was thought I ought to have done, which, I assured my master and the overseer, was no fault of mine; but no excuses were allowed. 'Hold your tongue, you impudent rascal,' met my every explanation. Slaveholders are so imperious when their passions are excited, as to construe every word of the slave into insolence. I could do nothing but submit to the agonizing infliction. Smarting still from the wounds, as well as from the consciousness of being whipped for no cause, I took advantage of the absence of my master, who had gone to church, to spend the time in the woods, and brood over my wretched lot. Oh, sir, I remember it well—and can never forget it."

"But this was five years ago; where have you been since?"

"I will try to tell you," said Madison. "Just four weeks after that Sabbath morning, I gathered up the few rags of clothing I had, and started, as I supposed, for the North and for freedom. I must not stop to describe my feelings on taking this step. It seemed like taking a leap into the dark. The thought of leaving my poor wife and two little children caused me indescribable anguish; but consoling myself with the reflection that once free, I could, possibly, devise ways and means to gain their freedom also, I nerved myself up to make the attempt. I started, but ill-luck attended me; for after being out a whole week, strange to say, I still found myself on my master's grounds; the third night after being out, a season of clouds and rain set in, wholly preventing me from seeing the North Star, which I had trusted as my guide, not dreaming that clouds might intervene between us.

"This circumstance was fatal to my project, for in losing my star, I lost my way; so when I supposed I was far towards the North, and had almost gained my freedom, I discovered myself at the very point from which I had started. It was a severe trial, for I arrived at home in great destitution; my feet were sore, and in travelling in the dark, I had dashed my foot against a stump, and started a nail, and lamed myself. I was wet and cold; one week had exhausted all my stores; and when I landed on my master's plantation, with all my work to do over again—hungry, tired, lame, and bewildered—I almost cursed the day that I was born. In this extremity I approached the quarters. I did so stealthily, although in my desperation I hardly cared whether

I was discovered or not. Peeping through the rents of the quarters, I saw my fellow-slaves seated by a warm fire, merrily passing away the time, as though their hearts knew no sorrow. Although I envied their seeming contentment, all wretched as I was, I despised the cowardly acquiescence in their own degradation which it implied, and felt a kind of pride and glory in my own desperate lot. I dared not enter the quarters—for where there is seeming contentment with slavery, there is certain treachery to freedom. I proceeded towards the great house, in the hope of catching a glimpse of my poor wife, whom I knew might be trusted with my secrets even on the scaffold. Just as I reached the fence which divided the field from the garden, I saw a woman in the yard, who in the darkness I took to be my wife; but a nearer approach told me it was not she. I was about to speak; had I done so, I would not have been here this night; for an alarm would have been sounded, and the hunters been put on my track. Here were hunger, cold, thirst, disappointment, and chagrin, confronted only by the dim hope of liberty. I tremble to think of that dreadful hour. To face the deadly cannon's mouth in warm blood unterrified, is, I think, a small achievement, compared with a conflict like this with gaunt starvation. The gnawings of hunger conquers by degrees, till all that a man has he would give in exchange for a single crust of bread. Thank God, I was not quite reduced to this extremity.

"Happily for me, before the fatal moment of utter despair, my good wife made her appearance in the yard. It was she; I knew her step. All was well now. I was, however, afraid to speak, lest I should frighten her. Yet speak I did; and, to my great joy, my voice was known. Our meeting can be more easily imagined than described. For a time hunger, thirst, weariness, and lameness were forgotten. But it was soon necessary for her to return to the house. She being a house-servant, her absence from the kitchen, if discovered, might have excited suspicion. Our parting was like tearing the flesh from my bones; yet it was the part of wisdom for her to go. She left me with the purpose of meeting me at midnight in the very forest where you last saw me. She knew the place well, as one of my melancholy resorts, and could easily find it, though the night was dark.

"I hastened away, therefore, and concealed myself, to await the arrival of my good angel. As I lay there among the leaves, I was strongly tempted to return again to the house of my master and give myself up; but remembering my solemn pledge on that memorable Sunday morning, I was able to linger out the two long hours between ten and midnight. I may well call them long hours. I have endured much hardship; I have encountered many perils; but the anxiety of those two hours, was the bitterest I ever experienced. True to her word, my wife came laden with provisions, and we sat down on the side of a log, at that dark and lonesome hour of the night. I cannot say we talked; our feelings were too great for that; yet we came to an understanding that I should make the woods my home, for if I gave myself up, I should be whipped and sold away; and if I started for the North, I should leave a wife doubly dear to me. We mutually determined, therefore, that I should remain in the vicinity. In the dismal swamps[1] I lived, sir, five long years—a cave for my home during the day. I wandered about at night with the wolf and the bear—sustained by the promise that my good Susan would meet me in the pine woods at least once a week. This promise was redeemed, I assure you, to the letter, greatly to my relief. I had partly become contented with my mode of life, and had made up my mind to spend my days there; but the wilderness that sheltered me thus long took fire, and refused longer to be my hiding-place.

"I will not harrow up your feelings by portraying the terrific scene of this awful conflagration. There is nothing to which I can liken it. It was horribly and indescribably grand. The whole world seemed on fire, and it appeared to me that the day of judgment had come; that the burning bowels of the earth had burst forth, and that the end of all things was at hand. Bears and wolves, scorched from their mysterious hiding-places in the earth, and all the wild inhabitants of the untrodden forest, filled with a common dismay, ran forth, yelling, howling, bewildered amidst the smoke and flame. The very heavens seemed to rain down fire through the towering trees; it was by the merest chance that I escaped the devouring element. Running before it, and stopping occasionally to take breath, I looked back to behold its frightful ravages, and to drink in its savage magnificence. It was awful, thrilling, solemn, beyond compare. When aided by the fitful wind, the merciless tempest of fire swept on, sparkling,

1 *dismal swamps* The Great Dismal Swamp spans southeastern Virginia and northeastern North Carolina. Thousands of fugitives from slavery made their homes in the Dismal Swamp, forming what are today sometimes referred to as maroon colonies.

creaking, cracking, curling, roaring, out-doing in its dreadful splendor a thousand thunderstorms at once. From tree to tree it leaped, swallowing them up in its lurid, baleful glare; and leaving them leafless, limbless, charred, and lifeless behind. The scene was overwhelming, stunning—nothing was spared—cattle, tame and wild, herds of swine and of deer, wild beasts of every name and kind—huge night-birds, bats, and owls, that had retired to their homes in lofty tree-tops to rest, perished in that fiery storm. The long-winged buzzard and croaking raven mingled their dismal cries with those of the countless myriads of small birds that rose up to the skies, and were lost to the sight in clouds of smoke and flame. Oh, I shudder when I think of it! Many a poor wandering fugitive, who, like myself, had sought among wild beasts the mercy denied by our fellow men, saw, in helpless consternation, his dwelling-place and city of refuge reduced to ashes forever. It was this grand conflagration that drove me hither; I ran alike from fire and from slavery."

After a slight pause (for both speaker and hearers were deeply moved by the above recital), Mr. Listwell, addressing Madison, said, "If it does not weary you too much, do tell us something of your journeyings since this disastrous burning—we are deeply interested in everything which can throw light on the hardships of persons escaping from slavery; we could hear you talk all night; are there no incidents that you could relate of your travels hither? or are they such that you do not like to mention them?"

"For the most part, sir, my course has been uninterrupted; and, considering the circumstances, at times even pleasant. I have suffered little for want[1] of food; but I need not tell you how I got it. Your moral code may differ from mine, as your customs and usages are different. The fact is, sir, during my flight, I felt myself robbed by society of all my just rights; that I was in an enemy's land, who sought both my life and my liberty. They had transformed me into a brute; made merchandise of my body, and, for all the purposes of my flight, turned day into night—and guided by my own necessities, and in contempt of their conventionalities, I did not scruple to take bread where I could get it."

---

1 *want* Lack.

"And just there you were right," said Mr. Listwell; "I once had doubts on this point myself, but a conversation with Gerrit Smith[1] (a man, by the way, that I wish you could see, for he is a devoted friend of your race, and I know he would receive you gladly) put an end to all my doubts on this point. But do not let me interrupt you."

"I had but one narrow escape during my whole journey," said Madison.

"Do let us hear of it," said Mr. Listwell.

"Two weeks ago," continued Madison, "after travelling all night, I was overtaken by daybreak, in what seemed to me an almost interminable wood. I deemed it unsafe to go farther, and, as usual, I looked around for a suitable tree in which to spend the day. I liked one with a bushy top, and found one just to my mind. Up I climbed, and hiding myself as well as I could, I, with this strap (pulling one out of his old coat-pocket) lashed myself to a bough, and flattered myself that I should get a *good night's* sleep that day; but in this I was soon disappointed. I had scarcely got fastened to my natural hammock, when I heard the voices of a number of persons, apparently approaching the part of the woods where I was. Upon my word, sir, I dreaded more these human voices than I should have done those of wild beasts. I was at a loss to know what to do. If I descended, I should probably be discovered by the men; and if they had dogs I should, doubtless, be '*treed*.' It was an anxious moment, but hardships and dangers have been the accompaniments of my life; and have, perhaps, imparted to me a certain hardness of character, which, to some extent, adapts me to them. In my present predicament, I decided to hold my place in the tree-top, and abide the consequences. But here I must disappoint you; for the men, who were all colored, halted at least a hundred yards from me, and began with their axes, in right good earnest, to attack the trees. The sound of their laughing axes was like the report[2] of as many well-charged pistols. By and by there came down at least a dozen trees with a terrible crash. They leaped upon the fallen trees with an air of victory. I could see no dog with them, and felt myself comparatively safe, though I could not forget the possibility that

1 *Gerrit Smith* Smith (1797–1874) was a prominent white abolitionist and a personal friend of Douglass's.

2 *report* Gunshot.

some freak or fancy might bring the axe a little nearer my dwelling than comported with my safety.

"There was no sleep for me that day, and I wished for night. You may imagine that the thought of having the tree attacked under me was far from agreeable, and that it very easily kept me on the look-out. The day was not without diversion. The men at work seemed to be a gay set; and they would often make the woods resound with that uncontrolled laughter for which we, as a race, are remarkable. I held my place in the tree till sunset—saw the men put on their jackets to be off. I observed that all left the ground except one, whom I saw sitting on the side of a stump, with his head bowed, and his eyes apparently fixed on the ground. I became interested in him. After sitting in the position to which I have alluded ten or fifteen minutes, he left the stump, walked directly towards the tree in which I was secreted, and halted almost under the same. He stood for a moment and looked around, deliberately and reverently took off his hat, by which I saw that he was a man in the evening of life, slightly bald and quite gray. After laying down his hat carefully, he knelt and prayed aloud, and such a prayer, the most fervent, earnest, and solemn, to which I think I ever listened. After reverently addressing the Almighty, as the all-wise, all-good, and the common Father of all mankind, he besought God for grace, for strength, to bear up under, and to endure, as a good soldier, all the hardships and trials which beset the journey of life, and to enable him to live in a manner which accorded with the gospel of Christ. His soul now broke out in humble supplication for deliverance from bondage. 'O thou,' said he, 'that hearest the raven's cry,[1] take pity on poor me! O deliver me! O deliver me! in mercy, O God, deliver me from the chains and manifold hardships of slavery! With thee, O Father, all things are possible.[2] Thou canst stand and measure the earth. Thou hast beheld and drove asunder the nations[3]—all power is in thy hand—thou didst say of old, "I have seen the affliction of my

---

1 *that hearest the raven's cry* See Psalm 147.9: "He giveth to the beast his food, and to the young ravens which cry."

2 *With thee … possible* See Matthew 19.26: "But Jesus beheld them, and said unto them, With men this is impossible; but with God all things are possible."

3 *Thou canst … the nations* See Habakkuk 3.6: "He stood, and measured the earth: he beheld, and drove asunder the nations."

people, and am come to deliver them"[1]—Oh look down upon our afflictions, and have mercy upon us.' But I cannot repeat his prayer, nor can I give you an idea of its deep pathos. I had given but little attention to religion, and had but little faith in it; yet, as the old man prayed, I felt almost like coming down and kneel[ing] by his side, and mingl[ing] my broken complaint with his.

"He had already gained my confidence; as how could it be otherwise? I knew enough of religion to know that the man who prays in secret is far more likely to be sincere than he who loves to pray standing in the street, or in the great congregation. When he arose from his knees, like another Zacheus,[2] I came down from the tree. He seemed a little alarmed at first, but I told him my story, and the good man embraced me in his arms, and assured me of his sympathy.

"I was now about out of provisions, and thought I might safely ask him to help me replenish my store. He said he had no money; but if he had, he would freely give it me. I told him I had *one dollar*; it was all the money I had in the world. I gave it to him, and asked him to purchase some crackers and cheese, and to kindly bring me the balance; that I would remain in or near that place, and would come to him on his return, if he would whistle. He was gone only about an hour. Meanwhile, from some cause or other, I know not what (but as you shall see very wisely), I changed my place. On his return I started to meet him; but it seemed as if the shadow of approaching danger fell upon my spirit, and checked my progress. In a very few minutes, closely on the heels of the old man, I distinctly saw *fourteen men*, with something like guns in their hands."

"Oh! the old wretch!" exclaimed Mrs. Listwell, "he had betrayed you, had he?"

"I think not," said Madison, "I cannot believe that the old man was to blame. He probably went into a store, asked for the articles for which I sent, and presented the bill I gave him; and it is so unusual

---

1 *I have seen ... deliver them* See Acts 7.34: "I have seen, I have seen the affliction of my people which is in Egypt, and I have heard their groaning, and am come down to deliver them. And now come, I will send thee into Egypt." These lines reference the enslavement of the Israelites in Egypt.

2 *Zacheus* Luke 19 relates the story of the tax collector Zacchaeus, who climbed a tree so as to be able to see Jesus as he passed through Jericho. Jesus called Zacchaeus down from the tree to greet him and invite himself to Zacchaeus' home, an honor that amazed the others in the crowd, who looked down on tax collectors as sinful.

for slaves in the country to have money, that fact, doubtless, excited suspicion, and gave rise to inquiry. I can easily believe that the truthfulness of the old man's character compelled him to disclose the facts; and thus were these blood-thirsty men put on my track. Of course I did not present myself; but hugged my hiding-place securely. If discovered and attacked, I resolved to sell my life as dearly as possible.

"After searching about the woods silently for a time, the whole company gathered around the old man; one charged him with lying, and called him an old villain; said he was a thief; charged him with stealing money; said if he did not instantly tell where he got it, they would take the shirt from his old back, and give him thirty-nine lashes.

"'I did *not* steal the money,' said the old man, 'it was given me, as I told you at the store; and if the man who gave it me is not here, it is not my fault.'

"'Hush! you lying old rascal; we'll make you smart for it. You shall not leave this spot until you have told where you got that money.'

"They now took hold of him, and began to strip him; while others went to get sticks with which to beat him. I felt, at the moment, like rushing out in the midst of them; but considering that the old man would be whipped the more for having aided a fugitive slave, and that, perhaps, in the *melée* he might be killed outright, I disobeyed this impulse. They tied him to a tree, and began to whip him. My own flesh crept at every blow, and I seem to hear the old man's piteous cries even now. They laid thirty-nine lashes on his bare back, and were going to repeat that number, when one of the company besought his comrades to desist. 'You'll kill the d—d old scoundrel! You've already whipt a dollar's worth out of him, even if he stole it!' 'O yes,' said another, 'let him down. He'll never tell us another lie, I'll warrant ye!' With this, one of the company untied the old man, and bid him go about his business.

"The old man left, but the company remained as much as an hour, scouring the woods. Round and round they went, turning up the underbrush, and peering about like so many bloodhounds. Two or three times they came within six feet of where I lay. I tell you I held my stick with a firmer grasp than I did in coming up to your house tonight. I expected to level one of them at least. Fortunately, however, I eluded their pursuit, and they left me alone in the woods.

"My last dollar was now gone, and you may well suppose I felt the loss of it; but the thought of being once again free to pursue my journey, prevented that depression which a sense of destitution causes; so swinging my little bundle on my back, I caught a glimpse of the *Great Bear*[1] (which ever points the way to my beloved star), and I started again on my journey. What I lost in money I made up at a hen-roost that same night, upon which I fortunately came."

"But you didn't eat your food raw? How did you cook it?" said Mrs. Listwell.

"O no, Madam," said Madison, turning to his little bundle; "I had the means of cooking." Here he took out of his bundle an old-fashioned tinder-box, and taking up a piece of a file, which he brought with him, he struck it with a heavy flint, and brought out at least a dozen sparks at once. "I have had this old box," said he, "more than five years. It is the *only* property saved from the fire in the dismal swamp. It has done me good service. It has given me the means of broiling many a chicken!"

It seemed quite a relief to Mrs. Listwell to know that Madison had, at least, lived upon cooked food. Women have a perfect horror of eating uncooked food.

By this time thoughts of what was best to be done about getting Madison to Canada began to trouble Mr. Listwell; for the laws of Ohio were very stringent against anyone who should aid, or who were found aiding a slave to escape through that State.[2] A citizen, for the simple act of taking a fugitive slave in his carriage, had just been stripped of all his property, and thrown penniless upon the world.[3] Notwithstanding this, Mr. Listwell was determined to see Madison safely on his way to Canada. "Give yourself no uneasiness," said he to Madison, "for if it cost my farm, I shall see you safely out of the

---

1 *Great Bear* The constellation today more widely known as the Big Dipper, two of whose stars form a line that points to the North Star.

2 *the laws … that State* Though Ohio had been established as a free state in 1803, shortly thereafter the state passed laws known as "Black Codes" or "Black Laws," forbidding residents from aiding any persons escaping slavery in another state, as well as restricting black immigration into the state and restricting the movement and employment of black people within the state. These laws were the result of pressures both from Ohio's slaveholding neighbor Kentucky and from anti-abolitionist Ohio residents; they were continually strengthened (and the penalties for violating them increased) over the following decades.

3 *A citizen … the world* The reference is unclear.

States, and on your way to a land of liberty. Thank God that there is *such* a land so near us! You will spend tomorrow with us, and tomorrow night I will take you in my carriage to the Lake. Once upon that, and you are safe."

"Thank you! thank you," said the fugitive; "I will commit myself to your care."

For the *first* time during *five* years, Madison enjoyed the luxury of resting his limbs on a comfortable bed, and inside a human habitation. Looking at the white sheets, he said to Mr. Listwell, "What, sir! you don't mean that I shall sleep in that bed?"

"Oh yes, oh yes."

After Mr. Listwell left the room, Madison said he really hesitated whether or not he should lie on the floor; for that was *far* more comfortable and inviting than any bed to which he had been used.

We pass over the thoughts and feelings, the hopes and fears, the plans and purposes, that revolved in the mind of Madison during the day that he was secreted at the house of Mr. Listwell. The reader will be content to know that nothing occurred to endanger his liberty, or to excite alarm. Many were the little attentions bestowed upon him in his quiet retreat and hiding-place. In the evening, Mr. Listwell, after treating Madison to a new suit of winter clothes, and replenishing his exhausted purse with five dollars, all in silver, brought out his two-horse wagon, well provided with buffaloes,[1] and silently started off with him to Cleveland. They arrived there without interruption, a few minutes before sunrise the next morning. Fortunately the steamer *Admiral* lay at the wharf, and was to start for Canada at nine o'clock. Here the last anticipated danger was surmounted. It was feared that just at this point the hunters of men might be on the look-out, and, possibly, pounce upon their victim. Mr. Listwell saw the captain of the boat; cautiously sounded him on the matter of carrying liberty-loving passengers, before he introduced his precious charge. This done, Madison was conducted on board. With usual generosity this true subject of the emancipating queen[2] welcomed Madison, and

---

1 *buffaloes* I.e., buffalo skins, for warmth.

2 *the emancipating queen* Slavery was abolished in most territories of the British Empire in 1834, three years prior to the accession of Queen Victoria to the throne; however, Britain and its colonies continued to be associated with abolitionism throughout Victoria's reign.

assured him that he should be safely landed in Canada, free of charge. Madison now felt himself no more a piece of merchandise, but a passenger, and, like any other passenger, going about his business, carrying with him what belonged to him, and nothing which rightfully belonged to anybody else.

Wrapped in his new winter suit, snug and comfortable, a pocket full of silver, safe from his pursuers, embarked for a free country, Madison gave every sign of sincere gratitude, and bade his kind benefactor farewell, with such a grip of the hand as bespoke a heart full of honest manliness, and a soul that knew how to appreciate kindness. It need scarcely be said that Mr. Listwell was deeply moved by the gratitude and friendship he had excited in a nature so noble as that of the fugitive. He went to his home that day with a joy and gratification which knew no bounds. He had done something "to deliver the spoiled out of the hands of the spoiler,"[1] he had given bread to the hungry, and clothes to the naked; he had befriended a man to whom the laws of his country forbade all friendship—and in proportion to the odds against his righteous deed, was the delightful satisfaction that gladdened his heart. On reaching home, he exclaimed, "*He is safe—he is safe—he is safe*"—and the cup of his joy was shared by his excellent lady. The following letter was received from Madison a few days after.

WINDSOR, CANADA WEST,[2] DEC. 16, 1840

My dear Friend—for such you truly are:

Madison is out of the woods at last; I nestle in the mane of the British lion, protected by his mighty paw from the talons and the beak of the American eagle. I am free, and breathe an atmosphere too pure for *slaves*, slave-hunters, or slaveholders. My heart is full. As

---

1 *to deliver ... the spoiler* See Jeremiah 21.12: "O house of David, thus saith the Lord; Execute judgment in the morning, and deliver him that is spoiled out of the hand of the oppressor, lest my fury go out like fire, and burn that none can quench it, because of the evil of your doings."

2 *CANADA WEST* A small anachronism: up until 1841, the two colonies of Canada were known as Upper and Lower Canada. The two were merged in 1841, with Upper Canada (now Ontario) becoming the province of Canada West and Lower Canada (now Quebec) becoming the province of Canada East. Windsor is the southernmost city in what is now Ontario.

many thanks to you, sir, and to your kind lady, as there are pebbles on the shores of Lake Erie; and may the blessing of God rest upon you both. You will never be forgotten by your profoundly grateful friend,

MADISON WASHINGTON

PART 3

——His head was with his heart,
And that was far away![1]

Childe Harold

Just upon the edge of the great road from Petersburg,[2] Virginia, to Richmond, and only about fifteen miles from the latter place, there stands a somewhat ancient and famous public tavern, quite notorious in its better days, as being the grand resort for most of the leading gamblers, horse-racers, cock-fighters, and slave-traders from all the country round about. This old rookery, the nucleus of all sorts of birds, mostly those of ill omen, has, like everything else peculiar to Virginia, lost much of its ancient consequence and splendor; yet it keeps up some appearance of gaiety and high life, and is still frequented, even by respectable travellers, who are unacquainted with its past history and present condition. Its fine old portico looks well at a distance, and gives the building an air of grandeur. A nearer view, however, does little to sustain this pretension. The house is large, and its style imposing, but time and dissipation, unfailing in their results, have made ineffaceable marks upon it, and it must, in the common course of events, soon be numbered with the things that were. The gloomy mantle of ruin is, already, outspread to envelop it, and its remains, even but now remind one of a human skull, after the flesh has mingled with the earth. Old hats and rags fill the places in the upper windows once occupied by large panes of glass, and the moulding boards along the roofing have dropped off from their places, leaving holes and crevices in the rented wall for bats and swallows to build their nests in. The platform of the portico, which fronts the highway, is a rickety affair; its planks are loose, and in some places entirely

1 *His head ... far away!* Slight misquotation from Lord Byron's 1812–18 poem *Childe Harold's Pilgrimage,* canto 4, stanza 141, lines 1–2; the original reads "eyes" instead of "heart."

2 *Petersburg* Approximately twenty miles south of Richmond.

gone, leaving effective mantraps in their stead for nocturnal ramblers. The wooden pillars, which once supported it, but which now hang as encumbrances, are all rotten, and tremble with the touch. A part of the stable, a fine old structure in its day, which has given comfortable shelter to hundreds of the noblest steeds of "the Old Dominion" at once, was blown down many years ago, and never has been, and probably never will be, rebuilt. The doors of the barn are in wretched condition; they will shut with a little human strength to help their worn out hinges, but not otherwise. The side of the great building seen from the road is much discolored in sundry places by slops poured from the upper windows, rendering it unsightly and offensive in other respects. Three or four great dogs, looking as dull and gloomy as the mansion itself, lie stretched out along the door-sills under the portico; and double the number of loafers, some of them completely rum-ripe, and others ripening, dispose themselves like so many sentinels about the front of the house. These latter understand the science of scraping acquaintance to perfection. They know everybody, and almost everybody knows them. Of course, as their title implies, they have no regular employment. They are (to use an expressive phrase) *hangers on*, or still better, they are what sailors would denominate *holders-on to the slack, in everybody's mess, and in nobody's watch*. They are, however, as good as the newspaper for the events of the day, and they sell their knowledge almost as cheap. Money they seldom have; yet they always have capital the most reliable. They make their way with a succeeding traveller by intelligence gained from a preceding one. All the great names of Virginia they know by heart, and have seen their owners often. The history of the house is folded in their lips, and they rattle off stories in connection with it, equal to the guides at Dryburgh Abbey.[1] He must be a shrewd man, and well skilled in the art of evasion, who gets out of the hands of these fellows without being at the expense of a treat.

It was at this old tavern, while on a second visit to the State of Virginia in 1841, that Mr. Listwell, unacquainted with the fame of the place, turned aside, about sunset, to pass the night. Riding up to the house, he had scarcely dismounted, when one of the half dozen

1 *Dryburgh Abbey* Ruined medieval abbey in southern Scotland, which became a popular tourist attraction in the nineteenth century.

barroom fraternity met and addressed him in a manner exceedingly bland[1] and accommodating.

"Fine evening, sir."

"Very fine," said Mr. Listwell. "This is a tavern, I believe?"

"O yes, sir, yes; although you may think it looks a little the worse for wear, it was once as good a house as any in Virginy. I make no doubt if ye spend the night here, you'll think it a good house yet; for there ain't a more accommodating man in the country than you'll find the landlord."

Listwell. "The most I want is a good bed for myself, and a full manger for my horse. If I get these, I shall be quite satisfied."

Loafer. "Well, I alloys like to hear a gentleman talk for his horse; and just becase the horse can't talk for itself. A man that don't care about his beast, and don't look arter it when he's travelling, ain't much in my eye anyhow. Now, sir, I likes a horse, and I'll guarantee your horse will be taken good care on here. That old stable, for all you see it looks so shabby now, once sheltered the great *Eclipse*,[2] when he run here agin *Batchelor* and *Jumping Jemmy*. Them was fast horses, but he beat 'em both."

Listwell. "Indeed."

Loafer. "Well, I rather reckon you've travelled a right smart distance today, from the look of your horse?"

Listwell. "Forty miles only."

Loafer. "Well! I'll be darned if that ain't a pretty good *only*. Mister, that beast of yours is a singed cat,[3] I warrant you. I never see'd a creature like that that wasn't good on the road. You've come about forty miles, then?"

Listwell. "Yes, yes, and a pretty good pace at that."

Loafer. "You're somewhat in a hurry, then, I make no doubt? I reckon I could guess if I would, what you're going to Richmond for? It wouldn't be much of a guess either; for it's rumored hereabouts, that there's to be the greatest sale of niggers[4] at Richmond tomorrow

---

1 *bland* Suave.

2 *Eclipse* Famous American racehorse (1814–47).

3 *singed cat* Idiom referring to a person or thing that is better than it looks.

4 *niggers* By the mid-nineteenth century, as the context here suggests, this word (today universally acknowledged to be an utterly unacceptable expression of racism) had firmly established itself in white American vernacular as an emphatically pejorative alternative to the then-more neutral term "negro."

that has taken place there in a long time; and I'll be bound you're a going there to have a hand in it."

Listwell. "Why, you must think, then, that there's money to be made at that business?"

Loafer. "Well, 'pon my honor, sir, I never made any that way myself; but it stands to reason that it's a money making business; for almost all other business in Virginia is dropped to engage in this. One thing is sartain, I never see'd a nigger-buyer yet that hadn't a plenty of money, and he wasn't as free with it as water. I has known one on 'em to treat as high as twenty times in a night; and, ginerally speaking, they's men of edication, and knows all about the government. The fact is, sir, I alloys like to hear 'em talk, bekase I alloys can learn something from them."

Listwell. "What may I call your name, sir?"

Loafer. "Well, now, they calls me Wilkes. I'm known all around by the gentlemen that comes here. They all knows old Wilkes."

Listwell. "Well, Wilkes, you seem to be acquainted here, and I see you have a strong liking for a horse. Be so good as to speak a kind word for mine to the hostler tonight, and you'll not lose anything by it."

Loafer. "Well, sir, I see you don't say much, but you've got an insight into things. It's alloys wise to get the good will of them that's acquainted about a tavern; for a man don't know when he goes into a house what may happen, or how much he may need a friend." Here the loafer gave Mr. Listwell a significant grin, which expressed a sort of triumphant pleasure at having, as he supposed, by his tact succeeded in placing so fine appearing a gentleman under obligations to him.

The pleasure, however, was mutual; for there was something so insinuating in the glance of this loquacious customer, that Mr. Listwell was very glad to get quit of him, and to do so more successfully, he ordered his supper to be brought to him in his private room, private to the eye, but not to the ear. This room was directly over the bar, and the plastering being off, nothing but pine boards and naked laths separated him from the disagreeable company below—he could easily hear what was said in the barroom, and was rather glad of the advantage it afforded, for, as you shall see, it furnished him important hints as to the manner and deportment he should assume during his stay at that tavern.

Mr. Listwell says he had got into his room but a few moments, when he heard the officious Wilkes below, in a tone of disappointment, exclaim, "Whar's that gentleman?" Wilkes was evidently expecting to meet with his friend at the barroom, on his return, and had no doubt of his doing the handsome thing. "He has gone to his room," answered the landlord, "and has ordered his supper to be brought to him."

Here someone shouted out, "Who is he, Wilkes? Where's he going?"

"Well, now, I'll be hanged if I know; but I'm willing to make any man a bet of this old hat agin a five dollar bill, that that gent is as full of money as a dog is of fleas. He's going down to Richmond to buy niggers, I make no doubt. He's no fool, I warrant ye."

"Well, he acts d—d strange," said another, "anyhow. I likes to see a man, when he comes up to a tavern, to come straight into the barroom, and show that he's a man among men. Nobody was going to bite him."

"Now, I don't blame him a bit for not coming in here. That man knows his business, and means to take care on his money," answered Wilkes.

"Wilkes, you're a fool. You only say that, becase you hope to get a few coppers out on him."

"You only measure my corn by your half-bushel, I won't say that you're only mad becase I got the chance of speaking to him first."

"O Wilkes! you're known here. You'll praise up anybody that will give you a copper; besides, 'tis my opinion that that fellow who took his long slab-sides upstairs, for all the world just like a half-scared woman, afraid to look honest men in the face, is a *Northerner*, and as mean as dishwater."

"Now what will you bet of that," said Wilkes.

The speaker said, "I make no bets with you, 'kase you can get that fellow upstairs there to say anything."

"Well," said Wilkes, "I am willing to bet any man in the company that *that* gentleman is a *nigger*-buyer. He didn't tell me so right down, but I reckon I knows enough about men to give a pretty clean guess as to what they are arter."

The dispute as to *who* Mr. Listwell was, what his business, where he was going, etc., was kept up with much animation for some time, and more than once threatened a serious disturbance of the peace. Wilkes had his friends as well as his opponents. After this sharp debate, the company amused themselves by drinking whiskey, and telling stories. The latter consisting of quarrels, fights, *rencontres*, and duels, in which distinguished persons of that neighborhood, and frequenters of that house, had been actors. Some of these stories were frightful enough, and were told, too, with a relish which bespoke the pleasure of the parties with the horrid scenes they portrayed. It would not be proper here to give the reader any idea of the vulgarity and dark profanity which rolled, as "a sweet morsel," under these corrupt tongues.[1] A more brutal set of creatures, perhaps, never congregated.

Disgusted, and a little alarmed withal, Mr. Listwell, who was not accustomed to such entertainment, at length retired, but not to sleep. He was *too* much wrought upon by what he had heard to rest quietly, and what snatches of sleep he got, were interrupted by dreams which were anything than pleasant. At eleven o'clock, there seemed to be several hundreds of persons crowding into the house. A loud and confused clamour, cursing and cracking of whips, and the noise of chains startled him from his bed; for a moment he would have given the half of his farm in Ohio to have been at home. This uproar was kept up with undulating course, till near morning. There was loud laughing—loud singing—loud cursing—and yet there seemed to be weeping and mourning in the midst of all. Mr. Listwell said he had heard enough during the forepart of the night to convince him that a buyer of men and women stood the best chance of being respected. And he, therefore, thought it best to say nothing which might undo the favorable opinion that had been formed of him in the barroom by at least one of the fraternity that swarmed about it. While he would not avow himself a purchaser of slaves, he deemed it not prudent to disavow it. He felt that he might, properly, refuse to cast such a pearl before parties which, to him, were worse than swine.[2] To reveal himself, and to impart a knowledge of his real character and sentiments would, to say the least, be imparting intelligence with the certainty of seeing it and himself both abused. Mr. Listwell confesses, that this reasoning did

---

1 *rolled … corrupt tongues* Reference to a line from Matthew Henry's Bible commentary, *Exposition of the Old and New Testaments*, Volume 8 (1708–10).

2 *cast … than swine* See Matthew 7.6: "Give not that which is holy unto the dogs, neither cast ye your pearls before swine, lest they trample them under their feet, and turn again and rend you."

not altogether satisfy his conscience, for, hating slavery as he did, and regarding it to be the immediate duty of every man to cry out against it, "without compromise and without concealment,"[1] it was hard for him to admit to himself the possibility of circumstances wherein a man might, properly, hold his tongue on the subject. Having as little of the spirit of a martyr as Erasmus,[2] he concluded, like the latter, that it was wiser to trust the mercy of God for his soul, than the humanity of slave-traders for his body. Bodily fear, not conscientious scruples, prevailed.

In this spirit he rose early in the morning, manifesting no surprise at what he had heard during the night. His quondam friend was soon at his elbow, boring him with all sorts of questions. All, however, directed to find out his character, business, residence, purposes, and destination. With the most perfect appearance of good nature and carelessness, Mr. Listwell evaded these meddlesome inquiries, and turned conversation to general topics, leaving himself and all that specially pertained to him, out of discussion. Disengaging himself from their troublesome companionship, he made his way towards an old bowling-alley, which was connected with the house, and which, like all the rest, was in very bad repair.

On reaching the alley Mr. Listwell saw, for the first time in his life, a slave-gang on their way to market. A sad sight truly. Here were one hundred and thirty human beings—children of a common Creator—guilty of no crime—men and women, with hearts, minds, and deathless spirits, chained and fettered, and bound for the market, in a Christian country—in a country boasting of its liberty, independence, and high civilization! Humanity converted into merchandise, and linked in iron bands, with no regard to decency or humanity! All sizes, ages, and sexes, mothers, fathers, daughters, brothers, sisters—all huddled together, on their way to market to be sold and separated from home, and from each other *forever*. And all to fill the pockets of men too lazy to work for an honest living, and who gain their fortune by plundering the helpless, and trafficking in the souls and sinews of men. As he gazed upon

1 *without compromise and without concealment* Slogan of the influential abolitionist newspaper *The National Anti-Slavery Standard*.

2 *Erasmus* Dutch Renaissance theologian who, though openly critical of the Catholic Church, was wary of religious partisanship and refused to align himself with the overt dissidence of the Protestant Reformation, thus escaping the persecution that many other early Protestants faced.

this revolting and heart-rending scene, our informant said he almost doubted the existence of a God of justice! And he stood wondering that the earth did not open and swallow up such wickedness.

In the midst of these reflections, and while running his eye up and down the fettered ranks, he met the glance of one whose face he thought he had seen before. To be resolved, he moved towards the spot. It was MADISON WASHINGTON! Here was a scene for the pencil! Had Mr. Listwell been confronted by one risen from the dead, he could not have been more appalled. He was completely stunned. A thunderbolt could not have struck him more dumb. He stood, for a few moments, as motionless as one petrified; collecting himself, he at length exclaimed, "*Madison! is that you?*"

The noble fugitive, but little less astonished than himself, answered cheerily, "O yes, sir, they've got me again."

Thoughtless of consequences for the moment, Mr. Listwell ran up to his old friend, placing his hands upon his shoulders, and looked him in the face! Speechless they stood gazing at each other as if to be doubly resolved that there was no mistake about the matter, till Madison motioned his friend away, intimating a fear lest the keepers should find him there, and suspect him of tampering with the slaves.

"They will soon be out to look after us. You can come when they go to breakfast, and I will tell you all."

Pleased with this arrangement, Mr. Listwell passed out of the alley; but only just in time to save himself, for, while near the door, he observed three men making their way to the alley. The thought occurred to him to await their arrival, as the best means of diverting the ever-ready suspicions of the guilty.

While the scene between Mr. Listwell and his friend Madison was going on, the other slaves stood as mute spectators—at a loss to know what all this could mean. As he left, he heard the man chained to Madison ask, "Who is that gentleman?"

"He is a friend of mine. I cannot tell you now. Suffice it to say he is a friend. You shall hear more of him before long, but mark me! whatever shall pass between that gentleman and me, in your hearing, I pray you will say nothing about it. We are all chained here together—ours is a common lot; and that gentleman is not less *your* friend than *mine*." At these words, all mysterious as they were, the unhappy company gave signs of satisfaction and hope. It seems that

Madison, by that mesmeric power which is the invariable accompaniment of genius, had already won the confidence of the gang, and was a sort of general-in-chief among them.

By this time the keepers arrived. A horrid trio, well fitted for their demoniacal work. Their uncombed hair came down over foreheads "*villainously low*,"[1] and with eyes, mouths, and noses to match. "Hallo! hallo!" they growled out as they entered. "Are you all there!"

"All here," said Madison.

"Well, well, that's right! your journey will soon be over. You'll be in Richmond by eleven today, and then you'll have an easy time on it."

"I say, gal, what in the devil are you crying about?" said one of them. "I'll give you something to cry about, if you don't mind." This was said to a girl, apparently not more than twelve years old, who had been weeping bitterly. She had, probably, left behind her a loving mother, affectionate sisters, brothers, and friends, and her tears were but the natural expression of her sorrow, and the only solace. But the dealers in human flesh have *no* respect for such sorrow. They look upon it as a protest against their cruel injustice, and they are prompt to punish it.

This is a puzzle not easily solved. *How* came he here? what can I do for him? may I not even now be in some way compromised in this affair? were thoughts that troubled Mr. Listwell, and made him eager for the promised opportunity of speaking to Madison.

The bell now sounded for breakfast, and keepers and drivers, with pistols and bowie-knives gleaming from their belts, hurried in, as if to get the best places. Taking the chance now afforded, Mr. Listwell hastened back to the bowling-alley. Reaching Madison, he said, "Now *do* tell me all about the matter. Do you know me?"

"Oh, yes," said Madison, "I know you well, and shall never forget you nor that cold and dreary night you gave me shelter. I must be short," he continued, "for they'll soon be out again. This, then, is the story in brief. On reaching Canada, and getting over the excitement of making my escape, sir, my thoughts turned to my poor wife, who had well deserved my love by her virtuous fidelity and undying affection for me. I could not bear the thought of leaving her in the

1 *villainously low* See Shakespeare's *The Tempest* 4.1.274–76: "We shall lose our time / And all be turned to barnacles or to apes / With foreheads villainous low."

cruel jaws of slavery, without making an effort to rescue her. First, I tried to get money to buy her; but oh! the process was *too slow.* I despaired of accomplishing it. She was in all my thoughts by day, and my dreams by night. At times I could almost hear her voice, saying, 'O Madison! Madison! will you then leave me here? can you leave me here to die? No! no! you will come! you will come!' I was wretched. I lost my appetite. I could neither work, eat, nor sleep, till I resolved to hazard my own liberty, to gain that of my wife! But I must be short. Six weeks ago I reached my old master's place. I laid about the neighborhood nearly a week, watching my chance, and, finally, I ventured upon the desperate attempt to reach my poor wife's room by means of a ladder. I reached the window, but the noise in raising it frightened my wife, and she screamed and fainted. I took her in my arms, and was descending the ladder, when the dogs began to bark furiously, and before I could get to the woods the white folks were roused. The cool night air soon restored my wife, and she readily recognized me. We made the best of our way to the woods, but it was now *too* late—the dogs were after us as though they would have torn us to pieces. It was all over with me now! My old master and his two sons ran out with loaded rifles, and before we were out of gunshot, our ears were assailed with '*Stop! stop! or be shot down.*' Nevertheless we ran on. Seeing that we gave no heed to their calls, they fired, and my poor wife fell by my side dead, while I received but a slight flesh wound. I now became desperate, and stood my ground, and awaited their attack over her dead body. They rushed upon me, with their rifles in hand. I parried their blows, and fought them 'till I was knocked down and overpowered."

"Oh! it was madness to have returned," said Mr. Listwell.

"Sir, I could not be free with the galling thought that my poor wife was still a slave. With her in slavery, my body, not my spirit, was free. I was taken to the house—chained to a ring-bolt—my wounds dressed. I was kept there three days. All the slaves, for miles around, were brought to see me. Many slave-holders came with their slaves, using me as proof of the completeness of their power, and of the impossibility of slaves getting away. I was taunted, jeered at, and berated by them, in a manner that pierced me to the soul. Thank God, I was able to smother my rage, and to bear it all with seeming composure. After my wounds were nearly healed, I was taken to a tree and stripped, and I received sixty lashes on my naked back. A few days after, I was sold to a slave-trader, and placed in this gang for the New Orleans market."

"Do you think your master would sell you to me?"

"O no, sir! I was sold on condition of my being taken South. Their motive is revenge."

"Then, then," said Mr. Listwell, "I fear I can do nothing for you. Put your trust in God, and bear your sad lot with the manly fortitude which becomes a man. I shall see you at Richmond, but don't recognize me." Saying this, Mr. Listwell handed Madison ten dollars; said a few words to the other slaves; received their hearty "God bless you," and made his way to the house.

Fearful of exciting suspicion by too long delay, our friend went to the breakfast table, with the air of one who half reproved the greediness of those who rushed in at the sound of the bell. A cup of coffee was all that he could manage. His feelings were too bitter and excited, and his heart was too full with the fate of poor Madison (whom he loved as well as admired) to relish his breakfast; and although he sat long after the company had left the table, he really did little more than change the position of his knife and fork. The strangeness of meeting again one whom he had met on two several occasions before, under extraordinary circumstances, was well calculated to suggest the idea that a supernatural power, a wakeful providence, or an inexorable fate, had linked their destiny together; and that no efforts of his could disentangle him from the mysterious web of circumstances which enfolded him.

On leaving the table, Mr. Listwell nerved himself up and walked firmly into the barroom. He was at once greeted again by that talkative chatterbox, Mr. Wilkes.

"Them's a likely set of niggers in the alley there," said Wilkes.

"Yes, they're fine looking fellows, one of them I should like to purchase, and for him I would be willing to give a handsome sum."

Turning to one of his comrades, and with a grin of victory, Wilkes said, "Aha, Bill, did you hear that? I told you I know'd that gentleman wanted to buy niggers, and would bid as high as any purchaser in the market."

"Come, come," said Listwell, "don't be too loud in your praise, you are old enough to know that prices rise when purchasers are plenty."

"That's a fact," said Wilkes, "I see you knows the ropes—and there's not a man in old Virginy whom I'd rather help to make a good bargain than you, sir."

Mr. Listwell here threw a dollar at Wilkes (which the latter caught with a dexterous hand), saying, "Take that for your kind good will." Wilkes held up the dollar to his right eye, with a grin of victory, and turned to the morose grumbler in the corner who had questioned the liberality of a man of whom he knew nothing.

Mr. Listwell now stood as well with the company as any other occupant of the barroom.

We pass over the hurry and bustle, the brutal vociferations of the slave-drivers in getting their unhappy gang in motion for Richmond; and we need not narrate every application of the lash to those who faltered in the journey. Mr. Listwell followed the train at a long distance, with a sad heart; and on reaching Richmond, left his horse at a hotel, and made his way to the wharf in the direction of which he saw the slave-coffle driven. He was just in time to see the whole company embark for New Orleans. The thought struck him that, while mixing with the multitude, he might do his friend Madison one last service, and he stepped into a hardware store and purchased three strong *files*. These he took with him, and standing near the small boat, which lay in waiting to bear the company by parcels to the side of the brig[1] that lay in the stream, he managed, as Madison passed him, to slip the files into his pocket, and at once darted back among the crowd.

All the company now on board, the imperious voice of the captain sounded, and instantly a dozen hardy seamen were in the rigging, hurrying aloft to unfurl the broad canvas of our Baltimore built American Slaver. The sailors hung about the ropes, like so many black cats, now in the round-tops, now in the cross-trees, now on the yard-arms; all was bluster and activity. Soon the broad fore topsail, the royal and top gallant sail were spread to the breeze. Round went the heavy windlass, clank, clank went the fall-bit—the anchors weighed—jibs, mainsails, and topsails hauled to the wind, and the long, low, black slaver, with her cargo of human flesh, careened and moved forward to the sea.

Mr. Listwell stood on the shore, and watched the slaver till the last speck of her upper sails faded from sight, and announced the limit

1 *brig* Ship.

of human vision. "Farewell! farewell! brave and true man! God grant that brighter skies may smile upon your future than have yet looked down upon your thorny pathway."

Saying this to himself, our friend lost no time in completing his business, and in making his way homewards, gladly shaking off from his feet the dust of Old Virginia.

Part 4

Oh, where's the slave so lowly
Condemn'd to chains unholy,
    Who could he burst
    His bonds at first
Would pine beneath them slowly?[1]

Moore.

——Know ye not
Who would be free, *themselves* must strike the blow.[2]

Childe Harold.

What a world of inconsistency, as well as of wickedness, is suggested by the smooth and gliding phrase, American Slave Trade; and how strange and perverse is that moral sentiment which loathes, execrates, and brands as piracy and as deserving of death the carrying away into captivity men, women, and children from the *African coast*;[3] but which is neither shocked nor disturbed by a similar traffic, carried on with the same motives and purposes, and characterized by even *more* odious peculiarities on the coast of our MODEL REPUBLIC. We execrate and hang the wretch guilty of this crime on the coast of Guinea, while we respect and applaud the guilty participators in this murderous business on the enlightened shores of the Chesapeake. The inconsistency is so flagrant and glaring, that it would seem to cast a doubt on the doctrine of the innate moral sense of mankind.

---

1 *Oh, where's … them slowly?* First stanza of Irish poet Thomas Moore's (1779–1852) "Oh, Where's the Slave."

2 *Know ye … the blow* See Byron's *Childe Harold's Pilgrimage*, 2.76.1–2.

3 *the carrying away … African coast* Reference to the Act Prohibiting Importation of Slaves (passed by the United States in 1807), which ended American participation in the international slave trade.

Just two months after the sailing of the Virginia slave brig, which the reader has seen move off to sea so proudly with her human cargo for the New Orleans market,[1] there chanced to meet, in the Marine Coffee-house at Richmond, a company of *ocean birds*, when the following conversation, which throws some light on the subsequent history, not only of Madison Washington, but of the hundred and thirty human beings with whom we last saw him chained.

"I say, shipmate, you had rather rough weather on your late passage to Orleans?" said Jack Williams, a regular old salt, tauntingly, to a trim, compact, manly looking person, who proved to be the first mate of the slave brig in question.

"Foul play, as well as foul weather," replied the firmly knit personage, evidently but little inclined to enter upon a subject which terminated so ingloriously to the captain and officers of the American slaver.

"Well, betwixt you and me," said Williams, "that whole affair on board of the *Creole* was miserably and disgracefully managed. Those black rascals got the upper hand of ye altogether; and, in my opinion, the whole disaster was the result of ignorance of the real character of *darkies* in general. With half a dozen *resolute* white men (I say it not boastingly), I could have had the rascals in irons in ten minutes, not because I'm so strong, but I know how to manage 'em. With my back against the *caboose*, I could, myself, have flogged a dozen of them; and had I been on board, by every monster of the deep, every black devil of 'em all would have had his neck stretched from the yardarm.[2] Ye made a mistake in yer manner of fighting 'em. All that is needed in dealing with a set of rebellious *darkies*, is to show that yer not afraid of 'em. For my own part, I would not honor a dozen niggers by pointing a gun at one on 'em—a good stout whip, or a stiff rope's end, is better than all the guns at Old Point[3] to quell a *nigger* insurrection. Why, sir, to take a gun to a *nigger* is the best way you can select to tell him you are afraid of him, and the best way of inviting his attack."

---

1 *New Orleans market* New Orleans became an important center of the internal slave trade in the nineteenth century, following the U.S.'s abolition of the international slave trade.

2 *yardarm* Horizontal spar that supports the sail; mutineers at sea were often executed by being hanged from the yardarm.

3 *Old Point* I.e., West Point, a major military academy in New York.

This speech made quite a sensation among the company, and a part of them indicated solicitude for the answer which might be made to it. Our first mate replied, "Mr. Williams, all that you've now said sounds very well *here* on shore, where, perhaps, you have studied negro character. I do not profess to understand the subject as well as yourself; but it strikes me, you apply the same rule in dissimilar cases. It is quite easy to talk of flogging niggers here on land, where you have the sympathy of the community, and the whole physical force of the government, State and national, at your command; and where, if a negro shall lift his hand against a white man, the whole community, with one accord, are ready to unite in shooting him down. I say, in such circumstances, it's easy to talk of flogging negroes and of negro cowardice; but, sir, I deny that the negro is, naturally, a coward, or that your theory of managing slaves will stand the test of *salt* water. It may do very well for an overseer, a contemptible hireling, to take advantage of fears already in existence, and which his presence has no power to inspire; to swagger about whip in hand, and discourse on the timidity and cowardice of negroes; for they have a smooth sea and a fair wind. It is one thing to manage a company of slaves on a Virginia plantation, and quite another thing to quell an insurrection on the lonely billows of the Atlantic, where every breeze speaks of courage and liberty. For the negro to act cowardly on shore, may be to act wisely; and I've some doubts whether *you*, Mr. Williams, would find it very convenient were you a slave in Algiers,[1] to raise your hand against the bayonets of a whole government."

"By George, shipmate," said Williams, "you're coming rather *too* near. Either I've fallen very low in your estimation, or your notions of negro courage have got up a buttonhole too high. Now I more than ever wish I'd been on board of that luckless craft. I'd have given ye practical evidence of the truth of my theory. I don't doubt there's some difference in being at sea. But a nigger's a nigger, on sea or land; and is a coward, find him where you will; a drop of blood from one on 'em will skeer a hundred. A knock on the nose, or a kick on the shin, will tame the wildest '*darkey*' you can fetch me. I say again, and will stand by it, I could, with half a dozen good men, put the whole

1 *slave in Algiers* During the eighteenth and early nineteenth centuries, pirates from Algiers were known to raid American ships in the Mediterranean and enslave their crews.

nineteen on 'em in irons, and have carried them safe to New Orleans too. Mind, I don't blame you, but I do say, and every gentleman here will bear me out in it, that the fault was somewhere, or them niggers would never have got off as they have done. For my part I feel ashamed to have the idea go abroad, that a ship load of slaves can't be safely taken from Richmond to New Orleans. I should like, merely to redeem the character of Virginia sailors, to take charge of a ship load on 'em tomorrow."

Williams went on in this strain, occasionally casting an imploring glance at the company for applause for his wit, and sympathy for his contempt of negro courage. He had, evidently, however, waked up the wrong passenger; for besides being in the right, his opponent carried that in his eye which marked him a man not to be trifled with.

"Well, sir," said the sturdy mate, "you can select your own method for distinguishing yourself—the path of ambition in this direction is quite open to you in Virginia, and I've no doubt that you will be highly appreciated and compensated for all your valiant achievements in that line; but for myself, while I do not profess to be a giant, I have resolved never to set my foot on the deck of a slave ship, either as officer, or common sailor again; I have got enough of it."

"Indeed! indeed!" exclaimed Williams, derisively.

"Yes, *indeed*," echoed the mate; "but don't misunderstand me. It is not the high value that I set upon my life that makes me say what I have said; yet I'm resolved never to endanger my life again in a cause which my conscience does not approve. I dare say *here* what many men *feel*, but *dare not speak*, that this whole slave-trading business is a disgrace and scandal to Old Virginia."

"Hold! hold on! shipmate," said Williams, "I hardly thought you'd have shown your colors so soon—I'll be hanged if you're not as good an abolitionist as Garrison[1] himself."

The mate now rose from his chair, manifesting some excitement. "What do you mean, sir," said he, in a commanding tone. "*That man does not live who shall offer me an insult with impunity*."[2]

The effect of these words was marked; and the company clustered around. Williams, in an apologetic tone, said, "Shipmate! keep your

1 *Garrison* Influential abolitionist William Lloyd Garrison (1805–79).

2 *That man … with impunity* Allusion to the well-known Latin phrase *Nemo me impune lacessit*, often translated as "No one provokes me with impunity."

temper. I mean't no insult. We all know that Tom Grant is no coward, and what I said about your being an abolitionist was simply this: you *might* have put down them black mutineers and murderers, but your conscience held you back."

"In that, too," said Grant, "you were mistaken. I did all that any man with equal strength and presence of mind could have done. The fact is, Mr. Williams, you underrate the courage as well as the skill of these negroes, and further, you do not seem to have been correctly informed about the case in hand at all."

"All I know about it is," said Williams, "that on the ninth day after you left Richmond, a dozen or two of the niggers ye had on board, came on deck and took the ship from you—had her steered into a British port, where, by the by, every woolly head of them went ashore and was free. Now I take this to be a discreditable piece of business, and one demanding explanation."

"There are a great many discreditable things in the world," said Grant. "For a ship to go down under a calm sky is, upon the first flush of it, disgraceful either to sailors or caulkers.[1] But when we learn, that by some mysterious disturbance in nature, the waters parted beneath, and swallowed the ship up, we lose our indignation and disgust in lamentation of the disaster, and in awe of the Power which controls the elements."

"Very true, very true," said Williams, "I should be very glad to have an explanation which would relieve the affair of its present discreditable features. I have desired to see you ever since you got home, and to learn from you a full statement of the facts in the case. To me the whole thing seems unaccountable. I cannot see how a dozen or two of ignorant negroes, not one of whom had ever been to sea before, and all of them were closely ironed between decks, should be able to get their fetters off, rush out of the hatchway in open daylight, kill two white men, the one the captain and the other their master, and then carry the ship into a British port, where every '*darkey*' of them was set free. There must have been great carelessness, or cowardice somewhere!"

The company which had listened in silence during most of this discussion, now became much excited. One said, I agree with Williams;

1 *caulkers* Workers who seal the wooden seams of a boat against leakage with oakum and melted tar.

and several said the thing looks black enough. After the temporary tumultuous exclamations had subsided—

"I see," said Grant, "how you regard this case, and how difficult it will be for me to render our ship's company blameless in your eyes. Nevertheless, I will state the fact precisely as they came under my own observation. Mr. Williams speaks of 'ignorant negroes,' and, as a general rule, they are ignorant; but had he been on board the *Creole* as I was, he would have seen cause to admit that there are exceptions to this general rule. The leader of the mutiny in question was just as shrewd a fellow as ever I met in my life, and was as well fitted to lead in a dangerous enterprise as any one white man in ten thousand. The name of this man, strange to say (ominous of greatness),[1] was Madison Washington. In the short time he had been on board, he had secured the confidence of every officer. The negroes fairly worshipped him. His manner and bearing were such that no one could suspect him of a murderous purpose. The only feeling with which we regarded him was, that he was a powerful, good-disposed negro. He seldom spake to anyone, and when he did speak, it was with the utmost propriety. His words were well chosen, and his pronunciation equal to that of any schoolmaster. It was a mystery to us *where* he got his knowledge of language; but as little was said to him, none of us knew the extent of his intelligence and ability till it was too late. It seems he brought three files with him on board, and must have gone to work upon his fetters the first night out; and he must have worked well at that; for on the day of the rising, he got the irons *off eighteen* besides himself.

"The attack began just about twilight in the evening. Apprehending a squall, I had commanded the second mate to order all hands on deck, to take in sail. A few minutes before this I had seen Madison's head above the hatchway, looking out upon the white-capped waves at the leeward. I think I never saw him look more good-natured. I stood just about midship, on the larboard side. The captain was pacing the quarter-deck on the starboard side, in company with Mr. Jameson, the owner of most of the slaves on board. Both were armed. I had just told the men to lay aloft, and was looking to see my orders

1 *ominous of greatness* In reference to the two celebrated Founders whose names Washington shares: James Madison (1751–1836) and George Washington (1732–99).

obeyed, when I heard the discharge of a pistol on the starboard side; and turning suddenly around, the very deck seemed covered with fiends from the pit. The nineteen negroes were all on deck, with their broken fetters in their hands, rushing in all directions. I put my hand quickly in my pocket to draw out my jack-knife; but before I could draw it, I was knocked senseless to the deck. When I came to myself (which I did in a few minutes, I suppose, for it was yet quite light), there was not a white man on deck. The sailors were all aloft in the rigging, and dared not come down. Captain Clarke and Mr. Jameson lay stretched on the quarter-deck—both dying—while Madison himself stood at the helm unhurt.

"I was completely weakened by the loss of blood, and had not recovered from the stunning blow which felled me to the deck; but it was a little too much for me, even in my prostrate condition, to see our good brig commanded by a *black murderer*. So I called out to the men to come down and take the ship, or die in the attempt. Suiting the action to the word, I started aft. You murderous villain, said I, to the imp at the helm, and rushed upon him to deal him a blow, when he pushed me back with his strong, black arm, as though I had been a boy of twelve. I looked around for the men. They were still in the rigging. Not one had come down. I started towards Madison again. The rascal now told me to stand back. 'Sir,' said he, 'your life is in my hands. I could have killed you a dozen times over during this last half hour, and could kill you now. You call me a *black murderer*. I am not a murderer. God is my witness that LIBERTY, not *malice*, is the motive for this night's work. I have done no more to those dead men yonder, than they would have done to me in like circumstances. We have struck for our freedom, and if a true man's heart be in you, you will honor us for the deed. We have done that which you applaud your fathers for doing, and if we are murderers, *so were they*.'

"I felt little disposition to reply to this impudent speech. By heaven, it disarmed me. The fellow loomed up before me. I forgot his blackness in the dignity of his manner, and the eloquence of his speech. It seemed as if the souls of both the great dead (whose names he bore) had entered him. To the sailors in the rigging he said: 'Men! the battle is over—your captain is dead. I have complete command of this vessel. All resistance to my authority will be in vain. My men have won their liberty, with no other weapons but their own broken fetters. We are nineteen in number. We do not thirst for your blood, we demand only our rightful freedom. Do not flatter yourselves that I am ignorant of chart or compass. I know both. We are now only about sixty miles from Nassau.[1] Come down, and do your duty. Land us in Nassau, and not a hair of your heads shall be hurt.'

"I shouted, *Stay where you are, men*—when a sturdy black fellow ran at me with a handspike, and would have split my head open, but for the interference of Madison, who darted between me and the blow. 'I know what you are up to,' said the latter to me. 'You want to navigate this brig into a slave port, where you would have us all hanged; but you'll miss it; before this brig shall touch a slave-cursed shore while I am on board, I will myself put a match to the magazine,[2] and blow her, and be blown with her, into a thousand fragments. Now I have saved your life twice within these last twenty minutes—for, when you lay helpless on deck, my men were about to kill you. I held them in check. And if you now (seeing I am your friend and not your enemy) persist in your resistance to my authority, I give you fair warning, YOU SHALL DIE.'

"Saying this to me, he cast a glance into the rigging where the terror-stricken sailors were clinging, like so many frightened monkeys, and commanded them to come down, in a tone from which there was no appeal; for four men stood by with muskets in hand, ready at the word of command to shoot them down.

"I now became satisfied that resistance was out of the question; that my best policy was to put the brig into Nassau, and secure the assistance of the American consul at that port. I felt sure that the authorities would enable us to secure the murderers, and bring them to trial.

"By this time the apprehended squall had burst upon us. The wind howled furiously—the ocean was white with foam, which, on account of the darkness, we could see only by the quick flashes of lightning that darted occasionally from the angry sky. All was alarm and confusion. Hideous cries came up from the slave women. Above the roaring billows a succession of heavy thunder rolled along, swelling the terrific din. Owing to the great darkness, and a sudden shift of

1 *Nassau* Capital city of the Bahamas, then a colony of the British Empire (in which slavery had been abolished).

2 *magazine* Storeroom where gunpowder is kept.

the wind, we found ourselves in the trough of the sea. When shipping a heavy sea over the starboard bow, the bodies of the captain and Mr. Jameson were washed overboard. For awhile we had dearer interests to look after than slave property. A more savage thunder-gust never swept the ocean. Our brig rolled and creaked as if every bolt would be started, and every thread of oakum would be pressed out of the seams. To the pumps! to the pumps! I cried, but not a sailor would quit his grasp. Fortunately this squall soon passed over, or we must have been food for sharks.

"During all the storm, Madison stood firmly at the helm—his keen eye fixed upon the binnacle.[1] He was not indifferent to the dreadful hurricane; yet he met it with the equanimity of an old sailor. He was silent but not agitated. The first words he uttered after the storm had slightly subsided, were characteristic of the man. 'Mr. mate, you cannot write the bloody laws of slavery on those restless billows. The ocean, if not the land, is free.' I confess, gentlemen, I felt myself in the presence of a superior man; one who, had he been a white man, I would have followed willingly and gladly in any honorable enterprise. Our difference of color was the only ground for difference of action. It was not that his principles were wrong in the abstract; for they are the principles of 1776. But I could not bring myself to recognize their application to one whom I deemed my inferior.

"But to my story. What happened now is soon told. Two hours after the frightful tempest had spent itself, we were plump at the wharf in Nassau. I sent two of our men immediately to our consul with a statement of facts, requesting his interference in our behalf. What he did, or whither he did anything, I don't know; but, by order of the authorities, a company of *black* soldiers came on board, for the purpose, as they said, of protecting the property. These impudent rascals, when I called on them to assist me in keeping the slaves on board, sheltered themselves adroitly under their instructions only to protect property—and said they did not recognize *persons* as *property*. I told them that by the laws of Virginia and the laws of the United States, the slaves on board were as much property as the barrels of flour in the hold. At this the stupid blockheads showed their *ivory*,[2]

1 *binnacle* Case in which a ship's compass is kept.
2 *ivory* I.e., their teeth.

rolled up their white eyes in horror, as if the idea of putting men on a footing with merchandise were revolting to their humanity. When these instructions were understood among the negroes, it was impossible for us to keep them on board. They deliberately gathered up their baggage before our eyes, and, against our remonstrances, poured through the gangway—formed themselves into a procession on the wharf—bid farewell to all on board, and, uttering the wildest shouts of exultation, they marched, amidst the deafening cheers of a multitude of sympathizing spectators, under the triumphant leadership of their heroic chief and deliverer, MADISON WASHINGTON."[1]

—1853

Each piece in *Autographs for Freedom* is accompanied by the signature of its author.

1 One detail left out of the conclusion to the story is that, while the majority of the ship's captives were set free, Washington and his fellow insurgents were held for several months on charges of mutiny. Following a trial at the British Admiralty Court, however, they were cleared of all charges; they were released in April 1842. Details of Washington's life following his release are unknown, though certain references from abolitionists in the 1840s who may have had contact with him suggest that he was still living in the Bahamas later in that decade.

In Context

Photographs of Frederick Douglass

Frederick Douglass was a great proponent of the new art of photography. He saw it as a fundamentally democratic medium as well as a crucial tool in the fight to end slavery and racial discrimination. Douglass used photography as a means to assert greater control over his public image as a black man, sitting for at least 160 distinct portraits over the course of his life (as identified by John Stauffer, Zoe Trodd, and Celeste-Marie Bernier in their 2015 *Picturing Frederick Douglass*). By contrast, there are only 126 photographs of Abraham Lincoln known to exist, and only 127 of Walt Whitman.

Daguerreotype taken c. 1841, artist unknown.
This is the first known photograph of Douglass.

Daguerreotype taken in July or August 1843, two years before the publication of Douglass's *Narrative*, artist unknown.

Daguerreotype taken in May 1848 by Edward White Gallery.

Daguerreotype taken c. 1853, two years before the publication of Douglass's second autobiography, *My Bondage and My Freedom.* Artist unknown.

Engraving of a photograph taken by John Howe Kent on 3 November 1882, used as the frontispiece to Douglass's revised third autobiography, *The Life and Times of Frederick Douglass* (1893).

Photograph taken on 31 October 1894 by Phineas C. Headley, Jr. and James E. Reed, a few months before Douglass's death. Douglass very rarely smiled in his photographs.

Portrait of Douglass seated with his second wife, Helen Pitts (right). Helen's sister, Eva Pitts, stands in the center. Taken c. 1884, shortly after their marriage, artist unknown.

Engraving used as the frontispiece to the first edition of Douglass's 1845 *Narrative*, artist unknown.

Cover of an 1847 anti-abolitionist pamphlet reprinting one of Douglass's speeches. The pamphlet described Douglass as a "presumptive negro" and as a "runaway slave from Baltimore," despite the fact that he had been manumitted some months before.

from *My Bondage and My Freedom*

This excerpt from Douglass's expanded 1855 autobiography provides an interesting point of comparison with the account provided in Chapter 10 of the *Narrative*.

Chapter 17
The Last Flogging

Sleep itself does not always come to the relief of the weary in body, and the broken in spirit; especially when past troubles only foreshadow coming disasters. The last hope had been extinguished. My master, who I did not venture to hope would protect me as *a man*, had even now refused to protect me as *his property*; and had cast me back, covered with reproaches and bruises, into the hands of a stranger to that mercy which was the soul of the religion he professed. May the reader never spend such a night as that allotted to me, previous to the morning which was to herald my return to the den of horrors from which I had made a temporary escape.

I remained all night—sleep I did not—at St. Michael's;[1] and in the morning (Saturday) I started off, according to the order of Master Thomas, feeling that I had no friend on earth, and doubting if I had one in heaven. I reached Covey's about nine o'clock; and just as I stepped into the field, before I had reached the house, Covey, true to his snakish habits, darted out at me from a fence corner, in which he had secreted himself, for the purpose of securing me. He was amply provided with a cowskin[2] and a rope; and he evidently intended to *tie me up*, and to wreak his vengeance on me to the fullest extent. I should have been an easy prey, had he succeeded in getting his hands upon me, for I had taken no refreshment since noon on Friday; and this, together with the pelting, excitement, and the loss of blood, had reduced my strength. I, however, darted back into the woods, before the ferocious hound could get hold of me, and buried myself in a thicket, where he lost sight of me. The corn-field afforded me cover,

1 *St. Michael's* Town in Maryland, home of Thomas Auld.
2 *cowskin* Whip made from cowhide.

in getting to the woods. But for the tall corn, Covey would have overtaken me, and made me his captive. He seemed very much chagrined that he did not catch me, and gave up the chase, very reluctantly; for I could see his angry movements, toward the house from which he had sallied, on his foray.

Well, now I am clear of Covey, and of his wrathful lash, for the present. I am in the wood, buried in its somber gloom, and hushed in its solemn silence; hid from all human eyes; shut in with nature and nature's God, and absent from all human contrivances. Here was a good place to pray; to pray for help for deliverance—a prayer I had often made before. But how could I pray? Covey could pray—Capt. Auld could pray—I would fain[1] pray; but doubts (arising partly from my own neglect of the means of grace, and partly from the sham religion which everywhere prevailed, cast in my mind a doubt upon all religion, and led me to the conviction that prayers were unavailing and delusive) prevented my embracing the opportunity, as a religious one. Life, in itself, had almost become burdensome to me. All my outward relations were against me; I must stay here and starve (I was already hungry), or go home to Covey's, and have my flesh torn to pieces, and my spirit humbled under the cruel lash of Covey. This was the painful alternative presented to me. The day was long and irksome. My physical condition was deplorable. I was weak, from the toils of the previous day, and from the want of food and rest; and had been so little concerned about my appearance, that I had not yet washed the blood from my garments. I was an object of horror, even to myself. Life, in Baltimore, when most oppressive, was a paradise to this. What had I done, what had my parents done, that such a life as this should be mine? That day, in the woods, I would have exchanged my manhood for the brutehood of an ox.

Night came. I was still in the woods, unresolved what to do. Hunger had not yet pinched me to the point of going home, and I laid myself down in the leaves to rest; for I had been watching for hunters all day, but not being molested during the day, I expected no disturbance during the night. I had come to the conclusion that Covey relied upon hunger to drive me home; and in this I was quite correct—the facts showed that he had made no effort to catch me, since morning.

---

1 *fain* Like to.

During the night, I heard the step of a man in the woods. He was coming toward the place where I lay. A person lying still has the advantage over one walking in the woods, in the day time, and this advantage is much greater at night. I was not able to engage in a physical struggle, and I had recourse to the common resort of the weak. I hid myself in the leaves to prevent discovery. But, as the night rambler in the woods drew nearer, I found him to be a *friend*, not an enemy; it was a slave of Mr. William Groomes, of Easton, a kind hearted fellow, named "Sandy." Sandy lived with Mr. Kemp that year, about four miles from St. Michael's. He, like myself, had been hired out by the year; but, unlike myself, had not been hired out to be broken. Sandy was the husband of a free woman, who lived in the lower part of "*Pot-pie Neck*,"[1] and he was now on his way through the woods, to see her, and to spend the Sabbath with her.

As soon as I had ascertained that the disturber of my solitude was not an enemy, but the good-hearted Sandy—a man as famous among the slaves of the neighborhood for his good nature, as for his good sense—I came out from my hiding place, and made myself known to him. I explained the circumstances of the past two days, which had driven me to the woods, and he deeply compassionated my distress. It was a bold thing for him to shelter me, and I could not ask him to do so; for, had I been found in his hut, he would have suffered the penalty of thirty-nine lashes on his bare back, if not something worse. But, Sandy was too generous to permit the fear of punishment to prevent his relieving a brother bondman from hunger and exposure; and, therefore, on his own motion, I accompanied him to his home, or rather to the home of his wife—for the house and lot were hers. His wife was called up—for it was now about midnight—a fire was made, some Indian meal was soon mixed with salt and water, and an ash cake[2] was baked in a hurry to relieve my hunger. Sandy's wife was not behind him in kindness—both seemed to esteem it a privilege to succor me; for, although I was hated by Covey and by my master, I was loved by the colored people, because *they* thought I was hated for my knowledge, and persecuted because I was feared. I was the *only* slave *now* in that region who could read and write. There had

1 *Pot-pie Neck* Local name for a section of the Tilghman peninsula in Talbot County, Maryland.

2 *Indian meal* I.e., cornmeal; *ash cake* Plain flatbread baked on hot ashes.

been one other man, belonging to Mr. Hugh Hamilton, who could read (his name was "Jim"), but he, poor fellow, had, shortly after my coming into the neighborhood, been sold off to the far south. I saw Jim ironed,[1] in the cart, to be carried to Easton for sale—pinioned[2] like a yearling for the slaughter. My knowledge was now the pride of my brother slaves; and, no doubt, Sandy felt something of the general interest in me on that account. The supper was soon ready, and though I have feasted since, with honorables, lord mayors and aldermen, over the sea, my supper on ash cake and cold water, with Sandy, was the meal, of all my life, most sweet to my taste, and now most vivid in my memory.

Supper over, Sandy and I went into a discussion of what was *possible* for me, under the perils and hardships which now overshadowed my path. The question was, must I go back to Covey, or must I now attempt to run away? Upon a careful survey, the latter was found to be impossible; for I was on a narrow neck of land, every avenue from which would bring me in sight of pursuers. There was the Chesapeake Bay to the right, and "Pot-pie" River to the left, and St. Michael's and its neighborhood occupying the only space through which there was any retreat.

I found Sandy an old adviser. He was not only a religious man, but he professed to believe in a system for which I have no name. He was a genuine African, and had inherited some of the so called magical powers, said to be possessed by African and eastern nations. He told me that he could help me; that, in those very woods, there was an herb, which in the morning might be found, possessing all the powers required for my protection (I put his thoughts in my own language); and that, if I would take his advice, he would procure me the root of the herb of which he spoke. He told me further, that if I would take that root and wear it on my right side, it would be impossible for Covey to strike me a blow; that with this root about my person, no white man could whip me. He said he had carried it for years, and that he had fully tested its virtues. He had never received a blow from a slaveholder since he carried it; and he never expected to receive one, for he always meant to carry that root as a protection. He knew Covey

---

1 *ironed* I.e., bound in iron cuffs or chains.

2 *pinioned* Having his arms and legs bound.

well, for Mrs. Covey was the daughter of Mr. Kemp; and he (Sandy) had heard of the barbarous treatment to which I was subjected, and he wanted to do something for me.

Now all this talk about the root, was, to me, very absurd and ridiculous, if not positively sinful. I at first rejected the idea that the simple carrying a root on my right side (a root, by the way, over which I walked every time I went into the woods), could possess any such magic power as he ascribed to it, and I was, therefore, not disposed to cumber my pocket with it. I had a positive aversion to all pretenders to "*divination*." It was beneath one of my intelligence to countenance such dealings with the devil, as this power implied. But, with all my learning—it was really precious little—Sandy was more than a match for me. "My book learning," he said, "had not kept Covey off me" (a powerful argument just then), and he entreated me, with flashing eyes, to try this. If it did me no good, it could do me no harm, and it would cost me nothing, anyway. Sandy was so earnest, and so confident of the good qualities of this weed, that, to please him, rather than from any conviction of its excellence, I was induced to take it. He had been to me the good Samaritan,[1] and had, almost providentially, found me, and helped me when I could not help myself; how did I know but that the hand of the Lord was in it? With thoughts of this sort, I took the roots from Sandy, and put them in my right hand pocket.

This was, of course, Sunday morning. Sandy now urged me to go home, with all speed, and to walk up bravely to the house, as though nothing had happened. I saw in Sandy too deep an insight into human nature, with all his superstition, not to have some respect for his advice; and perhaps, too, a slight gleam or shadow of his superstition had fallen upon me. At any rate, I started off toward Covey's, as directed by Sandy. Having, the previous night, poured my griefs into Sandy's ears, and got him enlisted in my behalf, having made his wife a sharer in my sorrows, and having, also, become well refreshed by sleep and food, I moved off, quite courageously, toward the much dreaded Covey's. Singularly enough, just as I entered his yard gate, I met him and his wife, dressed in their Sunday best—looking as smiling as angels—on

1 *good Samaritan* See Luke 10.33, in which Jesus tells a parable of a man who is beaten and left for dead by thieves, but is rescued and nursed back to health by a Samaritan. (In the Bible, the Samaritans are an ethnoreligious group who are often looked down upon by the Jews.)

their way to church. The manner of Covey astonished me. There was something really benignant in his countenance. He spoke to me as never before; told me that the pigs had got into the lot, and he wished me to drive them out; inquired how I was, and seemed an altered man. This extraordinary conduct of Covey, really made me begin to think that Sandy's herb had more virtue in it than I, in my pride, had been willing to allow; and, had the day been other than Sunday, I should have attributed Covey's altered manner solely to the magic power of the root. I suspected, however, that the *Sabbath*, and not the *root*, was the real explanation of Covey's manner. His religion hindered him from breaking the Sabbath, but not from breaking my skin. He had more respect for the *day* than for the *man*, for whom the day was mercifully given; for while he would cut and slash my body during the week, he would not hesitate, on Sunday, to teach me the value of my soul, or the way of life and salvation by Jesus Christ.

All went well with me till Monday morning; and then, whether the root had lost its virtue, or whether my tormentor had gone deeper into the black art than myself (as was sometimes said of him), or whether he had obtained a special indulgence, for his faithful Sabbath day's worship, it is not necessary for me to know, or to inform the reader; but, this much I *may* say—the pious and benignant smile which graced Covey's face on *Sunday*, wholly disappeared on *Monday*. Long before daylight, I was called up to go and feed, rub, and curry[1] the horses. I obeyed the call, and I would have so obeyed it, had it been made at an earlier hour, for I had brought my mind to a firm resolve, during that Sunday's reflection, viz:[2] to obey every order, however unreasonable, if it were possible, and, if Mr. Covey should then undertake to beat me, to defend and protect myself to the best of my ability. My religious views on the subject of resisting my master, had suffered a serious shock, by the savage persecution to which I had been subjected, and my hands were no longer tied by my religion. Master Thomas's indifference had severed the last link. I had now to this extent "backslidden" from this point in the slave's religious creed; and I soon had occasion to make my fallen state known to my Sunday-pious brother, Covey.

---

1 *curry* Brush.
2 *viz* Abbreviation for the Latin *videlicet*, meaning "namely" or "that is to say."

Whilst I was obeying his order to feed and get the horses ready for the field, and when in the act of going up the stable loft for the purpose of throwing down some blades, Covey sneaked into the stable, in his peculiar snake-like way, and seizing me suddenly by the leg, he brought me to the stable floor, giving my newly mended body a fearful jar. I now forgot my *roots,* and remembered my pledge to *stand up in my own defense.* The brute was endeavoring skillfully to get a slip-knot on my legs, before I could draw up my feet. As soon as I found what he was up to, I gave a sudden spring (my two day's rest had been of much service to me), and by that means, no doubt, he was able to bring me to the floor so heavily. He was defeated in his plan of tying me. While down, he seemed to think he had me very securely in his power. He little thought he was—as the rowdies say—"in" for a "rough and tumble" fight; but such was the fact. Whence came the daring spirit necessary to grapple with a man who, eight-and-forty hours before, could, with his slightest word, have made me tremble like a leaf in a storm, I do not know; at any rate, *I was resolved to fight,* and, what was better still, I was actually hard at it. The fighting madness had come upon me, and I found my strong fingers firmly attached to the throat of my cowardly tormentor; as heedless of consequences, at the moment, as though we stood as equals before the law. The very color of the man was forgotten. I felt as supple as a cat, and was ready for the snakish creature at every turn. Every blow of his was parried, though I dealt no blows in turn. I was strictly on the *defensive*, preventing him from injuring me, rather than trying to injure him. I flung him on the ground several times, when he meant to have hurled me there. I held him so firmly by the throat, that his blood followed my nails. He held me, and I held him.

All was fair, thus far, and the contest was about equal. My resistance was entirely unexpected, and Covey was taken all aback by it, for he trembled in every limb. "*Are you going to resist*, you scoundrel?" said he. To which, I returned a polite "*yes sir*"; steadily gazing my interrogator in the eye, to meet the first approach or dawning of the blow, which I expected my answer would call forth. But, the conflict did not long remain thus equal. Covey soon cried out lustily for help; not that I was obtaining any marked advantage over him, or was injuring him, but because he was gaining none over me, and was not able, single handed, to conquer me. He called for his cousin

Hughes, to come to his assistance, and now the scene was changed. I was compelled to give blows, as well as to parry them; and, since I was, in any case, to suffer for resistance, I felt (as the musty proverb goes) that "I might as well be hanged for an old sheep as a lamb." I was still *defensive* toward Covey, but *aggressive* toward Hughes; and, at the first approach of the latter, I dealt a blow, in my desperation, which fairly sickened my youthful assailant. He went off, bending over with pain, and manifesting no disposition to come within my reach again. The poor fellow was in the act of trying to catch and tie my right hand, and while flattering himself with success, I gave him the kick which sent him staggering away in pain, at the same time that I held Covey with a firm hand.

Taken completely by surprise, Covey seemed to have lost his usual strength and coolness. He was frightened, and stood puffing and blowing, seemingly unable to command words or blows. When he saw that poor Hughes was standing half bent with pain—his courage quite gone—the cowardly tyrant asked if I "meant to persist in my resistance." I told him "I *did mean to resist, come what might*"; that I had been by him treated like a *brute*, during the last six months; and that I should stand it *no longer*. With that, he gave me a shake, and attempted to drag me toward a stick of wood, that was lying just outside the stable door. He meant to knock me down with it; but, just as he leaned over to get the stick, I seized him with both hands by the collar, and, with a vigorous and sudden snatch, I brought my assailant harmlessly, his full length, on the *not over* clean ground—for we were now in the cow yard. He had selected the place for the fight, and it was but right that he should have all the advantages of his own selection.

By this time, Bill, the hired man, came home. He had been to Mr. Hemsley's, to spend the Sunday with his nominal wife, and was coming home on Monday morning, to go to work. Covey and I had been skirmishing from before daybreak, till now, that the sun was almost shooting his beams over the eastern woods, and we were still at it. I could not see where the matter was to terminate. He evidently was afraid to let me go, lest I should again make off to the woods; otherwise, he would probably have obtained arms from the house, to frighten me. Holding me, Covey called upon Bill for assistance. The scene here, had something comic about it. "Bill," who knew *precisely* what Covey wished him to do, affected ignorance, and pretended he did not know what to do. "What shall I do, Mr. Covey," said Bill. "Take hold of him—take hold of him!" said Covey. With a toss of his head, peculiar to Bill, he said, "indeed, Mr. Covey, I want to go to work." "*This is* your work," said Covey; "take hold of him." Bill replied, with spirit, "My master hired me here, to work, and *not* to help you whip Frederick." It was now my turn to speak. "Bill," said I, "don't put your hands on me." To which he replied, "My God! Frederick, I aint goin' to tech ye," and Bill walked off, leaving Covey and myself to settle our matters as best we might.

But, my present advantage was threatened when I saw Caroline (the slave-woman of Covey) coming to the cow yard to milk, for she was a powerful woman, and could have mastered me very easily, exhausted as I now was. As soon as she came into the yard, Covey attempted to rally her to his aid. Strangely—and, I may add, fortunately—Caroline was in no humor to take a hand in any such sport. We were all in open rebellion, that morning. Caroline answered the command of her master to "*take hold of me*," precisely as Bill had answered, but in *her*, it was at greater peril so to answer; she was the slave of Covey, and he could do what he pleased with her. It was *not* so with Bill, and Bill knew it. Samuel Harris, to whom Bill belonged, did not allow his slaves to be beaten, unless they were guilty of some crime which the law would punish. But, poor Caroline, like myself, was at the mercy of the merciless Covey; nor did she escape the dire effects of her refusal. He gave her several sharp blows.

Covey at length (two hours had elapsed) gave up the contest. Letting me go, he said—puffing and blowing at a great rate—"now, you scoundrel, go to your work; I would not have whipped you half so much as I have had you not resisted." The fact was, *he had not whipped me at all.* He had not, in all the scuffle, drawn a single drop of blood from me. I had drawn blood from him; and, even without this satisfaction, I should have been victorious, because my aim had not been to injure him, but to prevent his injuring me.

During the whole six months that I lived with Covey, after this transaction, he never laid on me the weight of his finger in anger. He would, occasionally, say he did not want to have to get hold of me again—a declaration which I had no difficulty in believing; and I had a secret feeling, which answered, "you need not wish to get hold of me again, for you will be likely to come off worse in a second fight than you did in the first."

Well, my dear reader, this battle with Mr. Covey—undignified as it was, and as I fear my narration of it is—was the turning point in my "*life as a slave*." It rekindled in my breast the smouldering embers of liberty; it brought up my Baltimore dreams, and revived a sense of my own manhood. I was a changed being after that fight. I was *nothing* before; I WAS A MAN NOW. It recalled to life my crushed self-respect and my self-confidence, and inspired me with a renewed determination to be A FREEMAN. A man, without force, is without the essential dignity of humanity. Human nature is so constituted, that it cannot *honor* a helpless man, although it can *pity* him; and even this it cannot do long, if the signs of power do not arise.

He only can understand the effect of this combat on my spirit, who has himself incurred something, hazarded something, in repelling the unjust and cruel aggressions of a tyrant. Covey was a tyrant, and a cowardly one, withal. After resisting him, I felt as I had never felt before. It was a resurrection from the dark and pestiferous tomb of slavery, to the heaven of comparative freedom. I was no longer a servile coward, trembling under the frown of a brother worm of the dust, but, my long-cowed spirit was roused to an attitude of manly independence. I had reached the point, at which I was *not afraid to die*. This spirit made me a freeman in *fact*, while I remained a slave in *form*. When a slave cannot be flogged he is more than half free. He has a domain as broad as his own manly heart to defend, and he is really "*a power on earth*."[1] While slaves prefer their lives, with flogging, to instant death, they will always find Christians enough, like unto Covey, to accommodate that preference. From this time, until that of my escape from slavery, I was never fairly whipped. Several attempts were made to whip me, but they were always unsuccessful. Bruises I did get, as I shall hereafter inform the reader; but the case I have been describing, was the end of the brutification to which slavery had subjected me.

The reader will be glad to know why, after I had so grievously offended Mr. Covey, he did not have me taken in hand by the

---

1 *a power on earth* See Mark 2.10 and Matthew 9.6: "the Son of man hath power on earth to forgive sins."

authorities; indeed, why the law of Maryland, which assigns hanging to the slave who resists his master, was not put in force against me; at any rate, why I was not taken up, as is usual in such cases, and publicly whipped, for an example to other slaves, and as a means of deterring me from committing the same offense again. I confess, that the easy manner in which I got off, was, for a long time, a surprise to me, and I cannot, even now, fully explain the cause.

The only explanation I can venture to suggest, is the fact, that Covey was, probably, ashamed to have it known and confessed that he had been mastered by a boy of sixteen. Mr. Covey enjoyed the unbounded and very valuable reputation, of being a first rate overseer and *negro breaker*. By means of this reputation, he was able to procure his hands for *very trifling* compensation, and with very great ease. His interest and his pride mutually suggested the wisdom of passing the matter by, in silence. The story that he had undertaken to whip a lad, and had been resisted, was, of itself, sufficient to damage him; for his bearing should, in the estimation of slaveholders, be of that imperial order that should make such an occurrence *impossible*. I judge from these circumstances, that Covey deemed it best to give me the go-by. It is, perhaps, not altogether creditable to my natural temper, that, after this conflict with Mr. Covey, I did, at times, purposely aim to provoke him to an attack, by refusing to keep with the other hands in the field, but I could never bully him to another battle. I had made up my mind to do him serious damage, if he ever again attempted to lay violent hands on me.

"Hereditary bondmen, know ye not
Who would be free, themselves must strike the blow?"[1]

—1855

---

1 *Hereditary bondmen … strike the blow* From English poet Lord Byron's *Childe Harold's Pilgrimage*, 2.76.1–2 (1812–18). Douglass frequently used this quotation in his speeches.

from *The Dred Scott Decision*

In the speech excerpted below, Frederick Douglass responds to the 1857 *Dred Scott* Supreme Court decision, which deemed that African Americans were not citizens and that the rights guaranteed by the U.S. Constitution did not apply to them. In his speech, which was given on 14 May 1857 to the American Anti-Slavery Society, Douglass assesses the impact of the *Dred Scott* decision on the abolitionist movement and disputes the decision's interpretation of the Constitution.

Mr. Chairman, Friends, and Fellow Citizens:

While four millions of our fellow countrymen are in chains—while men, women, and children are bought and sold on the auction-block with horses, sheep, and swine—while the remorseless slave-whip draws the warm blood of our common humanity—it is meet[1] that we assemble as we have done today, and lift up our hearts and voices in earnest denunciation of the vile and shocking abomination. It is not for us to be governed by our hopes or our fears in this great work; yet it is natural on occasions like this, to survey the position of the great struggle which is going on between slavery and freedom, and to dwell upon such signs of encouragement as may have been lately developed, and the state of feeling these signs or events have occasioned in us and among the people generally. It is a fitting time to take an observation to ascertain where we are, and what our prospects are. …

… We are now told, in tones of lofty exultation, that the day is lost—all lost—and that we might as well give up the struggle. The highest authority has spoken. The voice of the Supreme Court has gone out over the troubled waves of the national conscience, saying peace, be still.[2]

---

1 *meet* Appropriate.

2 *The voice … be still* See Mark 4.39, in which Jesus calms a storm on the Sea of Galilee: "And he arose, and rebuked the wind, and said unto the sea, Peace, be still. And the wind ceased, and there was a great calm."

This infamous decision of the slaveholding wing of the Supreme Court maintains that slaves are, within the contemplation of the Constitution of the United States, property; that slaves are property in the same sense that horses, sheep, and swine are property; that the old doctrine that slavery is a creature of local law is false; that the right of the slaveholder to his slave does not depend upon the local law, but is secured wherever the Constitution of the United States extends; that Congress has no right to prohibit slavery anywhere; that slavery may go in safety anywhere under the star-spangled banner; that colored persons of African descent have no rights that white men are bound to respect; that colored men of African descent are not and cannot be citizens of the United States.

You will readily ask me how I am affected by this devilish decision—this judicial incarnation of wolfishness? My answer is, and no thanks to the slaveholding wing of the Supreme Court, my hopes were never brighter than now.

I have no fear that the national conscience will be put to sleep by such an open, glaring, and scandalous tissue of lies as that decision is, and has been, over and over, shown to be.

The Supreme Court of the United States is not the only power in this world. It is very great, but the Supreme Court of the Almighty is greater. Judge Taney[1] can do many things, but he cannot perform impossibilities. He cannot bale out the ocean, annihilate the firm old earth, or pluck the silvery star of liberty from our Northern sky.[2] He may decide, and decide again; but he cannot reverse the decision of the Most High. He cannot change the essential nature of things—making evil good, and good evil.[3]

Happily for the whole human family, their rights have been defined, declared, and decided in a court higher than the Supreme Court. "There is a law," says Brougham, "above all the enactments of

---

1 *Judge Taney* Roger B. Taney, Chief Justice of the U.S. Supreme Court from 1836 to his death in 1864, in which capacity he wrote the majority decision in the *Dred Scott* case; he belonged to a slaveholding Maryland family.

2 *the silvery ... sky* Douglass refers to the North Star (Polaris), which enslaved people used as a navigation point when escaping to the North and which thus itself came to symbolize freedom (or the means of attaining freedom). Douglass named the first abolitionist newspaper he founded after his own escape from slavery *The North Star*.

3 *making ... evil* See Isaiah 5.20: "Woe unto them that call evil good, and good evil."

human codes, and by that law, unchangeable and eternal, man cannot hold property in man."[1] ...

Such a decision cannot stand. God will be true though every man be a liar. We can appeal from this hell-black judgment of the Supreme Court, to the court of common sense and common humanity. We can appeal from man to God. If there is no justice on earth, there is yet justice in heaven. You may close your Supreme Court against the black man's cry for justice, but you cannot, thank God, close against him the ear of a sympathising world, nor shut up the Court of Heaven. All that is merciful and just, on earth and in Heaven, will execrate and despise this edict of Taney.

If it were at all likely that the people of these free States would tamely submit to this demoniacal judgment, I might feel gloomy and sad over it, and possibly it might be necessary for my people to look for a home in some other country.[2] But as the case stands, we have nothing to fear.

In one point of view, we, the abolitionists and colored people, should meet this decision, unlooked for and monstrous as it appears, in a cheerful spirit. This very attempt to blot out forever the hopes of an enslaved people may be one necessary link in the chain of events preparatory to the downfall and complete overthrow of the whole slave system. ...

Come what will, I hold it to be morally certain that, sooner or later, by fair means or foul means, in quiet or in tumult, in peace or in blood, in judgment or in mercy, slavery is doomed to cease out of this otherwise goodly land, and liberty is destined to become the settled law of this Republic.

I base my sense of the certain overthrow of slavery, in part, upon the nature of the American government, the Constitution, the tendencies of the age, and the character of the American people; and this, notwithstanding the important decision of Judge Taney.

---

1 *There is ... in man* Douglass quotes, with some slight alterations, from a speech given in the British Parliament in 1830 by Henry Brougham, an antislavery British politician who helped pass the 1833 act that abolished slavery in the British Empire.

2 *my people ... other country* During the 1850s, in the wake of the Fugitive Slave Act and other perceived setbacks to the causes of abolition and black civil rights, support grew among African Americans for emigration out of the United States. Douglass himself strongly opposed black emigration.

I know of no soil better adapted to the growth of reform than American soil. I know of no country where the conditions for affecting great changes in the settled order of things, for the development of right ideas of liberty and humanity, are more favorable than here in these United States.

The very groundwork of this government is a good repository of Christian civilization. The Constitution, as well as the Declaration of Independence, and the sentiments of the founders of the republic, give us a platform broad enough, and strong enough, to support the most comprehensive plans for the freedom and elevation of all the people of this country, without regard to color, class, or clime.[1] …

Neither in the preamble nor in the body of the Constitution is there a single mention of the term slave or slave holder, slave master or slave state, neither is there any reference to the color, or the physical peculiarities of any part of the people of the United States. Neither is there anything in the Constitution standing alone, which would imply the existence of slavery in this country.

"We, the people"—not we, the white people—not we, the citizens, or the legal voters—not we, the privileged class, and excluding all other classes, but we, the people; not we, the horses and cattle, but we the people—the men and women, the human inhabitants of the United States, do ordain and establish this Constitution, etc.

I ask, then, any man to read the Constitution, and tell me where, if he can, in what particular that instrument affords the slightest sanction of slavery?

Where will he find a guarantee for slavery? Will he find it in the declaration that no person shall be deprived of life, liberty, or property, without due process of law? Will he find it in the declaration that the Constitution was established to secure the blessing of liberty? Will he find it in the right of the people to be secure in their persons and papers, and houses, and effects? Will he find it in the clause prohibiting the enactment by any state of a bill of attainder?[2]

---

1 *clime* I.e., place or region of origin.

2 *Will he … attainder* Douglass refers, respectively, to the so-called Due Process Clause in the Fifth Amendment to the Constitution; to the Preamble to the Constitution, which declares that the Constitution is established to "secure the Blessings of Liberty to ourselves and our Posterity"; to the Fourth Amendment's prohibition of "unreasonable searches and seizures"; and to the Constitution's mandate that neither the federal government (in Article

These all strike at the root of slavery, and any one of them, but faithfully carried out, would put an end to slavery in every state in the American Union. …

While this and much more can be said … in favor of the entire unconstitutionality of slavery, what have we on the other side?

How is the constitutionality of slavery made out, or attempted to be made out? …

The argument … is, that the Constitution comes down to us from a slaveholding period and a slaveholding people; and that, therefore, we are bound to suppose that the Constitution recognizes colored persons of African descent, the victims of slavery at that time, as debarred forever from all participation in the benefit of the Constitution and the Declaration of Independence, although the plain reading of both includes them in their beneficent range.

As a man, an American, a citizen, a colored man of both Anglo-Saxon[1] and African descent, I denounce this representation as a most scandalous and devilish perversion of the Constitution, and a brazen misstatement of the facts of history. …

The testimony of the church, and the testimony of the founders of this republic, from the Declaration downward, prove Judge Taney false; as false to history as he is to law.

Washington and Jefferson, and Adams, and Jay, and Franklin, and Rush,[2] and Hamilton, and a host of others, held no such degrading

---

I, Section 9, Clause 3) nor state governments (in Article I, Section 10, Clause 1) may pass bills of attainder—legislative acts whereby an individual or group are declared guilty of a crime and punished, often without trial.

1 *Anglo-Saxon* I.e., white. The term "Anglo-Saxon," which originally referred to the Germanic cultural group that settled in and ruled England in the early Middle Ages, was widely used in Britain and the United States in the nineteenth century to refer to white people inhabiting or stemming from England (or the British Isles more generally). In such contexts, the term often carried—and still carries—racist connotations of inherent racial superiority, although Douglass here uses it in a neutral, descriptive way.

2 *Jay* John Jay (1745–1829), American politician who was one of the founders of the United States; he favored the gradual abolition of slavery and, as governor of New York, helped pass a gradual emancipation law in 1799 that laid the groundwork for the ending of slavery in that state (though he also continued to enslave people himself into the early nineteenth century); *Rush* Benjamin Rush (1745–1813), American physician, politician, and signatory of the Declaration of Independence; he was a strong opponent of the slave trade and slavery and argued against ideas of black racial inferiority (though he also proposed that the "color" and "figure" of black people could be "cured").

views on the subject of slavery as are imputed by Judge Taney to the Fathers of the Republic.

All, at that time, looked for the gradual but certain abolition of slavery, and shaped the Constitution with a view to this grand result.

George Washington can never be claimed as a fanatic, or as the representative of fanatics. The slaveholders impudently use his name for the base purpose of giving respectability to slavery. Yet, in a letter to Robert Morris, Washington uses this language—language which, at this day, would make him a terror of the slaveholders, and the natural representative of the Republican Party.

"There is not a man living, who wishes more sincerely than I do, to see some plan adopted for the abolition of slavery; but there is only one proper and effectual mode by which it can be accomplished, and that is by Legislative authority; and this, as far as my suffrage will go, shall not be wanting."[1]

Washington only spoke the sentiment of his times. There were, at that time, abolition societies in the slave states—abolition societies in Virginia, in North Carolina, in Maryland, in Pennsylvania, and in Georgia—all slaveholding states. Slavery was so weak, and liberty so strong, that free speech could attack the monster to its teeth. Men were not mobbed and driven out of the presence of slavery, merely because they condemned the slave system. The system was then on its knees imploring to be spared, until it could get itself decently out of the world.

In the light of these facts, the Constitution was framed, and framed in conformity to it.

It may, however, be asked, if the Constitution were so framed that the rights of all the people were naturally protected by it, how happens it that a large part of the people have been held in slavery ever since its adoption? Have the people mistaken the requirements of their own Constitution?

---

1 *There is … wanting* Douglass quotes from a letter Washington wrote to Robert Morris, an English-born merchant who helped finance the American Revolution and later helped establish the U.S. financial system, on 12 April 1786. The full letter was written to assist an acquaintance of Washington's in his attempt to maintain ownership of one of his enslaved people, whom a committee of Philadelphia Quakers was seeking to liberate, and Washington goes on to condemn instances in which "slaves who are happy & content to remain with their present masters, are tampered with & seduced to leave them."

The answer is ready. The Constitution is one thing, its administration is another, and, in this instance, a very different and opposite thing. I am here to vindicate the law, not the administration of the law. It is the written Constitution, not the unwritten Constitution, that is now before us. If, in the whole range of the Constitution, you can find no warrant for slavery, then we may properly claim it for liberty.

Good and wholesome laws are often found dead on the statute book. We may condemn the practice under them and against them, but never the law itself. To condemn the good law with the wicked practice, is to weaken, not to strengthen our testimony. …

The Constitution knows all the human inhabitants of this country as "the people." It makes, as I have said before, no discrimination in favor of, or against, any class of the people, but is fitted to protect and preserve the rights of all, without reference to color, size, or any physical peculiarities. Besides, it has been shown by William Goodell[1] and others, that in eleven out of the old thirteen states, colored men were legal voters at the time of the adoption of the Constitution.

In conclusion, let me say, all I ask of the American people is that they live up to the Constitution, adopt its principles, imbibe its spirit, and enforce its provisions.

When this is done, the wounds of my bleeding people will be healed, the chain will no longer rust on their ankles, their backs will no longer be torn by the bloody lash, and liberty, the glorious birthright of our common humanity, will become the inheritance of all the inhabitants of this highly favored country.

—14 May 1857

---

1 *William Goodell* American journalist and abolitionist who devoted much effort, especially in his *Views of American Constitutional Law, in Its Bearing upon American Slavery* (1844), to showing that slavery was incompatible with the Constitution.

from *Self-Made Men*

Douglass first gave the following lecture in 1859; he repeated it many more times over the course of his career.

… I am here to speak to you of a peculiar type of manhood under the title of *Self-Made Men*. …

On the first point I may say that, by the term "self-made men," I mean especially what, to the popular mind, the term itself imports. Self-made men are the men who, under peculiar difficulties and without the ordinary helps of favoring circumstances, have attained knowledge, usefulness, power and position and have learned from themselves the best uses to which life can be put in this world, and in the exercises of these uses to build up worthy character. They are the men who owe little or nothing to birth, relationship, friendly surroundings; to wealth inherited or to early approved means of education; who are what they are, without the aid of any of the favoring conditions by which other men usually rise in the world and achieve great results. In fact they are the men who are not brought up but who are obliged to come up, not only without the voluntary assistance or friendly co-operation of society, but often in open and derisive defiance of all the efforts of society and the tendency of circumstances to repress, retard and keep them down. They are the men who, in a world of schools, academies, colleges and other institutions of learning, are often compelled by unfriendly circumstances to acquire their education elsewhere and, amidst unfavorable conditions, to hew out for themselves a way to success, and thus to become the architects of their own good fortunes. They are, in a peculiar sense, indebted to themselves for themselves. If they have travelled far, they have made the road on which they travelled. If they have ascended high, they have built their own ladder. From the depths of poverty such as these have often come. From the heartless pavements of large and crowded cities; barefooted, homeless, and friendless, they have come. From hunger, rags and destitution, they have come; motherless and fatherless, they have come, and may come. Flung overboard in the midnight storm on the broad and tempest-tossed ocean of life; left without ropes, planks, oars or life-preservers, they have bravely buffeted the frowning billows and have risen in safety and life where others, supplied with the best appliances for safety and success, have fainted, despaired and gone down forever.

Such men as these, whether found in one position or another, whether in the college or in the factory; whether professors or plowmen; whether Caucasian or Indian; whether Anglo-Saxon or Anglo-African, are self-made men and are entitled to a certain measure of respect for their success and for proving to the world the grandest possibilities of human nature, of whatever variety of race or color.

Though a man of this class need not claim to be a hero or to be worshiped as such, there is genuine heroism in his struggle and something of sublimity and glory in his triumph. Every instance of such success is an example and a help to humanity. It, better than any mere assertion, gives us assurance of the latent powers and resources of simple and unaided manhood. …

From these remarks it will be evident that, allowing only ordinary ability and opportunity, we may explain success mainly by one word and that word is WORK! WORK!! WORK!!! WORK!!!! Not transient and fitful effort, but patient, enduring, honest, unremitting and indefatigable work into which the whole heart is put, and which, in both temporal and spiritual affairs, is the true miracle worker. Everyone may avail himself of this marvelous power, if he will. There is no royal road to perfection. Certainly no one must wait for some kind of friend to put a springing board under his feet, upon which he may easily bound from the first round of their ladder onward and upward to its highest round. If he waits for this, he may wait long, and perhaps forever. He who does not think himself worth saving from poverty and ignorance by his own efforts, will hardly be thought worth the efforts of anybody else.

The lesson taught at this point by human experience is simply this, that the man who will get up will be helped up; and that the man who will not get up will be allowed to stay down. This rule may appear somewhat harsh, but in its general application and operation it is wise, just and beneficent. I know of no other rule which can be substituted for it without bringing social chaos. Personal independence is a virtue and it is the soul out of which comes the sturdiest manhood. But there can be no independence without a large share of self-dependence, and this virtue cannot be bestowed. It must be developed from within.

I have been asked "How will this theory affect the negro?" and "What shall be done in his case?" My general answer is "Give the negro fair play and let him alone. If he lives, well. If he dies, equally well. If he cannot stand up, let him fall down." …

I meant all that I said and a good deal more than some understand by fair play. It is not fair play to start the negro out in life, from nothing and with nothing, while others start with the advantage of a thousand years behind them. He should be measured, not by the heights others have obtained, but from the depths from which he has come. For any adjustment of the scale of comparison, fair play demands that to the barbarism from which the negro started shall be added two hundred years heavy with human bondage. Should the American people put a school house in every valley of the South and a church on every hillside and supply the one with teachers and the other with preachers, for a hundred years to come, they would not then have given fair play to the negro. …

—1859, 1893

Men of Color, to Arms!

Besides declaring the freedom of all enslaved people in areas of the South designated as being in rebellion against the federal government, President Lincoln's Emancipation Proclamation, issued on 1 January 1863, authorized the recruitment of African Americans to the U.S. Army. Foremost among the public figures who promptly began urging blacks to enlist was Frederick Douglass, who had been petitioning the government to allow black enlistment since the start of the Civil War. On 2 March 1863, Douglass issued the following call for recruits for the 54th Massachusetts Infantry Regiment, one of the first units of black troops (commanded by white officers) to be organized in the North in the wake of the Emancipation Proclamation. Two of Douglass's own sons were among the many who responded, and the 54th Massachusetts went on to win a reputation for battlefield heroism that paved the way for further mass African American recruitment.

When first the rebel cannon shattered the walls of Sumter and drove away its starving garrison,[1] I predicted that the war then and there inaugurated would not be fought out entirely by white men. Every month's experience during these dreary years has confirmed that opinion. A war undertaken and brazenly carried on for the perpetual enslavement of colored men, calls logically and loudly for colored men to help suppress it. Only a moderate share of sagacity was needed to see that the arm of the slave was the best defense against the arm of the slaveholder. Hence with every reverse to the national arms, with every exulting shout of victory raised by the slaveholding rebels, I have implored the imperiled nation to unchain against her foes her powerful black hand. Slowly and reluctantly that appeal is beginning to be heeded. Stop not now to complain that it was not heeded sooner. It may or it may not have been best that it should not. This is not the time to discuss that question. Leave it to the future. When the war is

1 *When first ... garrison* Reference to the First Battle of Fort Sumter on 12–13 April 1861, in which Confederate forces in Charleston, South Carolina, bombarded Fort Sumter, a federal military installation in Charleston harbor. Short on men and supplies, the garrison of the fort was forced to surrender. Although neither side suffered any casualties, these were the first shots fired between the South and the North.

over, the country is saved, peace is established, and the black man's rights are secured, as they will be, history with an impartial hand will dispose of that and sundry other questions. Action! action! not criticism, is the plain duty of this hour. Words are now useful only as they stimulate to blows. The office of speech now is only to point out when, where, and how to strike to the best advantage. There is no time to delay. The tide is at its flood that leads on to fortune. From East to West, from North to South, the sky is written all over with "now or never." Liberty won by white men would lack half its lustre. "Who would be free themselves must strike the blow." "Better even die free, than to live slaves." This is the sentiment of every brave colored man amongst us. There are weak and cowardly men in all nations. We have them among us. They will tell you that this is the "white man's war"; that you will be "no better off after than before the war"; that the getting of you into the army is to "sacrifice you on the first opportunity." Believe them not—cowards themselves, they do not wish to have their cowardice shamed by your brave example. Leave them to their timidity, or to whatever motive may hold them back.

I have not thought lightly of the words I am now addressing to you. The counsel I give comes of close observation of the great struggle now in progress—and of the deep conviction that this is your hour and mine.

In good earnest, then, and after the best deliberation, I, now, for the first time during this war, feel at liberty to call and counsel you to arms. By every consideration which binds you to your enslaved fellow countrymen, and the peace and welfare of your country; by every aspiration which you cherish for the freedom and equality of yourselves and your children; by all the ties of blood and identity which make us one with the brave black men now fighting our battles in Louisiana and in South Carolina,[1] I urge you to fly to arms, and smite with death the power that would bury the government and your liberty in the same hopeless grave. I wish I could tell you that the State of New York calls you to this high honor. For the moment her constituted authorities are silent on the subject. They will speak by and by, and doubtless on the right side; but we are not compelled

1 *the brave … South Carolina* Douglass refers to two black Union units which had already been formed in the South, the 1st Louisiana Native Guard and the 1st South Carolina Volunteers, both of which consisted largely or entirely of formerly enslaved people.

to wait for her. We can get at the throat of treason and slavery through the State of Massachusetts.

She was first in the War of Independence; first to break the chains of her slaves; first to make the black man equal before the law; first to admit colored children to her common schools, and she was first to answer with her blood the alarm cry of the nation—when its capital was menaced by rebels. You know her patriotic governor, and you know Charles Sumner[1]—I need add no more.

Massachusetts now welcomes you to arms as soldiers. She has but a small colored population from which to recruit. She has full leave of the general government to send one regiment to the war, and she has undertaken to do it. Go quickly and help fill up this first colored regiment from the North. I am authorized to assure you that you will receive the same wages,[2] the same rations, the same equipments, the same protection, the same treatment, and the same bounty[3] secured to the white soldiers. You will be led by able and skillful officers—men who will take special pride in your efficiency and success. They will be quick to accord to you all the honor you shall merit by your valor—and see that your rights and feelings are respected by other soldiers. I have assured myself on these points—and can speak with authority. More than twenty years of unswerving devotion to our common cause may give me some humble claim to be trusted at this momentous crisis.

I will not argue. To do so implies hesitation and doubt, and you do not hesitate. You do not doubt. The day dawns—the morning star is

---

1 *first to break ... the law* In legal cases decided in the years 1781–83, slavery was found to be inconsistent with the 1780 Massachusetts Constitution's declaration that "All men are born free and equal"; *first to admit ... schools* Massachusetts outlawed school assignment by race in 1855; *she was first ... rebels* The 6th Massachusetts Militia Regiment was the first unit of Union volunteers to arrive in Washington, D.C., at the start of the Civil War in April 1861; *her patriotic governor* John A. Andrew, abolitionist Governor of Massachusetts from 1861 to 1866; *Charles Sumner* U.S. senator for Massachusetts noted for his fervent opposition to slavery (1811–74).

2 *the same wages* In fact, the men of the 54th Massachusetts were paid only $7 a month, whereas white Union soldiers were paid $13 a month. When this was announced, the officers and enlisted men of the regiment chose to serve without pay as a protest. The disparity was remedied over a year later.

3 *bounty* Volunteers on both sides of the Civil War were frequently offered a monetary payment, or "bounty," as incentive to enlist; in the North, this could amount to up to $300. As with wages, the provision of bounties to African American volunteers was frequently unfair by comparison with those offered to white recruits.

bright upon the horizon! The iron gate of our prison stands half open. One gallant rush from the North will fling it wide open, while four millions of our brothers and sisters shall march out into liberty! The chance is now given you to end in a day the bondage of centuries, and to rise in one bound from social degradation to the plane of common equality with all other varieties of men. Remember Denmark Vesey of Charleston. Remember Nathaniel Turner of Southampton; remember Shields Green and Copeland, who followed noble John Brown, and fell as glorious martyrs for the cause of the slaves.[1] Remember that in a contest with oppression, the Almighty has no attribute which can take sides with oppressors.[2] The case is before you. This is our golden opportunity—let us accept it—and forever wipe out the dark reproaches unsparingly hurled against us by our enemies. Let us win for ourselves the gratitude of our country—and the best blessings of our posterity through all time. The nucleus of this first regiment is now in camp at Readville, a short distance from Boston. I will undertake to forward to Boston all persons adjudged fit to be mustered into this regiment who shall apply to me at any time within the next two weeks.

—1863

1 *Denmark Vesey … slaves* Douglass lists several African American organizers of, or participants in, armed resistance to slavery, all of whom were killed for their actions. Denmark Vesey helped plan an uprising by enslaved people in Charleston, South Carolina, in 1822; the plot was discovered and he was executed before the uprising could begin. Nat Turner, an enslaved man in Southampton County, Virginia, was hanged for leading an antislavery uprising in 1831. Shields Green, a fugitive enslaved man, and John A. Copeland, Jr., a free black man, were both hanged in 1859 for their participation in John Brown's failed raid on Harpers Ferry, Virginia.

2 *Remember … oppressors* In *Notes on the State of Virginia* (1781, published 1785), Thomas Jefferson wrote, regarding the possibility of a conflict between enslaved black people and white enslavers like himself, "The Almighty has no attribute which can take side with us in such a contest."

from *Composite Nation*

Douglass first gave the speech excerpted below in Boston in 1867; it became a part of his regular lecturing repertoire, and he continued to deliver it into the 1870s. The speech outlines the vision that Douglass—together with many other black and white activists—held during the Reconstruction era for how the United States could reinvent itself on a more equitable and inclusive basis. In particular, the speech argues strongly for the United States to welcome and incorporate Chinese immigrants, who began to arrive in the country in large numbers during the Gold Rush, and whose labor made possible (among other things) the completion of the transcontinental railroad in 1869. Despite Douglass's efforts, the anti-Asian racism and hostility to Chinese immigration that his speech identified and criticized only gained strength in subsequent decades, culminating in the 1882 Chinese Exclusion Act, which prohibited all immigration of Chinese laborers to the U.S.

… The simple organization of a people into a national body, composite[1] or otherwise, is of itself an impressive fact. As an original proceeding, it marks the point of departure of a people, from the darkness and chaos of unbridled barbarism, to the wholesome restraints of public law and society. It implies a willing surrender and subjection of individual aims and ends, often narrow and selfish, to the broader and better ones that arise out of society as a whole. It is both a sign and a result of civilization. …

Without undue vanity or unjust depreciation of others, we may claim to be, in many respects, the most fortunate of nations. We stand in relation to all others, as youth to age. Other nations have had their day of greatness and glory; we are yet to have our day, and that day is coming. The dawn is already upon us. It is bright and full of promise. Other nations have reached their culminating point. We are at the beginning of our ascent. They have apparently exhausted the conditions essential to their further growth and extension, while we are abundant in all the material essential to further national growth and greatness. …

1 *composite* In this context, comprising people of multiple races or ethnicities.

There are clouds, wind, smoke and dust and noise, overhead and around, and there always will be; but no genuine thunder, with destructive bolt, menaces from any quarter of the sky.

The real trouble with us was never our system or form of government, or the principles underlying it; but the peculiar composition of our people, the relations existing between them and the compromising spirit which controlled the ruling power of the country.

We have for a long time hesitated to adopt and carry out the only principle which can solve that difficulty and give peace, strength and security to the republic, *and that is* the principle of absolute *equality*.

We are a country of all extremes, ends and opposites; the most conspicuous example of composite nationality in the world. Our people defy all the ethnological and logical classifications. In races we range all the way from black to white, with intermediate shades which, as in the apocalyptic vision, no man can name a number.[1]

In regard to creeds and faiths, the condition is no better, and no worse. Differences both as to race and to religion are evidently more likely to increase than to diminish.

We stand between the populous shores of two great oceans. Our land is capable of supporting one fifth of all the globe. Here, labor is abundant and better remunerated than anywhere else. All moral, social and geographical causes conspire to bring to us the peoples of all other over-populated countries.

Europe and Africa are already here, and the Indian was here before either. He stands today between the two extremes of black and white, too proud to claim fraternity with either, and yet too weak to withstand the power of either. Heretofore the policy of our government has been governed by race pride, rather than by wisdom.

Until recently, neither the Indian nor the negro has been treated as a part of the body politic. No attempt has been made to inspire either with a sentiment of patriotism, but the hearts of both races have been diligently sown with the dangerous seeds of discontent and hatred.

The policy of keeping the Indians to themselves has kept the tomahawk and scalping knife busy upon our borders, and has cost us largely in blood and treasure.

---

1 *as in ... number* See Revelation 7.9 (the Book of Revelation is also called the Apocalypse of John): "After this I beheld, and lo, a great multitude, which no man could number, of all nations, and kindreds, and people, and tongues, stood before the throne."

Our treatment of the negro has lacked humanity and filled the country with agitation and ill-feeling, and brought the nation to the verge of ruin.

Before the relations of these two races are satisfactorily settled, and in despite of all opposition, a new race is making its appearance within our borders, and claiming attention.

It is estimated that not less than one hundred thousand Chinamen[1] are now within the limits of the United States. Several years ago every vessel, large or small, of steam or sail, bound to our Pacific coast and hailing from the Flowery Kingdom,[2] added to the number and strength of this new element of our population.

Men differ widely as to the magnitude of this potential Chinese immigration. The fact that by the late treaty with China[3] we bind ourselves to receive immigrants from that country only as the subjects of the Emperor, and by the construction, at least, are bound not to naturalize them, and the further fact that Chinamen themselves have a superstitious devotion to their country and an aversion to permanent location in any other, contracting even to have their bones carried back, should they die abroad, and from the fact that many have returned to China, and the still more stubborn fact that resistance to their coming has increased rather than diminished, it is inferred that we shall never have a large Chinese population in America. This, however, is not my opinion.

It may be admitted that these reasons, and others, may check and moderate the tide of immigration; but it is absurd to think that they will do more than this. Counting their number now by the thousands, the time is not remote when they will count them by the millions. The Emperor's hold upon the Chinamen may be strong, but the Chinaman's hold upon himself is stronger.

---

1 *Chinamen* Term for Chinese people or people of Chinese descent, now considered derogatory.

2 *Flowery Kingdom* Archaic name for China, based on a translation of the Chinese *hwa kwo*.

3 *the late … China* Reference to the 1868 Burlingame Treaty between the United States and China (named after Anson Burlingame, the former U.S. Minister to China, who gave up his post in 1867 to help China negotiate a new treaty with the U.S.). The treaty, which aimed to re-establish U.S.–China relations on a more equitable footing, included provisions that guaranteed Chinese the right to free immigration to and travel within the U.S.; however, the text of the treaty emphasized that "nothing herein contained shall be held to confer naturalization … upon the subjects of China in the United States."

Treaties against naturalization, like all other treaties, are limited by circumstances. As to the superstitious attachment of the Chinese to China, that, like all other superstitions, will dissolve in the light and heat of truth and experience. The Chinaman may be a bigot, but it does not follow that he will continue to be one tomorrow. He is a man, and will be very likely to act like a man. He will not be long in finding out that a country which is good enough to live in is good enough to die in, and that a soil that was good enough to hold his body while alive, will be good enough to hold his bones when he is dead.

Those who doubt a large immigration should remember that the past furnishes no criterion as a basis of calculation. We live under new and improved conditions of migration, and these conditions are constantly improving.

America is no longer an obscure and inaccessible country. Our ships are in every sea, our commerce is in every port, our language is heard all around the globe, steam and lightning have revolutionized the whole domain of human thought, changed all geographical relations, make a day of the present seem equal to a thousand years of the past, and the continent that Columbus only conjectured four centuries ago is now the center of the world.

I believe that Chinese immigration on a large scale will yet be our irrepressible fact. The spirit of race pride will not always prevail.

The reasons for this opinion are obvious; China is a vastly overcrowded country. Her people press against each other like cattle in a rail car. Many live upon the water and have laid out streets upon the waves.

Men, like bees, want room. When the hive is overflowing, the bees will swarm, and will be likely to take up their abode where they find the best prospect for honey. In matters of this sort, men are very much like bees. Hunger will not be quietly endured, even in the Celestial Empire,[1] when it is once generally known that there is bread enough and to spare[2] in America. What Satan said of Job is true of the

1 *Celestial Empire* Name for China, based on a literal translation of the Chinese term *Tiāncháo*.

2 *bread … to spare* See Luke 15.17, in Jesus' Parable of the Prodigal Son, in which the younger son of a wealthy father, after having squandered his inheritance and being reduced to poverty and hunger in a foreign country, recalls that his father's hired servants "have bread enough and to spare."

Chinaman, as well as of other men, "All that a man hath will he give for his life."[1] They will come here to live, where they know the means of living are in abundance.

The same mighty forces which have swept to our shores the overflowing population of Europe; which have reduced the people of Ireland three millions below its normal standard; will operate in a similar manner upon the hungry population of China and other parts of Asia. Home has its charms, and native land has its charms, but hunger, oppression, and destitution will dissolve these charms and send men in search of new countries and new homes.

Not only is there a Chinese motive behind this probable immigration, but there is also an American motive which will play its part, and which will be all the more active and energetic because there is in it an element of pride, of bitterness and revenge.

Southern gentlemen who led in the late rebellion have not parted with their convictions at this point, any more than at any other. They want to be independent of the negro. They believed in slavery and they believe in it still. They believed in an aristocratic class, and they believe in it still, and though they have lost slavery, one element essential to such a class, they still have two important conditions to the reconstruction of that class. They have intelligence, and they have land. Of these, the land is the more important. They cling to it with all the tenacity of a cherished superstition. They will neither sell to the negro, nor let the carpetbagger[2] have it in peace, but are determined to hold it for themselves and their children forever.

They have not yet learned that when a principle is gone, the incident must go also; that what was wise and proper under slavery is foolish and mischievous in a state of general liberty; that the old bottles are worthless when the new wine has come;[3] but they have found that land is a doubtful benefit, where there are no hands to till it.

---

1 *What Satan ... life* See Job 2.4.

2 *carpetbagger* Term for Northerners who moved to the Southern states during the Reconstruction era, either to promote Republican political goals—including the equality and enfranchisement of African Americans—or to pursue business and political opportunities on their own behalf. The term quickly became derogatory, especially as used by white Southerners.

3 *the old bottles ... has come* See Matthew 9.17: "Neither do men put new wine into old bottles; else the bottles break, and the wine runneth out, and the bottles perish: but they put new wine into new bottles, and both are preserved."

Hence these gentlemen have turned their attention to the Celestial Empire. They would rather have laborers who will work for nothing; but as they cannot get the negro on these terms, they want Chinamen, who, they hope, will work for next to nothing.…

The Chinese in themselves have first rate recommendations. They are industrious, docile, cleanly, frugal; they are dexterous of hand, patient of toil, marvelously gifted in the power of imitation, and have but few wants. Those who have carefully observed their habits in California say they subsist upon what would be almost starvation to others.

The conclusion of the whole will be that they will want to come to us, and as we become more liberal, we shall want them to come, and what we want will naturally be done.

They will no longer halt upon the shores of California. They will burrow no longer in her exhausted and deserted gold mines, where they have gathered wealth from barrenness, taking what others left. They will turn their backs not only upon the Celestial Empire but upon the golden shores of the Pacific, and the wide waste of waters whose majestic waves spoke to them of home and country. They will withdraw their eyes from the glowing West and fix them upon the rising sun. They will cross the mountains, cross the plains, descend our rivers, penetrate to the heart of the country and fix their homes with us forever.

Assuming then that immigration already has a foothold and will continue for many years to come, we have a new element in our national composition which is likely to exercise a large influence upon the thought and the action of the whole nation.

The old question as to what shall be done with the negro will have to give place to the greater question "What shall be done with the Mongolian,"[1] and perhaps we shall see raised one even still greater, namely, "What will the Mongolian do with both the negro and the white?"

Already has the matter taken this shape in California and on the Pacific coast generally. Already has California assumed a bitterly unfriendly attitude toward the Chinaman.[2] Already has she driven

---

1 *Mongolian* In this context, a racial term, today considered archaic and offensive, that was often used in the nineteenth century to characterize East Asian people.

2 *Already … Chinaman* Widespread white Californian hostility towards Chinese immigrants arose almost as soon as large numbers of Chinese first began to arrive in California

them from her altars of justice. Already has she stamped them as outcasts and handed them over to popular contempt and vulgar jest. Already are they the constant victims of cruel harshness and brutal violence. Already have our Celtic brothers, never slow to execute the behests of popular prejudice against the weak and defenseless, recognized in the heads of these people fit targets for their shilalahs.[1] Already, too, are their associations formed in avowed hostility to the Chinese.

In all this there is, of course, nothing strange. Repugnance to the presence and influence of foreigners is an ancient feeling among men. It is peculiar to no particular race or nation. It is met with, not only in the conduct of one nation toward another, but in the conduct of the inhabitants of different parts of the same country, sometimes of the same city, and even of the same village. "Lands intersected by a narrow frith abhor each other. Mountains interposed, make enemies of nations."[2] To the Hindu, every man not twice born is Mleeka.[3] To the Greek, every man not speaking Greek is a barbarian. To the Jew, everyone not circumcised is a gentile. To the Mohametan, everyone not believing in the Prophet is a kaffer.[4]

---

during the Gold Rush (1848–55). Chinese immigrants were subjected to frequent assault and to such punitive measures as the Foreign Miners' Tax (1850), which drove most Chinese away from gold mining and into enclaves in the cities; later, California banned the immigration of any person "of the Chinese or Mongolian races" outright, although this law was struck down by the State Supreme Court.

1 *shilalahs* Douglass's spelling of "shillelagh," the Irish name for a walking stick that doubles as a club or cudgel.

2 *Lands … nations* See Book II, lines 16–18, of *The Task* (1785), a long poem by the English poet William Cowper. The passage from which these lines are taken is a condemnation of slavery that was frequently quoted by abolitionists; *frith* I.e., firth, a narrow body of water.

3 *To the Hindu … Mleeka* In Hindu tradition, an individual is considered to be "twice-born" if they have experienced a second, intellectual and spiritual "birth," in addition to their physical birth, by being initiated into religious instruction. Being twice-born was frequently—though not invariably—considered to be an attribute of members of the upper castes of Hindu society. *Mleeka* is Douglass's rendering of a word in Sanskrit, an ancient Indian language considered sacred in Hindu religion, that is better transliterated *mleccha,* meaning "foreigner" or "barbarian." Unlike being twice-born, which is a religious designation, *mleccha* was an ethnic and linguistic designation.

4 *Mohametan* I.e., Muslim; *the Prophet* I.e., the Prophet Muhammad; *kaffer* Arabic term, today typically transliterated *kafir,* used in the Islamic tradition to designate someone who does not believe in the tenets of Islam, one of the foremost of which is that Muhammad was the final prophet of the one God. By the nineteenth century, the term [continued …]

I need not repeat here the multitude of reproachful epithets expressive of the same sentiment among ourselves. All who are not to the manor born[1] have been made to feel the lash and sting of these reproachful names. …

Nature has two voices, the one high, the other low; one is in sweet accord with reason and justice, and the other apparently at war with both. The more men know of the essential nature of things, and of the true relation of mankind, the freer they are from prejudice of every kind. The child is afraid of the giant form of his own shadow. This is natural, but he will part with his fears when he is older and wiser. So ignorance is full of prejudice, but it will disappear with enlightenment. But I pass on.

I have said that the Chinese will come, and have given some reasons why we may expect them in very large numbers in no very distant future. Do you ask if I would favor such immigration? I answer, *I would.* "Would you admit them as witnesses in our courts of law?" *I would.* "Would you have them naturalized, and have them invested with all the rights of American citizenship?" *I would.* "Would you allow them to vote?" *I would.* "Would you allow them to hold office?" *I would.*

But are there not reasons against all this? Is there not such a law or principle as that of self-preservation? Does not every race owe something to itself? Should it not attend to the dictates of common sense? Should not a superior race protect itself from contact with inferior ones? Are not the white people the owners of this continent? Have they not the right to say what kind of people shall be allowed to come here and settle? Is there not such a thing as being more generous than wise? In the effort to promote civilization may we not corrupt and destroy what we have? Is it best to take on board more passengers than the ship will carry?

To all of this and more I have one among many answers, altogether satisfactory to me, though I cannot promise that it will be so to you.

I submit that this question of Chinese immigration should be settled upon higher principles than those of a cold and selfish

---

had also evolved into a designation for sub-Saharan African Indigenous peoples; in the twentieth century, the term's use in this context came to be almost exclusively pejorative, and today it is regarded, especially in South Africa, as extremely offensive.

1 *to … born* I.e., born into or given easy access to a privileged identity or position in life.

expediency. There are such things in the world as human rights. They rest upon no conventional foundation, but are external, universal and indestructible.

Among these is the right of locomotion;[1] the right of migration; the right which belongs to no particular race, but belongs alike to all and to all alike. It is the right you assert by staying here, and your fathers asserted by coming here. It is this great right that I assert for the Chinese and the Japanese, and for all other varieties of men equally with yourselves, now and forever. I know of no rights of race superior to the rights of humanity, and when there is a supposed conflict between human and national rights, it is safe to go to the side of humanity. I have great respect for the blue-eyed and light-haired races of America. They are a mighty people. In any struggle for the good things of this world, they need have no fear. They have no need to doubt that they will get their full share.

But I reject the arrogant and scornful theory by which they would limit migratory rights, or any other essential human rights, to themselves, and which would make them the owners of this great continent to the exclusion of all other races of men.

I want a home here not only for the negro, the mulatto[2] and the Latin races, but I want the Asiatic to find a home here in the United States, and feel at home here, both for his sake and for ours. Right wrongs no man. If respect is had to majorities, the fact that only one-fifth of the population of the globe is white and the other four-fifths are colored, ought to have some weight and influence in disposing of this and similar questions. …

I close these remarks as I began. If our action shall be in accordance with the principles of justice, liberty, and perfect human equality, no eloquence can adequately portray the greatness and grandeur of the future of the republic.

We shall spread the network of our science and our civilization over all who seek their shelter, whether from Asia, Africa, or the Isles of the Sea. We shall mould them all, each after his kind, into Americans;

1 *locomotion* I.e., movement.

2 *mulatto* Mixed-race. In the nineteenth century, "mulatto" was a term commonly used to classify individuals with one white parent and one parent of African descent; it is today considered archaic and offensive.

Indian and Celt, negro and Saxon, Latin and Teuton,[1] Mongolian and Caucasian, Jew and gentile, all shall here bow to the same law, speak the same language, support the same government, enjoy the same liberty, vibrate with the same national enthusiasm, and seek the same national ends.

—1867, REVISED 1869

---

1 *Saxon* The term "Saxon"—or, in more extended form, "Anglo-Saxon"—originally referred to the Germanic cultural group that settled in and ruled England in the early Middle Ages; it was widely used in the nineteenth century, in both Britain and the United States, to refer to white people inhabiting or stemming from England (or the British Isles more generally). In such contexts, the term often carried—and still carries—racist connotations of inherent racial superiority, though Douglass here uses it in a neutral, descriptive way; *Teuton* Germanic, Northern European. Today this term is considered dated and, like "Anglo-Saxon," is compromised by its frequent racist connotations.

from *Oration in Memory of Abraham Lincoln, Delivered at the Unveiling of the Freedmen's Monument*

The speech excerpted below was Frederick Douglass's keynote address at the dedication of the Emancipation Memorial, a statue in Washington, D.C., celebrating Abraham Lincoln's role in ending American slavery. The monument was funded by contributions from formerly enslaved people ("freedmen")—hence its alternate nineteenth-century name, the Freedmen's Monument. (Images of the statue can be seen in the "In Context" section that follows the excerpt.) Douglass's speech is noteworthy for its nuanced, multifaceted assessment of Lincoln's attitudes and actions regarding race and slavery, which balances recognition of Lincoln's pivotal contributions with acknowledgment of his limitations as, first and foremost, "the white man's President." Douglass also went on to criticize the memorial itself, in remarks that he reportedly added impromptu to the speech and later published in the Washington, D.C. *National Republican* (this published text can also be found in the "In Context" section below).

Friends and Fellow Citizens:

I warmly congratulate you upon the highly interesting object which has caused you to assemble in such numbers and spirit as you have today. This occasion is, in some respects, remarkable. Wise and thoughtful men of our race who shall come after us and study the lesson of our history in the United States; who shall survey the long and dreary spaces over which we have traveled, who shall count the links in the great chain of events by which we have reached our present position, will make a note of this occasion. They will think of it and speak of it with a sense of manly pride and complacency.[1] …

We stand today at the national center to perform something like a national act—an act which is to go into history; and we are here where every pulsation of the national heart can be heard, felt, and

1 *complacency* Satisfaction.

reciprocated. A thousand wires, fed with thought and winged with lightning, put us in instantaneous communication with the loyal and true men all over this country.

Few facts could better illustrate the vast and wonderful change which has taken place in our condition as a people than the fact of our assembling here for the purpose we have today. Harmless, beautiful, proper, and praiseworthy as this demonstration is, I cannot forget that no such demonstration would have been tolerated here twenty years ago. The spirit of slavery and barbarism, which still lingers to blight and destroy in some dark and distant parts of our country, would have made our assembling here the signal and excuse for opening upon us all the floodgates of wrath and violence. That we are here in peace today is a compliment and a credit to American civilization and a prophecy of still greater national enlightenment and progress in the future. I refer to the past, not in malice, for this is no day for malice, but simply to place more distinctly in front the gratifying and glorious change which has come both to our white fellow-citizens and ourselves, and to congratulate all upon the contrast between now and then—the new dispensation of freedom with its thousand blessings to both races, and the old dispensation of slavery with its ten thousand evils to both races, white and black. In view, then, of the past, the present, and the future, with the long and dark history of our bondage behind us, and with liberty, progress, and enlightenment before us, I again congratulate you upon this auspicious day and hour.

Friends and fellow citizens, the story of our presence here is soon and easily told. We are here in the District of Columbia, here in the city of Washington, the most luminous point of American territory … to express, as best we may, by appropriate forms and ceremonies, our grateful sense of the vast, high, and preeminent services rendered to ourselves, to our race, to our country, and to the whole world by Abraham Lincoln. …

… First things are always interesting, and this is one of our first things. It is the first time that, in this form and manner, we have sought to do honor to an American great man, however deserving and illustrious. I commend the fact to notice; let it be told in every part of the republic; let men of all parties and opinions hear it; let those who despise us, not less than those who respect us, know that now and here, in the spirit of liberty, loyalty, and gratitude, … we, the colored people, newly emancipated and rejoicing in our blood-bought freedom, near the close of the first century in the life of this republic, have now and here unveiled, set apart, and dedicated a monument of enduring granite and bronze, in every line, feature, and figure of which the men of this generation may read, and those of after-coming generations may read, something of the exalted character and great works of Abraham Lincoln, the first martyr President of the United States.

Fellow citizens, in what we have said and done today, and in what we may say and do hereafter, we disclaim everything like arrogance and assumption. We claim for ourselves no superior devotion to the character, history, and memory of the illustrious name whose monument we have here dedicated today. We fully comprehend the relation of Abraham Lincoln both to ourselves and to the white people of the United States. Truth is proper and beautiful at all times and in all places, and it is never more proper and beautiful in any case than when speaking of a great public man whose example is likely to be commended for honor and imitation long after his departure to the solemn shades—the silent continents of eternity. It must be admitted, truth compels me to admit, even here in the presence of the monument we have erected to his memory, Abraham Lincoln was not, in the fullest sense of the word, either our man or our model. In his interests, in his associations, in his habits of thought, and in his prejudices, he was a white man.

He was pre-eminently the white man's President, entirely devoted to the welfare of white men. He was ready and willing at any time during the first years of his administration to deny, postpone, and sacrifice the rights of humanity in the colored people to promote the welfare of the white people of this country. In all his education and feeling he was an American of the Americans. He came into the Presidential chair upon one principle alone, namely, opposition to the extension of slavery. His arguments in furtherance of this policy had their motive and mainspring in his patriotic devotion to the interests of his own race. To protect, defend, and perpetuate slavery in the states where it existed Abraham Lincoln was not less ready than any other President to draw the sword of the nation. He was ready to execute all the supposed constitutional guarantees of the United States Constitution in favor of the slave system anywhere inside the slave states. He was willing to pursue, recapture, and send back the fugitive slave to his master, and to suppress a slave rising for liberty, though his guilty master were already in arms against the government. The race to which we belong were not the special objects of his consideration. Knowing this, I concede to you, my white fellow citizens, a pre-eminence in this worship at once full and supreme. First, midst, and last, you and yours were the objects of his deepest affection and his most earnest solicitude. You are the children of Abraham Lincoln. We are at best only his stepchildren; children by adoption, children by force of circumstances and necessity. To you it especially belongs to sound his praises, to preserve and perpetuate his memory, to multiply his statues, to hang his pictures high upon your walls, and commend his example, for to you he was a great and glorious friend and benefactor. ... But while in the abundance of your wealth, and in the fullness of your just and patriotic devotion, you do all this, we entreat you to despise not the humble offering we this day unveil to view; for while Abraham Lincoln saved for you a country, he delivered us from a bondage, according to Jefferson, one hour of which was worse than ages of the oppression your fathers rose in rebellion to oppose.[1]

Fellow citizens, ours is no new-born zeal and devotion—merely a thing of this moment. The name of Abraham Lincoln was near and dear to our hearts in the darkest and most perilous hours of the republic. We were no more ashamed of him when shrouded in clouds of darkness, of doubt, and defeat than when we saw him crowned with victory, honor, and glory. Our faith in him was often taxed and strained to the uttermost, but it never failed. When he tarried long in the mountain;[2] when he strangely told us that we were the cause

---

1 *a bondage ... oppose* In a 1786 letter, Thomas Jefferson wrote: "What a stupendous, what an incomprehensible machine is man! who can endure toil, famine, stripes, imprisonment or death itself in vindication of his own liberty, and the next moment ... inflict on his fellow men a bondage, one hour of which is fraught with more misery than ages of that which he rose in rebellion to oppose."

2 *tarried ... mountain* See Deuteronomy 1.6–8, in which Moses (whose final address to the Israelites is traditionally believed to comprise the Book of Deuteronomy) describes how God commanded the Israelites to stop delaying their entry into the Promised Land after their escape from slavery in Egypt: "The Lord our God spake unto us in Horeb, saying, Ye have dwelt long enough in this mount: ... go in and possess the land which the Lord sware unto your fathers, Abraham, Isaac, and Jacob, to give unto them and to their seed after them."

of the war;[1] when he still more strangely told us that we were to leave the land in which we were born;[2] when he refused to employ our arms in defence of the Union; when, after accepting our services as colored soldiers, he refused to retaliate our murder and torture as colored prisoners;[3] when he told us he would save the Union if he could with slavery;[4] when he revoked the Proclamation of Emancipation of General Frémont;[5] when he refused to remove the popular commander of the Army of the Potomac, in the days of its inaction and defeat, who was more zealous in his efforts to protect slavery than to suppress rebellion;[6] when we saw all this, and more, we were at times grieved,

---

1 *when he ... the war* On 14 August 1862, Lincoln told a delegation of African Americans to the White House, "But for your race among us there could not be war[.] ... [W]ithout the institution of Slavery and the colored race as a basis, the war could not have an existence."

2 *when he ... were born* For much of his political career, Lincoln supported the resettlement, or "colonization," of free African Americans outside of the United States—a cause that enjoyed broad popularity among white Americans during the first half of the nineteenth century but was condemned by many African Americans and abolitionists. The explicit aim of Lincoln's August 1862 meeting with an African American delegation referred to in the previous footnote was to enlist African American commitment to this project.

3 *when, after accepting ... colored prisoners* After the Emancipation Proclamation authorized the recruitment of black troops into the Union Army, the Confederacy declared that all black soldiers taken prisoner would be treated as slave insurrectionists and executed or enslaved. In response, Lincoln issued a general order decreeing that "for every soldier of the United States killed in violation of the laws of war, a rebel soldier shall be executed; and for every one enslaved by the enemy or sold into slavery, a rebel soldier shall be placed at hard labor on the public works." Lincoln himself, however, helped ensure that this order was never carried out, even after several occasions in which Confederates massacred surrendered black troops.

4 *when he ... with slavery* In a famous letter of 22 August 1862, Lincoln stated, "If I could save the Union without freeing *any* slave I would do it, and if I could save it by freeing *all* the slaves I would do it; and if I could save it by freeing some and leaving others alone I would also do that."

5 *when he ... Frémont* On 30 August 1861, Union General John C. Frémont, in his capacity as commander of the military Department of the West, issued an order proclaiming the emancipation of all enslaved people held by Confederate supporters in Missouri (a slave state that remained in the Union). Fearing that the proclamation would alienate Missouri and the other slaveholding Union "border states," and that it would imply that the North was fighting for emancipation rather than the preservation of the Union, Lincoln ordered Frémont to rescind the proclamation and later had him removed from command.

6 *when he ... rebellion* The commander of the Union Army of the Potomac (the main Union army in the vicinity of Washington, D.C.) was, for much of 1861 and 1862, George McClellan. He was popular with his troops for his role in making the army a well-trained and efficient force but was widely criticized for being reluctant to fight and overly cautious on the battlefield. McClellan opposed any government interference with slavery and (like many other white Northerners) held racist views of African Americans; [continued ...]

stunned, and greatly bewildered; but our hearts believed while they ached and bled. Nor was this, even at that time, a blind and unreasoning superstition. Despite the mist and haze that surrounded him; despite the tumult, the hurry, and confusion of the hour, we were able to take a comprehensive view of Abraham Lincoln, and to make reasonable allowance for the circumstances of his position. We saw him, measured him, and estimated him; not by stray utterances to injudicious and tedious delegations, who often tried his patience; not by isolated facts torn from their connection; not by any partial and imperfect glimpses, caught at inopportune moments; but by a broad survey, in the light of the stern logic of great events, and in view of that "divinity which shapes our ends, rough hew them how we will,"[1] we came to the conclusion that the hour and the man of our redemption had somehow met in the person of Abraham Lincoln. It mattered little to us what language he might employ on special occasions; it mattered little to us, when we fully knew him, whether he was swift or slow in his movements; it was enough for us that Abraham Lincoln was at the head of a great movement, and was in living and earnest sympathy with that movement, which, in the nature of things, must go on until slavery should be utterly and forever abolished in the United States.

When, therefore, it shall be asked what we have to do with the memory of Abraham Lincoln, or what Abraham Lincoln had to do with us, the answer is ready, full, and complete. Though he loved Caesar less than Rome,[2] though the Union was more to him than our freedom or our future, under his wise and beneficent rule we saw ourselves gradually lifted from the depths of slavery to the heights of liberty and manhood; under his wise and beneficent rule, and by measures approved and vigorously pressed by him, we saw that the handwriting of ages, in the form of prejudice and proscription, was rapidly fading from the face of our whole country; under his rule, and in due time, about as soon after all as the country could tolerate

---

however, despite McClellan's poor battlefield record and refusal (in his own words) to "fight for the abolitionists," Lincoln long refrained from removing him from command.

1 *divinity ... we will* See Shakespeare's *Hamlet* 5.2.10–11.

2 *he loved ... Rome* See Shakespeare's *Julius Caesar* 3.2.23–24, in which Brutus explains why he helped to assassinate Julius Caesar: "not that I loved Caesar less, but that I loved Rome more."

the strange spectacle, we saw our brave sons and brothers laying off the rags of bondage, and being clothed all over in the blue uniforms of the soldiers of the United States; under his rule we saw two hundred thousand of our dark and dusky people responding to the call of Abraham Lincoln, and with muskets on their shoulders, and eagles on their buttons, timing their high footsteps to liberty and union under the national flag; under his rule we saw the independence of the black republic of Haiti, the special object of slaveholding aversion and horror, fully recognized, and her minister, a colored gentleman, duly received here in the city of Washington;[1] under his rule we saw the internal slave trade, which so long disgraced the nation, abolished, and slavery abolished in the District of Columbia;[2] under his rule we saw for the first time the law enforced against the foreign slave trade, and the first slave-trader hanged like any other pirate or murderer;[3] under his rule, assisted by the greatest captain of our age,[4] and his inspiration, we saw the Confederate States, based upon the idea that our race must be slaves, and slaves forever, battered to pieces and scattered to the four winds; under his rule, and in the fullness of time, we saw Abraham Lincoln, after giving the slaveholders three months' grace in which to save their hateful slave system, penning the immortal paper, which, though special in its language,

---

1 *we saw … Washington* The U.S. refused to grant diplomatic recognition to Haiti, the nation created by the successful revolution of the enslaved black population of the French colony of Saint-Domingue, for over fifty years after Haiti attained its independence in 1804, in deference to the belief of Southern slaveholders that recognizing Haiti would embolden enslaved African Americans to resist slavery. After Southern secession removed this obstacle, the Lincoln administration formally recognized Haiti on 12 July 1862; the first Haitian ambassador to the U.S. was accredited on 3 March 1863.

2 *slavery … District of Columbia* President Lincoln signed the District of Columbia Compensated Emancipation Act, which ended slavery in the District of Columbia and provided partial compensation for former slaveholders, on 16 April 1862.

3 *we saw … murderer* Participation in the international slave trade was illegal in the United States from 1808 and was made a capital offense in 1820. However, the few people ever convicted of slaving between 1808 and 1860 only received light sentences (and were usually able to avoid them). Nathaniel Gordon, a Portland, Maine-based trader in enslaved people who was captured with a cargo of enslaved Africans in August 1860, was the first and only person executed in the U.S. for illegal slave-trading; he was hanged on 21 February 1862 after President Lincoln refused to pardon him.

4 *the greatest … age* I.e., Ulysses S. Grant, who rose to supreme command of all Union armies by the end of the Civil War and subsequently served two terms as President (1869–77); he was in the audience for Douglass's speech.

was general in its principles and effect, making slavery forever impossible in the United States.[1] Though we waited long, we saw all this and more....

I have said that President Lincoln was a white man, and shared the prejudices common to his countrymen towards the colored race. Looking back to his times and to the condition of his country, we are compelled to admit that this unfriendly feeling on his part may be safely set down as one element of his wonderful success in organizing the loyal American people for the tremendous conflict before them, and bringing them safely through that conflict. His great mission was to accomplish two things: first, to save his country from dismemberment and ruin; and, second, to free his country from the great crime of slavery. To do one or the other, or both, he must have the earnest sympathy and the powerful cooperation of his loyal fellow-countrymen. Without this primary and essential condition to success his efforts must have been vain and utterly fruitless. Had he put the abolition of slavery before the salvation of the Union, he would have inevitably driven from him a powerful class of the American people and rendered resistance to rebellion impossible. Viewed from the genuine abolition ground, Mr. Lincoln seemed tardy, cold, dull, and indifferent; but measuring him by the sentiment of his country, a sentiment he was bound as a statesman to consult, he was swift, zealous, radical, and determined.

Though Mr. Lincoln shared the prejudices of his white fellow-countrymen against the negro, it is hardly necessary to say that in his heart of hearts he loathed and hated slavery.[2] The man who could say,

---

1 *we saw ... United States* In the so-called Preliminary Emancipation Proclamation, issued on 22 September 1862, Lincoln announced that, as of 1 January 1863, all enslaved people in states that remained in arms against the federal government would be declared free. The final version of the Proclamation that took effect on 1 January 1863 was a military order that was issued solely under the auspices of Lincoln's authority as commander-in-chief, and it applied only to enslaved people in ten Confederate states; the status of enslaved people in the four slaveholding Union "border states" and in the Union-occupied state of Tennessee (as well as in certain other designated areas) was not affected by it. Despite its limited initial applicability, however, the Proclamation was a crucial first step towards the eventual legal abolition of slavery nationwide.

2 [Douglass's note] "I am naturally anti-slavery. If slavery is not wrong, nothing is wrong. I cannot remember when I did not so think and feel."—*Letter of Mr. Lincoln to Mr. Hodges, of Kentucky*, April 4, 1864. [Douglass quotes from a letter Lincoln sent to Albert Hodges, the editor of a Kentucky newspaper, summarizing a conversation Lincoln had had with

"Fondly do we hope, fervently do we pray, that this mighty scourge of war shall soon pass away, yet if God wills it continue till all the wealth piled by two hundred years of bondage shall have been wasted, and each drop of blood drawn by the lash shall have been paid for by one drawn by the sword, the judgments of the Lord are true and righteous altogether,"[1] gives all needed proof of his feeling on the subject of slavery. He was willing, while the South was loyal, that it should have its pound of flesh, because he thought that it was so nominated in the bond;[2] but farther than this no earthly power could make him go.

... Few great public men have ever been the victims of fiercer denunciation than Abraham Lincoln was during his administration. He was often wounded in the house of his friends.[3] Reproaches came thick and fast upon him from within and from without, and from opposite quarters. He was assailed by abolitionists; he was assailed by slaveholders; he was assailed by the men who were for peace at any price; he was assailed by those who were for a more vigorous prosecution of the war; he was assailed for not making the war an abolition war; and he was most bitterly assailed for making the war an abolition war.

But now behold the change: the judgment of the present hour is, that taking him for all in all, measuring the tremendous magnitude of the work before him, considering the necessary means to ends, and surveying the end from the beginning, infinite wisdom has seldom sent any man into the world better fitted for his mission than Abraham Lincoln. His birth, his training, and his natural endow-

---

Hodges and two other Kentucky politicians, in which Lincoln described how his view of the relationship between his personal feelings about slavery and his sense of his constitutional responsibility as President had shifted during and because of the Civil War.]

1 *Fondly ... altogether* Douglass quotes (with some slight alterations) what was, in 1876, already becoming a famous passage from Lincoln's Second Inaugural Address.

2 *its pound ... the bond* Reference to Shakespeare's play *The Merchant of Venice* (1596–99), in which the Jewish moneylender Shylock demands, as the collateral for a loan ("bond") he extends to the merchant Antonio, a pound of Antonio's flesh should Antonio default. Douglass is suggesting that, to Lincoln, tolerance of the cruelty of Southern slavery was a hateful but accepted condition of the agreement between Northern and Southern states that created the U.S., in the same way that Shylock's cruel demand for a pound of Antonio's flesh was a hateful but accepted condition of his agreement with Antonio.

3 *He was ... friends* See Zechariah 13.6: "And one shall say unto him, What are these wounds in thine hands? Then he shall answer, Those with which I was wounded in the house of my friends." In the Christian tradition, this verse has sometimes been interpreted as foreshadowing the betrayal and crucifixion of Jesus.

ments, both mental and physical, were strongly in his favor. Born and reared among the lowly, a stranger to wealth and luxury, compelled to grapple single-handed with the flintiest hardships of life, from tender youth to sturdy manhood, he grew strong in the manly and heroic qualities demanded by the great mission to which he was called by the votes of his countrymen. ... [W]hether in his flatboat on the Mississippi River, or at the fireside of his frontier cabin, he was a man of work. A son of toil himself, he was linked in brotherly sympathy with the sons of toil in every loyal part of the republic. This very fact gave him tremendous power with the American people, and materially contributed not only to selecting him to the presidency, but in sustaining his administration of the government. ...

... Abraham Lincoln was clear in his duty, and had an oath in heaven.[1] He calmly and bravely heard the voice of doubt and fear all around him, but he had an oath in heaven, and there was not power enough on earth to make this honest boatman, backwoodsman, and broad-handed splitter of rails evade or violate that sacred oath. He had not been schooled in the ethics of slavery; his plain life had favored his love of truth. He had not been taught that treason and perjury were the proof of honor and honesty. His moral training was against his saying one thing when he meant another. The trust that Abraham Lincoln had in himself and in the people was surprising and grand, but it was also enlightened and well founded. He knew the American people better than they knew themselves, and his truth was based upon this knowledge.

Fellow citizens, the fourteenth day of April, 1865, of which this is the eleventh anniversary, is now and will ever remain a memorable day in the annals of this republic. It was on the evening of this day, while a fierce and sanguinary rebellion was in the last stages of its desolating power, while its armies were broken and scattered before the invincible armies of Grant and Sherman, while a great nation, torn and rent by war, was already beginning to raise to the skies loud anthems of joy at the dawn of peace, it was startled, amazed, and overwhelmed by the crowning crime of slavery—the assassination of Abraham Lincoln. It was a new crime—a pure act of malice. No

---

1 *an oath in heaven* Another reference to *The Merchant of Venice*; see 4.1.236, in which Shylock refuses to accept three times the amount of money he loaned Antonio in lieu of a pound of Antonio's flesh: "An oath, an oath, I have an oath in heaven!"

purpose of the rebellion was to be served by it. It was the simple gratification of a hell-black spirit of revenge. But it has done good after all. It has filled the country with a deeper abhorrence of slavery and a deeper love for the great liberator.

Had Abraham Lincoln died from any of the numerous ills to which flesh is heir;[1] had he reached that good old age of which his vigorous constitution and his temperate habits gave promise; had he been permitted to see the end of his great work; had the solemn curtain of death come down but gradually, we should still have been smitten with a heavy grief, and treasured his name lovingly. But, dying as he did die, by the red hand of violence, killed, assassinated, taken off without warning, not because of personal hate—for no man who knew Abraham Lincoln could hate him—but because of his fidelity to union and liberty, he is doubly dear to us, and his memory will be precious forever.

Fellow citizens, I end, as I began, with congratulations. We have done a good work for our race today. In doing honor to the memory of our friend and liberator we have been doing highest honors to ourselves and those who come after us; we have been fastening to ourselves a name and fame imperishable and immortal; we have also been defending ourselves from a blighting scandal. When now it shall be said that the colored man is soulless, that he has no appreciation of benefits or benefactors; when the foul reproach of ingratitude is hurled at us, and it is attempted to scourge us beyond the range of human brotherhood, we may calmly point to the monument we have this day erected to the memory of Abraham Lincoln.

—14 April 1876

1 *the numerous ... heir* See *Hamlet* 3.1.70–71 (in the famous "To be, or not to be" soliloquy), in which Hamlet refers to "the thousand natural shocks / That flesh is heir to."

In Context

The Emancipation Memorial ("Freedmen's Monument")

The Emancipation Memorial in Lincoln Park, Washington, D.C., was and remains a source of controversy. The memorial was paid for primarily, if not solely, by financial contributions from formerly enslaved people, beginning with a recently emancipated Virginian woman, Charlotte Scott, who reportedly donated the first five dollars she earned as a free woman for the building of a monument to Lincoln shortly after his assassination. African American supporters of the project such as Douglass and Henry Highland Garnet, however, disagreed about the nature and purpose of the planned monument: should its primary goal be to memorialize Lincoln or to edify formerly enslaved people? And while African Americans paid for the monument, white Americans designed it. The white sculptor Harriet Hosmer initially proposed a grand design that would include a statue of Lincoln at the center surrounded by smaller statues of several African Americans, including black Civil War soldiers, but this was rejected as too expensive. The design ultimately chosen was the work of Thomas Ball, another white sculptor, who had initially come up with it after learning of Lincoln's assassination; the African American figure was modeled on a formerly enslaved man named Archer Alexander, one of the last escapees from slavery to be captured under the 1850 Fugitive Slave Act.

Douglass followed his keynote speech at the memorial's dedication with a letter to the editor of the Washington, D.C. *National Republican*, given below, in which he criticized the memorial's design. Douglass's expressed desire, in that letter, to see "another monument" in Lincoln Park was realized in 1974, when a memorial to the African American educator and women's- and civil-rights activist Mary McLeod Bethune was built in the park (the Emancipation Memorial was rotated to face it). More recently, the Emancipation Memorial has been criticized for not depicting African Americans as agents in their own liberation; participants in the 2020 Black Lives Matter protests called for the monument's removal, and the congressional delegate for Washington, D.C., Eleanor Holmes Norton, introduced a bill to this effect in February 2021.

Nineteenth-century image of the Emancipation Memorial.

Frederick Douglass, Letter to the Editor of the *National Republican* (19 April 1876)

Sir: Admirable as is the monument by Mr. Ball in Lincoln Park, it does not, as it seems to me, tell the whole truth, and perhaps no one monument could be made to tell the whole truth of any subject which it might be designed to illustrate. The mere act of breaking the negro's chains was the act of Abraham Lincoln, and is beautifully expressed in this monument. But the act by which the negro was made a citizen of the United States and invested with the elective franchise was pre-eminently the act of President U. S. Grant,[1] and this is nowhere seen in the Lincoln monument. The negro here, though rising, is still on his knees and nude. What I want to see before I die is a monument representing the negro, not couchant[2] on his knees like a four-footed animal, but erect on his feet like a man. There is room in Lincoln Park for another monument, and I throw out this suggestion to the end that it may be taken up and acted upon.

The Emancipation Memorial today.

1 *the act by which … U. S. Grant* The Fourteenth and Fifteenth Amendments to the U.S. Constitution, guaranteeing the citizenship and voting rights (respectively) of African Americans, were ratified in 1868 and 1870; the Fifteenth Amendment was ratified during the presidency of Ulysses S. Grant (1869–77), but the Fourteenth was ratified during the presidency of Andrew Johnson (1865–69).

2 *couchant* Lying down or crouching, usually with head upraised.

from *Life and Times of Frederick Douglass*

In the first and second versions of his autobiography, Douglass had left unexplained any of the details of his escape from slavery, on the grounds—as he explains in Chapter 11 of the *Narrative*—that telling the story would probably cause "difficulties" for those who helped him and "would most undoubtedly induce greater vigilance on the part of slaveholders." It was only in 1881, sixteen years after the passing of the Thirteenth Amendment, that Douglass decided it would be safe to tell the story of his escape in greater detail than had ever been revealed to the reading public before. This material from Douglass's third and final autobiography, *Life and Times of Frederick Douglass*, is included below, reproducing text from the revised and expanded 1893 edition.

FROM PART I

FROM CHAPTER 20
APPRENTICESHIP LIFE

... [A]fter three years spent in the country, roughing it in the field, and experiencing all sorts of hardships, I was again permitted to return to Baltimore, the very place of all others, short of a free State, where I most desired to live. The three years spent in the country had made some difference in me, and in the household of Master Hugh. "Little Tommy" was no longer little Tommy, and I was not the slender lad who had left the Eastern Shore just three years before. The loving relations between Master Tommy and myself were broken up. He was no longer dependent on me for protection, but felt himself a *man*, and had other and more suitable associates. In childhood he had considered me scarcely inferior to himself—certainly quite as good as any other boy with whom he played; but the time had come when his *friend* must be his slave. So we were cold to each other, and parted. It was a sad thing to me, that, loving each other as we had done, we must now take different roads. To him a thousand avenues were open. Education had made him acquainted with all the treasures of the world and liberty had flung open the gates thereunto; but I who had attended him seven years; who had watched over him with the care of a big brother, fighting his battles in the street and shielding him from harm to an extent which induced his mother to say, "Oh, Tommy is always safe when he is with Freddy"—I must be confined to a single condition. He had grown and become a *man*: I, though grown to the stature of manhood, must all my life remain a minor—a mere boy. Thomas Auld, junior, obtained a situation on board the brig *Tweed*, and went to sea. I have since heard of his death. There were few persons to whom I was more sincerely attached than to him.

Very soon after I went to Baltimore to live, Master Hugh succeeded in getting me hired to Mr. William Gardiner,[1] an extensive ship-builder on Fell's Point. … At the end of eight months Master Hugh refused longer to allow me to remain with Gardiner. The circumstance which led to this refusal was the committing of an outrage upon me, by the white apprentices of the ship-yard. The fight was a desperate one, and I came out of it shockingly mangled. I was cut and bruised in sundry places, and my left eye was nearly knocked out of its socket. The facts which led to this brutal outrage upon me illustrate a phase of slavery which was destined to become an important element in the overthrow of the slave system, and I may therefore state them with some minuteness. That phase was this—the conflict of slavery with the interests of white mechanics and laborers. In the country this conflict was not so apparent; but in cities, such as Baltimore, Richmond, New Orleans, Mobile, etc., it was seen pretty clearly. The slaveholders, with a craftiness peculiar to themselves, by encouraging the enmity of the poor laboring white man against the blacks, succeeded in making the said white man almost as much a slave as the black slave himself. The difference between the white slave and the black slave was this: the latter belonged to one slaveholder, while the former belonged to the slaveholders collectively. The white slave had taken from him by indirection what the black slave had taken from him directly and without ceremony. Both were plundered, and by the same plunderers. The slave was robbed by his master of all his earnings, above what was required for his bare physical necessities, and the white laboring man was robbed by the slave system of the just results of his labor, because he was flung into competition

1 *William Gardiner* Spelled "Gardner" in Douglass's *Narrative* (1845).

with a class of laborers who worked without wages. The slaveholders blinded them to this competition by keeping alive their prejudice against the slaves as *men*—not against them as *slaves*. They appealed to their pride, often denouncing emancipation as tending to place the white working man on an equality with negroes, and by this means they succeeded in drawing off the minds of the poor whites from the real fact, that by the rich slave-master they were already regarded as but a single remove from equality with the slave. The impression was cunningly made that slavery was the only power that could prevent the laboring white man from falling to the level of the slave's poverty and degradation. To make this enmity deep and broad between the slave and the poor white man, the latter was allowed to abuse and whip the former without hindrance. But, as I have said, this state of affairs prevailed *mostly* in the country. In the city of Baltimore there were not unfrequent murmurs that educating slaves to be mechanics might, in the end, give slave-masters power to dispense altogether with the services of the poor white man. But with characteristic dread of offending the slaveholders, these poor white mechanics in Mr. Gardiner's ship-yard, instead of applying the natural, honest remedy for the apprehended evil, and objecting at once to work there by the side of slaves, made a cowardly attack upon the free colored mechanics, saying they were eating the bread which should be eaten by American freemen, and swearing that they, the mechanics, would not work with them. The feeling was *really* against having their labor brought into competition with that of the colored freeman, and aimed to prevent him from serving himself, in the evening of life, with the trade with which he had served his master, during the more vigorous portion of his days. Had they succeeded in driving the black freemen out of the ship-yard, they would have determined also upon the removal of the black slaves. The feeling was, about this time, very bitter toward all colored people in Baltimore (1836), and they—free and slave—suffered all manner of insult and wrong.

… In the conflict which ended my stay at Mr. Gardiner's I was beset by four of them [white laborers] at once—Ned North, Ned Hayes, Bill Stewart, and Tom Humphreys. Two of them were as large as myself, and they came near killing me, in broad daylight. One came in front, armed with a brick; there was one at each side and one behind, and they closed up all around me. I was struck on all sides;

and while I was attending to those in front I received a blow on my head from behind, dealt with a heavy hand-spike. I was completely stunned by the blow, and fell heavily on the ground among the timbers. Taking advantage of my fall they rushed upon me and began to pound me with their fists. With a view of gaining strength, I let them lay on for awhile after I came to myself. They had done me little damage, so far; but finally getting tired of that sport I gave a sudden surge, and despite their weight I rose to my hands and knees. Just as I did this one of their number planted a blow with his boot in my left eye, which for a time seemed to have burst my eye-ball. When they saw my eye completely closed, my face covered with blood, and I staggering under the stunning blows they had given me, they left me. As soon as I gathered strength I picked up the hand-spike and madly enough attempted to pursue them; but here the carpenters interfered and compelled me to give up my pursuit. It was impossible to stand against so many.

Dear reader, you can hardly believe the statement, but it is true and therefore I write it down; that no fewer than fifty white men stood by and saw this brutal and shameful outrage committed, and not a man of them all interposed a single word of mercy. There were four against one, and that one's face was beaten and battered most horribly, and no one said, "that is enough"; but some cried out, "Kill him! kill him! kill the d——n nigger![1] knock his brains out! he struck a white person!" I mention this inhuman outcry to show the character of the men and the spirit of the times at Gardiner's ship-yard; and, indeed, in Baltimore generally, in 1836. As I look back to this period, I am almost amazed that I was not murdered outright, so murderous was the spirit which prevailed there. On two other occasions while there I came near losing my life. On one of these, I was driving bolts in the hold through the keelson, with Hayes. In its course the bolt bent. Hayes cursed me and said that it was my blow which bent the bolt. I denied this and charged it upon him. In a fit of rage he seized an adze and darted toward me. I met him with a maul and parried his blow, or I should have lost my life.

---

1 *nigger* By the mid-nineteenth century, as the context here suggests, this word (today universally acknowledged to be an utterly unacceptable expression of racism) had firmly established itself in white American vernacular as an emphatically pejorative alternative to the then-more neutral term "negro."

After the united attack of North, Stewart, Hayes, and Humphreys, finding that the carpenters were as bitter toward me as the apprentices, and that the latter were probably set on by the former, I found my only chance for life was in flight. I succeeded in getting away without an additional blow. To strike a white man was death by lynch law, in Gardiner's ship-yard; nor was there much of any other law toward the colored people at that time in any other part of Maryland.

After making my escape from the ship-yard I went straight home and related my story to Master Hugh; and to his credit I say it, that his conduct, though he was not a religious man, was every way more humane than that of his brother Thomas, when I went to him in a somewhat similar plight, from the hands of his "Brother Edward Covey."[1] Master Hugh listened attentively to my narration of the circumstances leading to the ruffianly assault, and gave many evidences of his strong indignation at what was done. He was a rough but manly-hearted fellow, and at this time his best nature showed itself.

The heart of my once kind mistress Sophia was again melted in pity towards me. My puffed-out eye and my scarred and blood-covered face moved the dear lady to tears. She kindly drew a chair by me, and with friendly and consoling words, she took water and washed the blood from my face. No mother's hand could have been more tender than hers. She bound up my head and covered my wounded eye with a lean piece of fresh beef. It was almost compensation for all I suffered, that it occasioned the manifestation once more of the originally characteristic kindness of my mistress. Her affectionate heart was not yet dead, though much hardened by time and circumstances.

As for Master Hugh, he was furious, and gave expression to his feelings in the forms of speech usual in that locality. He poured curses on the whole of the ship-yard company, and swore that he would have satisfaction. His indignation was really strong and healthy; but unfortunately it resulted from the thought that his rights of property, in my person, had not been respected, more than from any sense of the outrage perpetrated upon me as a *man*. I had reason to think this

---

1 *Brother Edward Covey* In his first *Narrative*, Douglass describes his time working under the brutal overseer Edward Covey, which results in a violent confrontation in which Douglass overcomes him; Douglass continues to live with Covey for several months after this incident, but is never physically abused by him again.

from the fact that he could, himself, beat and mangle when it suited him to do so.

Bent on having satisfaction, as he said, just as soon as I got a little the better of my bruises Master Hugh took me to Esquire Watson's office on Bond Street, Fell's Point, with a view to procuring the arrest of those who had assaulted me. He gave to the magistrate an account of the outrage as I had related it to him, and seemed to expect that a warrant would at once be issued for the arrest of the lawless ruffians. Mr. Watson heard all that he had to say, then coolly inquired, "Mr. Auld, who saw this assault of which you speak?" "It was done, sir, in the presence of a ship-yard full of hands." "Sir," said Mr. Watson, "I am sorry, but I cannot move in this matter, except upon the oath of white witnesses." "But here's the boy; look at his head and face," said the excited Master Hugh; "*they* show *what* has been done." But Watson insisted that he was not authorized to do anything, unless white witnesses of the transaction would come forward and testify to what had taken place. He could issue no warrant, on my word, against white persons, and if I had been killed in the presence of a *thousand blacks*, their testimony combined would have been insufficient to condemn a single murderer. Master Hugh was compelled to say, for once, that this state of things was *too* bad, and he left the office of the magistrate disgusted.

Of course it was impossible to get any white man to testify against my assailants. The carpenters saw what was done; but the actors were but the agents of their malice, and did only what the carpenters sanctioned. They had cried with one accord, "Kill the nigger! kill the nigger!" Even those who may have pitied me, if any such were among them, lacked the moral courage to volunteer their evidence. The slightest show of sympathy or justice toward a person of color was denounced as abolitionism; and the name of abolitionist subjected its hearer to frightful liabilities. "D——n abolitionists," and "kill the niggers," were the watch-words of the foul-mouthed ruffians of those days. Nothing was done, and probably would not have been, had I been killed in the affray. The laws and the morals of the Christian city of Baltimore afforded no protection to the sable[1] denizens of that city.

---

1 *sable* I.e., dark-skinned.

Master Hugh, on finding that he could get no redress for the cruel wrong, withdrew me from the employment of Mr. Gardiner and took me into his own family, Mrs. Auld kindly taking care of me and dressing my wounds until they were healed and I was ready to go to work again.

While I was on the Eastern Shore, Master Hugh had met with reverses which overthrew his business and had given up ship-building in his own yard, on the City Block, and was now acting as foreman of Mr. Walter Price. The best that he could do for me was to take me into Mr. Price's yard, and afford me the facilities there for completing the trade which I began to learn at Gardiner's. Here I rapidly became expert in the use of caulkers'[1] tools, and in the course of a single year, I was able to command the highest wages paid to journeymen caulkers in Baltimore.

The reader will observe that I was now of some pecuniary value to my master. During the busy season I was bringing six and seven dollars per week. I have sometimes brought him as much as nine dollars a week, for wages were a dollar and a half per day.

After learning to caulk, I sought my own employment, made my own contracts, and collected my own earnings—giving Master Hugh no trouble in any part of the transactions to which I was a party.

Here, then, were better days for the Eastern Shore *slave*. I was free from the vexatious assaults of the apprentices at Gardiner's; free from the perils of plantation life and once more in favorable condition to increase my little stock of education, which had been at a dead stand since my removal from Baltimore. I had on the Eastern Shore been only a teacher, when in company with other slaves, but now there were colored persons here who could instruct me. Many of the young caulkers could read, write, and cipher. Some of them had high notions about mental improvement, and the free ones on Fell's Point organized what they called the "East Baltimore Mental Improvement Society." To this society, notwithstanding it was intended that only free persons should attach themselves, I was admitted, and was several times assigned a prominent part in its debates. I owe much to the society of these young men.

1 *caulkers* Workers who seal the wooden seams of a boat against leakage with oakum and melted tar.

The reader already knows enough of the *ill* effects of good treatment on a slave to anticipate what was now the case in my improved condition. It was not long before I began to show signs of disquiet with slavery, and to look around for means to get out of it by the shortest route. I was living among *freemen*, and was in all respects equal to them by nature and attainments. *Why should I be a slave?* There was *no* reason why I should be the thrall of any man. Besides, I was now getting, as I have said, a dollar and fifty cents per day. I contracted for it, worked for it, collected it; it was paid to me, and it was *rightfully* my own; and yet upon every returning Saturday night, this money—my own hard earnings, every cent of it,—was demanded of me and taken from me by Master Hugh. He did not earn it; he had no hand in earning it; why, then should he have it? I owed him nothing. He had given me no schooling, and I had received from him only my food and raiment; and for these, my services were supposed to pay from the first. The right to take my earnings was the right of the robber. He had the power to compel me to give him the fruits of my labor, and this *power* was his only right in the case. I became more and more dissatisfied with this state of things, and in so becoming I only gave proof of the same human nature which every reader of this chapter in my life—slaveholder, or non-slaveholder—is conscious of possessing.

To make a contented slave, you must make a thoughtless one. It is necessary to darken his moral and mental vision, and, as far as possible, to annihilate his power of reason. He must be able to detect no inconsistencies in slavery. The man who takes his earnings must be able to convince him that he has a perfect right to do so. It must not depend upon mere force: the slave must know no higher law than his master's will. The whole relationship must not only demonstrate to his mind its necessity, but its absolute rightfulness. If there be one crevice through which a single drop can fall, it will certainly rust off the slave's chain.

from Second Part

Chapter 1
Escape from Slavery

In the first narrative of my experience in slavery, written nearly forty years ago, and in various writings since, I have given the public what I considered very good reasons for withholding the manner of my escape. In substance these reasons were, first, that such publication at any time during the existence of slavery might be used by the master against the slave, and prevent the future escape of any who might adopt the same means that I did. The second reason was, if possible, still more binding to silence—for publication of details would certainly have put in peril the persons and property of those who assisted. Murder itself was not more sternly and certainly punished in the State of Maryland than was the aiding and abetting the escape of a slave. Many colored men, for no other crime than that of giving aid to a fugitive slave, have, like Charles T. Torrey,[1] perished in prison. The abolition of slavery in my native State[2] and throughout the country, and the lapse of time, render the caution hitherto observed no longer necessary. But, even since the abolition of slavery, I have sometimes thought it well enough to baffle curiosity by saying that while slavery existed there were good reasons for not telling the manner of my escape, and since slavery had ceased to exist there was no reason for telling it. I shall now, however, cease to avail myself of this formula, and, as far as I can, endeavor to satisfy this very natural curiosity. I should perhaps have yielded to that feeling sooner, had there been anything very heroic or thrilling in the incidents connected with my escape, for I am sorry to say I have nothing of that sort to tell; and yet the courage that could risk betrayal and the bravery which was ready to encounter death if need be, in pursuit of freedom, were essential features in the undertaking. My success was due to address rather than to courage; to good luck rather than to bravery. My means of escape were provided for me by the very men who were making laws

---

1 *Charles T. Torrey* Influential white abolitionist and one of the first operators of the Underground Railroad, who was jailed for his activities in 1846 and died there of tuberculosis a few months thereafter. Approximately 400 enslaved people were freed due to his direct efforts.

2 *my native State* Maryland.

to hold and bind me more securely in slavery. It was the custom in the State of Maryland to require of the free colored people to have what were called free papers. This instrument they were required to renew very often, and by charging a fee for this writing, considerable sums from time to time were collected by the State. In these papers the name, age, color, height and form of the free man were described, together with any scars or other marks upon his person which could assist in his identification. This device of slaveholding ingenuity, like other devices of wickedness, in some measure defeated itself—since more than one man could be found to answer the same general description. Hence many slaves could escape by personating the owner of one set of papers; and this was often done as follows: A slave nearly or sufficiently answering the description set forth in the papers, would borrow or hire them till he could by their means escape to a free state, and then, by mail or otherwise, return them to the owner. The operation was a hazardous one for the lender as well as for the borrower. A failure on the part of the fugitive to send back the papers would imperil his benefactor, and the discovery of the papers in possession of the wrong man would imperil both the fugitive and his friend. It was therefore an act of supreme trust on the part of a freeman of color thus to put in jeopardy his own liberty that another might be free. It was, however, not unfrequently bravely done, and was seldom discovered. I was not so fortunate as to sufficiently resemble any of my free acquaintances as to answer the description of their papers. But I had one friend—a sailor—who owned a sailor's protection, which answered somewhat the purpose of free papers—describing his person and certifying to the fact that he was a free American sailor. The instrument had at its head the American eagle, which at once gave it the appearance of an authorized document. This protection did not, when in my hands, describe its bearer very accurately. Indeed, it called for a man much darker than myself, and close examination of it would have caused my arrest at the start. In order to avoid this fatal scrutiny on the part of the railroad official, I had arranged with Isaac Rolls, a hackman,[1] to bring my baggage to the train just on the moment of starting, and jumped upon the car myself when the train was already in motion. Had I

---

1 *hackman* Person hired to drive carriages and transport goods.

gone into the station and offered to purchase a ticket, I should have been instantly and carefully examined, and undoubtedly arrested. In choosing this plan upon which to act, I considered the jostle of the train, and the natural haste of the conductor in a train crowded with passengers, and relied upon my skill and address[1] in playing the sailor as described in my protection, to do the rest. One element in my favor was the kind feeling which prevailed in Baltimore and other seaports at the time, towards "those who go down to the sea in ships."[2] "Free trade and sailors' rights"[3] expressed the sentiment of the country just then. In my clothing I was rigged out in sailor style. I had on a red shirt and a tarpaulin hat and black cravat, tied in sailor fashion, carelessly and loosely about my neck. My knowledge of ships and sailor's talk came much to my assistance, for I knew a ship from stem to stern, and from keelson to cross-trees, and could talk sailor like an "old salt." On sped the train, and I was well on the way to Havre de Grace before the conductor came into the negro car to collect tickets and examine the papers of his black passengers. This was a critical moment in the drama. My whole future depended upon the decision of this conductor. Agitated I was while this ceremony was proceeding, but still, externally at least, I was apparently calm and self-possessed. He went on with his duty—examining several colored passengers before reaching me. He was somewhat harsh in tone and peremptory in manner until he reached me, when, strangely enough, and to my surprise and relief, his whole manner changed. Seeing that I did not readily produce my free papers, as the other colored persons in the car had done, he said to me in a friendly contrast with that observed towards the others: "I suppose you have your free papers?" To which I answered: "No, sir; I never carry my free papers to sea with me." "But you have something to show that you are a free man, have you not?" "Yes, sir," I answered; "I have a paper with the American eagle on it, that will carry me round the world." With this I drew from my deep sailor's pocket my seaman's protection, as before described. The merest glance at the paper satisfied him, and he took my fare

1 *address* Manner of speaking, deportment.

2 *those who … in ships* See Psalm 107.23–24: "They that go down to the sea in ships, that do business in great waters; These see the works of the Lord, and his wonders in the deep."

3 *Free trade and sailors' rights* Well-known slogan of the War of 1812, written upon a flag flown by Captain David Porter.

and went on about his business. This moment of time was one of the most anxious I ever experienced. Had the conductor looked closely at the paper, he could not have failed to discover that it called for a very different looking person from myself, and in that case it would have been his duty to arrest me on the instant and send me back to Baltimore from the first station. When he left me with the assurance that I was all right, though much relieved, I realized that I was still in great danger: I was still in Maryland, and subject to arrest at any moment. I saw on the train several persons who would have known me in any other clothes, and I feared they might recognize me, even in my sailor "rig," and report me to the conductor, who would then subject me to a closer examination, which I knew well would be fatal to me.

Though I was not a murderer fleeing from justice, I felt, perhaps, quite as miserable as such a criminal. The train was moving at a very high rate of speed for that time of railroad travel, but to my anxious mind, it was moving far too slowly. Minutes were hours, and hours were days during this part of my flight. After Maryland I was to pass through Delaware—another slave State, where slave-catchers generally awaited their prey, for it was not in the interior of the State, but on its borders, that these human hounds were most vigilant and active. The border lines between slavery and freedom were the dangerous ones, for the fugitives. The heart of no fox or deer, with hungry hounds on his trail, in full chase, could have beaten more anxiously or noisily than did mine from the time I left Baltimore till I reached Philadelphia. The passage of the Susquehanna River at Havre de Grace was at that time made by ferry-boat, on board of which I met a young colored man by the name of Nichols, who came very near betraying me. He was a "hand" on the boat, but instead of minding his business, he insisted upon knowing me, and asking me dangerous questions as to where I was going, and when I was coming back, etc. I got away from my old and inconvenient acquaintance as soon as I could decently do so, and went to another part of the boat. Once across the river I encountered a new danger. Only a few days before I had been at work on a revenue cutter,[1] in Mr. Price's ship-yard, under

---

1 *revenue cutter* Vessel built for customs officers, whose purpose is to guard the coast and catch smugglers.

the care of Captain McGowan. On the meeting at this point of the two trains, the one going south stopped on the track just opposite to the one going north, and it so happened that this Captain McGowan sat at a window where he could see me very distinctly, and would certainly have recognized me had he looked at me but for a second. Fortunately, in the hurry of the moment, he did not see me, and the trains soon passed each other on their respective ways. But this was not the only hair-breadth escape. A German blacksmith, whom I knew well, was on the train with me, and looked at me very intently, as if he thought he had seen me somewhere before in his travels. I really believe he knew me, but had no heart to betray me. At any rate he saw me escaping and held his peace.

The last point of imminent danger, and the one I dreaded most, was Wilmington. Here we left the train and took the steamboat for Philadelphia. In making the change I again apprehended arrest, but no one disturbed me, and I was soon on the broad and beautiful Delaware, speeding away to the Quaker City.[1] On reaching Philadelphia in the afternoon I inquired of a colored man how I could get on to New York? He directed me to the Willow Street depot, and thither I went, taking the train that night. I reached New York Tuesday morning, having completed the journey in less than twenty-four hours. Such is briefly the manner of my escape from slavery—and the end of my experience as a slave. Other chapters will tell the story of my life as a freeman.

FROM CHAPTER II
SECESSION AND WAR

THE BLACK MAN AT THE WHITE HOUSE[2]

My efforts to secure just and fair treatment for the colored soldiers did not stop at letters and speeches. At the suggestion of my friend,

1 *the Quaker City* I.e., Philadelphia, which has strong historical connections to the Quakers, having been founded by Quaker leader William Penn (1644–1718).

2 In August 1863, Douglass met with Abraham Lincoln at the White House to petition for the equal treatment of black soldiers in the U.S. Army. He recounted the story of that meeting both in speeches (see the In Context material below) and in his final autobiography in 1881.

Major Stearns,[1] ... I was induced to go to Washington and lay the complaints of my people before President Lincoln and the Secretary of War;[2] and to urge upon them such action as should secure to the colored troops then fighting for the country a reasonable degree of fair play. I need not say that at the time I undertook this mission it required much more nerve than a similar one would require now. The distance then between the black man and the white American citizen[3] was immeasurable. I was an ex-slave, identified with a despised race, and yet I was to meet the most exalted person in this great republic. It was altogether an unwelcome duty, and one from which I would gladly have been excused. I could not know what kind of a reception would be accorded me. I might be told to go home and mind my business, and leave such questions as I had come to discuss to be managed by the men wisely chosen by the American people to deal with them. Or I might be refused an interview altogether. Nevertheless, I felt bound to go, and my acquaintance with Senators Charles Sumner, Henry Wilson, Samuel Pomeroy, Secretary Salmon P. Chase, Secretary William H. Seward, and Assistant Secretary of War Charles A. Dana[4] encouraged me to hope at least for a civil reception. My confidence was fully justified in the result. I shall never forget my first interview with this great man. I was accompanied to the executive mansion and introduced to President Lincoln by Senator Pomeroy. The room in which he received visitors was the one now used by the President's secretaries. I entered it with a moderate estimate of my own consequence, and yet there I was to talk with, and even to advise, the head man of a great nation. Happily for me, there was no vain pomp and ceremony about him. I was never more quickly or more completely put at ease in the presence of a great man than in that of Abraham Lincoln. He was seated, when I entered, in a low arm-chair with his feet extended on the floor, surrounded by a large number of documents and several busy secretaries. The room bore

---

1 *Major Stearns* George Luther Stearns (1809–67), white abolitionist who worked during the Civil War as a recruiter of black soldiers for the U.S. Army.

2 *Secretary of War* Edwin Stanton (1814–69).

3 *the black ... American citizen* Douglass's wording here alludes to the 1857 Supreme Court ruling (*Dred Scott v. Sanford*) determining that no black person, whether free or enslaved, could be considered a U.S. citizen.

4 *Senators ... Dana* Various significant Republican Party members and abolitionists.

the marks of business, and the persons in it, the President included, appeared to be much over-worked and tired. Long lines of care were already deeply written on Mr. Lincoln's brow, and his strong face, full of earnestness, lighted up as soon as my name was mentioned. As I approached and was introduced to him he arose and extended his hand, and bade me welcome. I at once felt myself in the presence of an honest man—one whom I could love, honor, and trust without reserve or doubt. Proceeding to tell him who I was and what I was doing, he promptly, but kindly, stopped me, saying, "I know who you are, Mr. Douglass; Mr. Seward has told me all about you. Sit down. I am glad to see you." I then told him the object of my visit: that I was assisting to raise colored troops; that several months before I had been very successful in getting men to enlist, but that now it was not easy to induce the colored men to enter the service, because there was a feeling among them that the government did not, in several respects, deal fairly with them. Mr. Lincoln asked me to state particulars. I replied that there were three particulars which I wished to bring to his attention. First, that colored soldiers ought to receive the same wages as those paid to white soldiers. Second, that colored soldiers ought to receive the same protection when taken prisoners, and be exchanged as readily and on the same terms as any other prisoners, and if Jefferson Davis should shoot or hang colored soldiers in cold blood the United States government should, without delay, retaliate in kind and degree upon Confederate prisoners in its hands. Third, when colored soldiers, seeking the "bubble reputation at the cannon's mouth,"[1] performed great and uncommon service on the battlefield, they should be rewarded by distinction and promotion precisely as white soldiers are rewarded for like services.

Mr. Lincoln listened with patience and silence to all I had to say. He was serious and even troubled by what I had said and by what he had evidently before thought upon the same points. He, by his silent listening not less than by his earnest reply to my words, impressed me with the solid gravity of his character.

He began by saying that the employment of colored troops at all was a great gain to the colored people; that the measure could not have been successfully adopted at the beginning of the war; that the

1 *seeking … mouth* See Shakespeare's *As You Like It* 2.7.159–60.

wisdom of making colored men soldiers was still doubted; that their enlistment was a serious offense to popular prejudice; that they had larger motives for being soldiers than white men; that they ought to be willing to enter the service upon any condition; that the fact that they were not to receive the same pay as white soldiers seemed a necessary concession to smooth the way to their employment at all as soldiers; but that ultimately they would receive the same. On the second point, in respect to equal protection, he said the case was more difficult. Retaliation was a terrible remedy, and one which it was very difficult to apply; that, if once begun, there was no telling where it would end; that if he could get hold of the Confederate soldiers who had been guilty of treating colored soldiers as felons he could easily retaliate, but the thought of hanging men for a crime perpetrated by others was revolting to his feelings. He thought that the rebels themselves would stop such barbarous warfare; that less evil would be done if retaliation were not resorted to and that he had already received information that colored soldiers were being treated as prisoners of war. In all this I saw the tender heart of the man rather than the stern warrior and commander-in-chief of the American army and navy, and, while I could not agree with him, I could but respect his humane spirit.

On the third point he appeared to have less difficulty, though he did not absolutely commit himself. He simply said that he would sign any commission to colored soldiers whom his Secretary of War should commend to him. Though I was not entirely satisfied with his views, I was so well satisfied with the man and with the educating tendency of the conflict that I determined to go on with the recruiting.

From the President I went to see Secretary Stanton. The manner of no two men could be more widely different. I was introduced by Assistant Secretary Dana, whom I had known many years before at "Brook Farm," Mass.,[1] and afterward as managing editor of the New York *Tribune*. Every line in Mr. Stanton's face told me that my communication with him must be brief, clear, and to the point; that he might turn his back upon me as a bore at any moment; that politeness was not one of his weaknesses. His first glance was that of a man who

---

1 *many years … Mass.* Assistant Secretary of War Charles A. Dana lived between 1841 and 1846 at the Transcendentalist utopian community Brook Farm.

says: "Well, what do you want? I have no time to waste upon you or anybody else, and I shall waste none. Speak quick, or I shall leave you." The man and the place seemed alike busy. Seeing I had no time to lose, I hastily went over the ground I had gone over to President Lincoln. As I ended I was surprised by seeing a changed man before me. Contempt and suspicion and brusqueness had all disappeared from his face and manner, and for a few minutes he made the best defense that I had then heard from anybody of the treatment of colored soldiers by the government. I was not satisfied, yet I left in the full belief that the true course to the black man's freedom and citizenship was over the battle-field, and that my business was to get every black man I could into the Union armies. Both the President and Secretary of War assured me that justice would ultimately be done my race, and I gave full faith and credit to their promise. On assuring Mr. Stanton of my willingness to take a commission, he said he would make me assistant adjutant to General Thomas,[1] who was then recruiting and organizing troops in the Mississippi valley. He asked me how soon I could be ready. I told him in two weeks, and that my commission might be sent to me at Rochester. For some reason, however, my commission never came. The government, I fear, was still clinging to the idea that positions of honor in the service should be occupied by white men, and that it would not do to inaugurate just then the Policy of perfect equality. I wrote to the department for my commission, but was simply told to report to General Thomas. This was so different from what I expected and from what I had been promised that I wrote to Secretary Stanton that I would report to General Thomas on receipt of my commission, but it did not come, and I did not go to the Mississippi valley as I had fondly hoped. I knew too much of camp life and the value of shoulder straps in the army to go into the service without some visible mark of my rank. I have no doubt that Mr. Stanton in the moment of our meeting meant all he said, but thinking the matter over he felt that the time had not then come for a step so radical and aggressive. Meanwhile my three sons were in the service, Lewis and Charles … in the Massachusetts regiments, and Frederick recruiting colored troops in the Mississippi valley.

—1881, 1893

---

1 *General Thomas* U.S. Army general George Henry Thomas (1816–70).

In Context

The Black Man at the White House

By early 1864 Douglass had begun to speak in public lectures about his meeting with Lincoln; the *Chicago Tribune* for 28 February 1864 describes a speech given at Bryan Hall in aid of the Ladies' Freedmen's Aid Society, during which "[t]he visit paid by [Douglass] to the President was humorously described." The full text of that speech (which was delivered at other locations as well that season, as the *Hartford Courant* advertisement reproduced below attests) is no longer extant, but the *Tribune's* brief report suggests that this earlier account of the meeting with Lincoln differed somewhat in tone from that published in *Life and Times*.

from "The Black Man at the White House: Frederick Douglass at Bryan Hall; Lecture in Aid of the 'Ladies' Freedmen's Aid Society,'" *Chicago Tribune* (28 February 1864)

Notwithstanding the disagreeable change in the weather, Bryan Hall was comfortably filled yesterday afternoon by an enthusiastic audience, drawn thither to hear the second lecture of the eloquent champion of his own oppressed race—Fred. Douglass. … The lecture was a fine effort, and was listened to with deep attention, and frequently called forth loud and enthusiastic applause. Mr. Douglass was introduced to the audience by Rev. Robert Collyer, after a short and impressive prayer by that gentleman.

Mr. Douglass then commenced his lecture by referring to the mutability of all human institutions, whose greatest permanence is only obtained when they nearest approach justice and truth, which are eternal. Nothing could better illustrate the uncertainties of worldly institutions than the present state of our republic. … All the teachings of the hour assert that only righteousness exalteth a nation, and there is no repose for us unless by some saving justice to those who have been oppressed these many years. There can be no permanent peace for this country unless all the rights for the negro are given him. … The visit paid by the speaker to the President was humorously described, and that portion of it relative to the crowds of patriots waiting to serve the country without [it] interfering with their personal interests, brought down the house in long, continued applause. He paid a graceful compliment to Abraham Lincoln for his kind reception, and characterized him as one of the men of the age, and somewhat ahead of the people. …

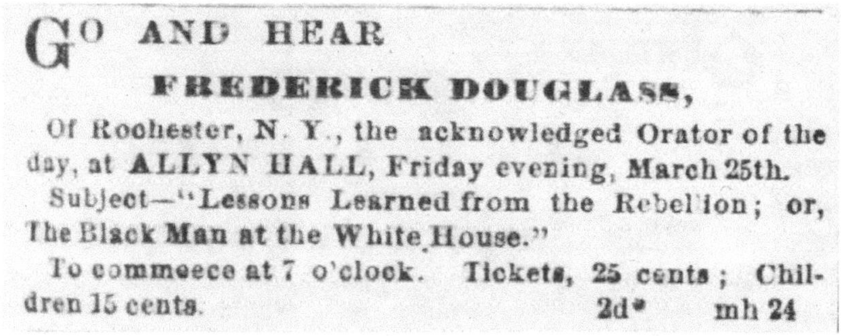
GO AND HEAR

FREDERICK DOUGLASS,

Of Roohester, N. Y., the acknowledged Orator of the day, at ALLYN HALL, Friday evening, March 25th.

Subject—"Lessons Learned from the Rebellion; or, The Black Man at the White House."

To commeece at 7 o'clock. Tickets, 25 cents; Children 15 cents. 2d* mh 24

Advertisement, *Hartford Courant*, 25 March 1864.

From the Publisher

A name never says it all, but the word "Broadview" expresses a good deal of the philosophy behind our company. We are open to a broad range of academic approaches and political viewpoints. We pay attention to the broad impact book publishing and book printing has in the wider world; for some years now we have used 100% recycled paper for most titles. Our publishing program is internationally oriented and broad-ranging. Our individual titles often appeal to a broad readership too; many are of interest as much to general readers as to academics and students.

Founded in 1985, Broadview remains a fully independent company owned by its shareholders—not an imprint or subsidiary of a larger multinational.

To order our books or obtain up-to-date information, please visit broadviewpress.com.

broadview press
www.broadviewpress.com

This book is made of paper from well-managed FSC® - certified forests, recycled materials, and other controlled sources.

MIX
Paper from responsible sources
FSC® C103567
FSC www.fsc.org

PCF

BIO GAS ENERGY

PERMANENT